The Myths of
Measurement and
Meritocracy

The Myths of Measurement and Meritocracy

Why Accountability Metrics in Higher Education Are Unfair and Increase Inequality

J. M. Beach

ROWMAN & LITTLEFIELD
Lanham • Boulder • New York • London

Published by Rowman & Littlefield
An imprint of The Rowman & Littlefield Publishing Group, Inc.
4501 Forbes Boulevard, Suite 200, Lanham, Maryland 20706
www.rowman.com
6 Tinworth Street, London, SE11 5AL, United Kingdom

British Library Cataloguing in Publication Information Available

Library of Congress Cataloging-in-Publication Data

Name: Beach, J. M. (Josh M.) author.
Title: The myths of measurement and meritocracy : why accountability metrics in higher
    education are unfair and increase inequality / J.M. Beach.
Description: Lanham : The Rowman and Littlefield Publishing Group, 2021. | Includes
    bibliographical references and index. | Summary: "This book examines the idea of
    educational accountability in higher education"—Provided by publisher.
Identifiers: LCCN 2021015403 | ISBN 9781475862249 (cloth) | ISBN 9781475862256
    (paperback) | ISBN 9781475862263 (epub)
Subjects: LCSH: Educational accountability—United States. | Education, Higher—
    United States. | Educational equalization—United States. | Educational evaluation—
    United States.
Classification: LCC LB2806.22 .B44 2021 | DDC 379.1/58—dc23
LC record available at https://lccn.loc.gov/2021015403

For Virginia, who graciously put up with long hours
and many years of research and writing.

And for David Labaree, a scholar without parallel, who inspired my
path to teaching when I was an undergraduate, and who was a guiding
light for this project. Thank you for your support of both books.

"If you can't measure it, you can't manage it."—Robert S. Kaplan and David P. Norton, *The Balanced Scorecard*

"It is wrong to suppose that if you can't measure it, you can't manage it—a costly myth."—W. Edwards Deming, *The New Economics*

"Not everything that is important is measurable, and much that is measurable is unimportant."—Jerry Z. Muller, *The Tyranny of Metrics*

"Measuring the wrong thing is often worse than measuring nothing, because you get what you measure."—Jeffrey Pfeffer, *Leadership BS*

"We must measure what matters. The starting point has to be deciding what matters most."—Daniel Koretz, *The Testing Charade: Pretending to Make Schools Better*

Praise for *The Myths of Measurement and Accountability*

"Beach argues that the accountability movement, which has already done so much damage to American public schools, is now coming after higher education as well, and he shows that this effort is not only based on faulty measures but also promises to lay waste to a system that is the envy of the world."—David F. Labaree, professor emeritus at the Graduate School of Education, Stanford University, and author of *How to Succeed in School Without Really Learning*, *Someone Has to Fail*, and *A Perfect Mess*

"'Playing school' is endemic throughout K–12 and higher education. Evaluation—both of students and of educators—is how we score the game. In this scholarly exploration of the sociology, economics, philosophy, and history of contemporary education, Josh Beach explores how and why the scoring rules became bogus and antithetical to supporting learning and improving teaching, rewarding behavior that undermines learning. The current quagmire arose from the postwar push for 'scientific' management—and viewing education as a consumer product—enabled by questionable measurement practices, irrational reverence for numbers, and a generous helping of the equivocation fallacy (e.g., conflating students' response to the prompt, 'how effective was the instructor?' with actual teaching effectiveness). I recommend this book to anyone who relies on, is subjected to, or engages in the evaluation of teaching and learning."—Philip B. Stark, associate dean for the Division of Mathematical and Physical Sciences and professor of statistics, University of California at Berkeley

"This book is thoughtful, well-informed, and passionately argued."—Jack Schneider, assistant professor of education at the University of Massachusetts at Lowell, co-editor of *History of Education Quarterly*, director of research at Massachusetts Consortium for Innovative Education Assessment, and author of *Beyond Test Scores*, *Excellence for All* and *A Wolf at the Schoolhouse Door*

"Beach has done an amazing job of blending the wisdom of many of the world's most thoughtful educators with his own ideas about what makes for better schooling. Both volumes deal with issues of assessment and accountability, and the desperate need for more humane systems of using these tools and ideas. These highly readable and well referenced books both inform and stimulate."—David C. Berliner, Regents' Professor Emeritus at Arizona State University and author of *50 Myths and Lies That Threaten America's Public Schools*, *Collateral Damage*, and *The Manufactured Crisis*

"In this book, part two of his series, Beach focuses on higher education policy, exposing the inequities of opportunity that stem from an overreliance on accountability metrics for evaluating educational quality. Collectively, this two-part series delivers a well-researched evidenced based argument for why it is past time we abandon the overreliance and narrow use of tests and measurement systems for holding educators accountable throughout the K–20 educational pipeline."—Sharon L. Nichols, professor of educational psychology at the University of Texas at San Antonio and author of *Collateral Damage: How High-Stakes Testing Corrupts America's Schools* and *Educational Policies and Youth in the 21st Century*

"J. M. Beach, in his densely researched book *The Myths of Measurement and Meritocracy*, shows how the educational assessment enterprise has been marked by a lack of rigor, by poor theory, and by unclear intentions. Too many assessment metrics have become a veneer bearing no relationship to the experience that lies behind it. They promote schooling rather than education, endurance rather than learning, obedience rather than enthusiasm. And Beach, because of his belief in the real and enduring promise of education, is not satisfied with this mismeasured chimera. Beach's book serves as a warning to teachers, administrators, and families alike: don't believe everything you see just because it's stated with two digits after the decimal point. 'In order to make data meaningful, you need an accurate theory,' Beach writes. And educational assessment has often been dragged forward by misshapen and mechanistic theoretical models that do not bear scrutiny. Good teachers produce good learning. Good learning is shown by good grades. Good students will recognize good teaching. An accumulation of good grades leads to a good degree. A good degree will lead to a good job, and a good job to a good life. Beach carefully shows the disconnect in each link of this causal chain, the rickety Rube Goldberg device that looks clever but would never in fact work."—Herb Childress, partner at Teleidoscope Group, former dean of research and assessment at Boston Architectural College, director of the University Writing Program at Duke University, and the author of *The Adjunct Underclass* and *The PhDictionary*

Contents

Foreword   xiii

Preface   xvii

Introduction   xxi

1   Public Opinion Surveys: From Managing the Herd to Consumer
    Satisfaction   1

2   The Premise of Student Evaluation Surveys: Measuring Teacher
    Effectiveness   13

3   Pressured to Please: The Negotiated Compromise of Playing
    School   27

4   A Question of Validity: Student Surveys Don't Measure
    Teaching or Learning   43

5   Predictably Irrational: The Cognitive Miser and the Limits of
    Consumer Choice   59

6   Are Students Capable of Evaluating Teaching or Learning?: An
    Investigation of the "Fox Effect"   69

7   Signaling or Human Capital?: Credentialism, Degree Inflation,
    and Socioeconomic Inequality   91

8   The Myth of Meritocracy: The Cautionary Examples of Ancient
    China and Modern South Korea   125

Conclusion   139

References 147

Preview of *Can We Measure What Matters Most?* 171

Index 173

About the Author 181

Foreword

David Labaree, Professor Emeritus, Graduate School of Education, Stanford University

In this book, J. M. Beach argues that the accountability movement, which has already done so much damage to American public schools, is now coming after higher education as well, and he shows that this effort is not only based on faulty measures but also promises to lay waste to a system that is the envy of the world.

The idea that a system of education should be held accountable to the public is in itself hardly problematic. Of course it should. We need to know that higher education is fulfilling the goals we set for it and having a beneficial impact of both the individuals who enroll in it and the society in which they live and work. The problem is in the metrics used to measure institutional effectiveness, including such things as student evaluations of their teachers, tests of student knowledge acquisition, graduation rates, and income levels after graduation.

A key problem with these metrics is that they narrow the aims for higher education to a few outcomes that are readily measurable but not very important. We want this system to produce competent citizens for our democracy, productive workers for our economy, and social opportunity for people from all walks of life. None of the current metrics captures these broader outcomes that we want to see from our system of colleges and universities.

In the first volume of this series, Beach explores the problem of accountability for American public schools, and many of the dysfunctions that arise from holding these institutions accountable also apply to higher education. One is that teaching and learning in colleges and universities, as in elementary and secondary school, requires the mutual cooperation of teacher and student. Teachers can't make students learn; they need to encourage them to learn, which is much more difficult to carry out and impossible to standardize. Another is that the system of higher education is astonishingly complex and radically decentralized, with some 4,000 degree-granting institutions operating independently and largely under campus-level control. These campuses vary considerably in governance, program focus, selectivity, funding, and degrees offered, which undercuts the likelihood that any standards of performance would apply to all.

But the American system of higher education has some core characteristics that mark it off from elementary and secondary schooling and further confound efforts to apply accountability measures across the board.

First, whereas attendance at the lower levels of schooling is mandated by law, college attendance is purely voluntary. A college can't count on having students enroll; it has to induce them to do so. And in a crowded higher education market, it has to compete effectively with other colleges who are also marketing their wares. Exacerbating the stakes in this competition is the fact that public and private colleges alike are heavily dependent on student tuition and fees to maintain financial viability. For most of U.S. history, state funding has fallen far short of covering college costs, and this has become increasingly true in the last 50 years, as the share of college budgets covered by state appropriations has been steadily declining.

A major consequence of this situation is that, much more than the school system, the higher education system has to be highly sensitive to consumer preferences. Colleges are compelled to be adept at figuring out what students want and giving it to them. If they don't, the college down the road will do so, so they need to keep attuned to current trends and keep ahead of the curve. Think of how the college dorm room with bunk beds and a bathroom down the hall has turned into a suite of rooms with hotel amenities. Look at the growth of food courts to replace the cafeteria and elaborate athletic facilities to replace the lowly gym.

As early at the 1880s colleges realized they needed more than academics to keep the consumer happy, so they encouraged fraternities and sororities and intercollegiate athletics in order to rev up campus social life. These elements not only attracted and retained students, but they also built a loyalty to the institution that would pay off in having loyal alumni who would send their children to the alma mater and make generous donations to the annual fundraising campaign. Think of all of the ways that American students and alumni display the college logo, on sweatshirts and caps and bumper stickers and yard signs on game days. Students at European universities don't wear the brand the way that American students do. The reason is that here college is not where you go; it's who you are.

With the student-consumer as king of campus, colleges also need to be worried about demanding too much studiousness from their clientele. Party schools build more loyalty than academic rigor and stringent grading. With student course evaluations playing such an important role in college accountability, it's no wonder that grades on campus have inflated so much, with the average grade moving from C to something more like A–. Low grades don't make for happy campers and future donors.

In addition to consumerism, the US higher education system has another trait that distinguishes it from other systems around the world. It's a system without a plan. No one could have designed a system as fiendishly complex as this: public, private, religious, and for-profit; associate, bachelor's, master's, professional, and doctoral degrees; residential and commuter; urban and rural; teaching-focused and research-focused; selective and open access.

The present system emerged organically in the early 19th century as a collection of private colleges with corporate charters and only occasional state funding. Each operated as an independent enterprise with a private board of governors and a president as CEO, whose job was to negotiate a path toward viability through the crowded college market. When states began opening public institutions, they followed the model of independence and self sufficiency laid out by their private predecessors, since they too had to function without reliable state funding.

The result was the evolution of a system whose vulnerabilities in the 19th century turned into strengths in the twentieth. The forced autonomy that came from underfunding made these institutions into a formidable array of competitors who figured out how to survive and thrive in a demanding environment. Relatively free of control from the state, they were able to adapt quickly to changing market conditions, pursuing opportunities as they emerged—for new programs of study, lines of research, funding prospects, donor bases, and avenues for excellence, which would draw in the best students and faculty and enhance the brand.

What makes the system so effective today is that it has never had to be held accountable to a monolithic regime of metrics set by the state. Emergent rather than planned, arising from the bottom up rather than imposed from the top down, the system has assumed a dominant position in the global ecology of higher education. Accountability could kill it.

Preface

We Aren't Measuring
What Matters Most

What do students learn in school? In the 21st century, this question has become a political dilemma for countries all across the globe. It is a deceptively simple question, but there has never been an easy answer.

The problem of measuring student learning appears to express an educational problem: What and how much do students learn? And yet, when you investigate the educational accountability movement, especially in the United States where it began, you realize that the preoccupation with student learning is not about education. Calls for accountability have always been more focused on politics and economics (Labaree 1997b).

The accountability movement in schools, which started in the United States in the early 20th century, and spread across the world a century later, is not about education. It is about furthering a neoliberal political agenda, which has sought the economic transformation of all institutions and the state. Economic efficiency and organizational accountability have been two of the central political agendas of neoliberal reformers (Senge [1990] 2006, xii). One of the main political slogans of neoliberalism has been, "If you can't measure it, you can't manage it" (Kaplan and Norton 1996, 21).

This book is the companion volume to *Can We Measure What Matters Most? Why Educational Accountability Metrics Lower Student Learning and Demoralize Teachers*. I wrote these books because I believe that public intellectuals, academics, policy makers, school administrators, and teachers need to ask critical questions about what has been done over the past century in the monumental, expensive, and futile effort to keep schools "accountable."

Over the course of the 20th century, the traditional faith in the sacred value of schooling, which was broadly shared by all classes and cultures for thousands of years, was slowly dissolved. Now there is a new orthodoxy. We have given up traditional ideals about inculcating the young and replaced them with neoliberal accountability programs focused on standardized tests and ritualized schooling (Schneider 2017; Ravitch 2010).

I focused the companion book on the history of educational accountability metrics. In that book I discuss how accountability measurements have not only failed to deliver meaningful reforms, but also how their unintended consequences have made schooling much worse for many students.

In this book I investigate if schools actually educate most of their students in terms of developing useful knowledge or skills, which is supposedly the main purpose of schooling. In particular, I want to focus on adolescents in high school and college. I'll also investigate whether schooling, in particular higher education, is an equitable and meritocratic institution that promotes teaching and learning. I want to know if schooling actually helps most students, especially the most socially and economically disadvantaged, become successful in life, specifically in terms of the labor market.

Most people believe that students learn in schools because student learning is supposedly the primary institutional purpose of schools. Most people also believe that schooling helps students succeed in life and the labor market, especially the most disadvantaged.

But what if students don't learn much in schools? What if schools were never designed to produce student learning? What if schools don't help most students, either personally or economically? What if schools aren't meritocratic institutions? What if schooling actually exacerbates inequality and makes the lives of the disadvantaged even worse?

I'll be investigating the modern myth that schools are functional institutions that train students for success by giving them human capital in terms of giving students useful knowledge and skills. Contrary to popular belief, when you study the historical record, you will find that educational institutions have mostly *schooled* students rather than educated them. In most cultures, the primary purpose of schooling has been memorizing traditional rituals, signaling social status, and awarding symbolic credentials, not producing meaningful student learning or skills.

So, if students and teachers are just playing school, and if accountability metrics are only measuring the empty ritual of playing school, then how are accountability measurements going to make schools more efficient or effective? Is it even possible to make schools effective, or are these institutions naturally ineffective because of their traditional, symbolic function?

In particular, I will be examining the invalidity of three important accountability measurements that have become institutionalized standards in high school and higher education: grades, student evaluation surveys, and the labor market value of credentials. I chose these measurements because they are some of the most important examples of educational accountability standards in the 21st century, especially in terms of the institutional assessment of high school and higher education.

I also chose these measurements because most academic studies of the accountability movement have focused on standardized tests and the No Child Left Behind legislation, which I touched upon in the first volume. I want to get beyond that narrow and overly-discussed frame of reference. Instead, I want to look at how accountability measurements have been transforming higher education, the pinnacle of public schooling, mostly for the worse (see, for example, Ravitch 2010; Koretz 2017; Schneider 2017). But more importantly, these metrics clearly demonstrate the dangerous invalidity and irrationality of most accountability measurements being used in schools.

Like the first volume in this series, this book is deeply personal. While I have studied the research on school reform and the accountability movement for over a decade, I wrote this book from the lens of a teacher and a student. I have been a student in one way or another for most of my life, and I have been an educator for over twenty years, teaching in three countries: the U.S., South Korea, and China.

As an instructor, I have taught a diverse range of students from preschool to university to training professional teachers. As a teacher, I have also been the object of many types of accountability measurements. I have personally suffered the unfair consequences of meaningless metrics. And from what I have seen, I am deeply skeptical about what schools, and the reformers of schools, can actually accomplish using accountability measurements.

But while I am skeptical of school reform, I continue to believe in the transformative power of *education* because I have seen its effect on my own life, on the life of my son, and on the lives of many of my students. For accountability measurements to work, whether it be in schools or any other organization or business, we have to measure what actually matters rather than just measuring what is easiest or cheapest or most politically expedient.

Thus, as professor of education Daniel Koretz (2017) has argued, "The starting point has to be deciding what matters most" (220). I hope this book raises some deep questions about what should matter most when it comes to education and schooling, and what we should and should not be measuring if we want our schools, and the lives of students, to improve.

Introduction

Investigating the Myths of Measurement and the Meritocracy of Higher Education

Many scholars and pundits have pointed out that universal access to public schooling and higher education in the United States has never come with "the assurance of quality or equality in students' educational experiences and outcomes" (Peurach et al. 2019, 35; see also Brint and Karabel 1989; Grubb and Lazerson 2004; Beach 2011a). By the late 1960s, many people began to complain that government social programs, including public schools and higher education, cost a lot of money, but don't really do much for individuals or society. (Drucker 1969, 212–13).

Milton Friedman ([1962] 2002), the Nobel Prize winning economist and neoliberal philosopher, famously argued that schooling was a waste of tax dollars. Friedman lamented that Americans were "getting so little per dollar spent" on education because public schools were not being held accountable for measurable results (105). Friedman argued that public schools were an inefficient investment, implying that tax dollars would be better spent elsewhere.

A couple of years later, business professor and neoliberal philosopher Peter F. Drucker (1969) echoed Friedman's concerns, saying "The growing resistance to the cost of education indicates that the public is beginning to be concerned with what it gets for its money. . . . We clearly are not at all convinced that we are getting our money's worth for what we spend on it" (312). While Friedman and Drucker caused a lot of shock and dismay with their criticisms about the inefficiency of public schooling, they were actually reiterating an old and established mantra that had become conventional wisdom by the middle of the 20th century.

Friedman and Drucker were neoliberal reformers who believed that tradi-tional inequalities were relics of the past that were eliminated by the meri-tocratic marketplace in the 20th century, which enabled anyone to succeed if they were willing to work hard enough in school and in the labor market. Since World War II, neoliberals have wanted to completely transform the whole of society and the state in the U.S. by re-creating all institutions with market principles.

The anthropologist and historian David Harvey (2005) wrote a highly acclaimed history of neoliberalism as a political movement. He explained that neoliberal reformers believed that "if markets do not exist (in areas such as land, water, education, health care, social security, or environmental pollu-tion) then they must be created, by state action if necessary" (2).

In terms of educational reform over the past century, neoliberal reformers have transformed schools into business-like organizations, which are now justified on market principles. Schools are now seen as economic organiza-tions instead of moral or cultural institutions. All across the world, the neo-liberal model of schooling has become a new "secular faith" (Wolf 2002, x). Economist W. Norton Grubb and historian Marvin Lazerson (2004) derisively called it, "The Educational Gospel" (vii; see also Birnbaum 2000, xii; Sandel 2012; Sandel 2020; Wolf 2002).

Neoliberal schools have become credential factories that process students and supposedly produce human capital, which is a private good which enables personal wealth. Schools also supposedly contribute to national eco-nomic growth by producing human capital, via the hidden hand of the market (Labaree 1997b; Birnbaum 2000, 91; Markovits 2019; Grubb and Lazerson 2004; Wolf 2002). Rather than developing human beings, students are now considered consumers with clear preferences who buy educational products and services, which are investments that will pay students dividends in the labor market.

School administrators have become highly-paid, corporate managers who evaluate the efficiency of their educational factories, control their workforce, and raise performance-based capital. Teachers have been reduced to low-paid service providers who seek to please their customers. Most teachers in higher education are poorly paid gig workers on short-term contracts.

As employees, teachers have two functions. They are supposed to follow the orders of their supervisors, who are supposedly experts at keeping schools productive and economically efficient. Teachers are also supposed to please their customers. What do students want? Students want entertaining theater that requires no effort and no learning.

For the most part, teachers do not teach. And schools, especially institu-tions of higher education, are no longer educational organizations.

Schools are now business-like organizations. Schools are expected to satisfy customers and stakeholders by demonstrating their effectiveness with measurable outcomes. Rather than rely on antiquated beliefs that schools do what they're supposed to do, modern school managers believe that schools must measure the quantity and quality of the products their credential factories produce so as to justify their precarious budgets, which are increasingly predicated upon performance-based funding (Schneider 2017; Dougherty et al. 2016).

Thus, school administrators now follow the popular advice of business professor Andy Grove (2015), who famously declared, "a measurement—any measurement—is better than none" (17). Since the 20th century, demonstrating the effectiveness of schools with accountability measurements has become the conventional wisdom all across the globe.

While institutions of higher education in the U.S. have never been exempt from the criticisms of the educational accountability movement, which started in the late 19th century in the U.S., it wasn't until the 1990s that national accountability reforms were mandated for colleges and universities. These accountability efforts focused first on community colleges (Beach 2011a), and only recently in the past two decades, have they been applied to all colleges and research universities (Spellings Commission 2006; Labaree 2010; Keeling and Hersh 2012).

However, reform efforts in higher education have been mostly focused on public, non-selective institutions. These schools receive the most public money and they have had the worst performance metrics, largely because they serve more disadvantaged students and because they receive less funding and have few resources than elite schools. Several critics have noted that non-selective colleges and universities in the U.S. have become "dropout factories" (Kirp 2019, 4, 11) because most students who attend these schools drop out and never earn a degree, many leaving with thousands of dollars of student debt.

Early in the 1990s, the National Governors Association (1991) announced that institutions of higher education would be treated no differently than public K–12 schools. The NGA declared, "The public has a right to know what it is getting for its expenditure of tax resources. . . . They have a right to know that their resources are being wisely invested and committed" (3).

Over the next twenty years the public was shocked when academic researchers and government agencies found "little consistent evidence to suggest that either postsecondary education in general or the type of institution attended in particular had a differential effect on knowledge acquisition for different kinds of students" (Pascarella and Terenzini 2005, 134; Keeling and Hersh 2012, 27).

The Spellings Commission (2006) on the Future of Higher Education noted the "lack of useful data and accountability" metrics by colleges and universities, which meant that there was "no solid evidence" for student learning or other outcomes (4, 13).

To make matters worse, there was no agreement about what to measure, how to measure, or how to compare the data that could be found. According to the Spellings Commission, no one actually knew which colleges or universities "do a better job than others of not only graduating students but of teaching them what they need to learn" (vii).

The lack of evidence on the outcomes and efficiency of higher education shocked many critics, like Donald Levine, a former dean of the University of Chicago, who complained: "The scandal of higher education in our time is that so little attention gets paid, in institutions that claim to provide an education, to what it is that college educators claim to be providing" (qtd. in Delbanco 2007).

Over the last decade, and for the first time, according to historian and sociologist David Labaree (2010), educational reformers have been trying to create uniform academic standards and measurements, modeled on the No Child Left Behind legislation, that extend from K–12 schools all the way to higher education (Schwartz-Chrismer, Hodge and Saintil 2006; Koretz 2017).

Colleges, universities, and community colleges are now spending large amounts of money to collect vast quantities of data in order to evaluate if teachers are doing their jobs. They are also trying to evaluate if "students learn the content of the academic curriculum" (Labaree 2010, 187–88, 206; Birnbaum 2000, 84). Institutions of higher education are having to prove their worth and justify their existence, just like K–12 schools have had to do since the 1970s.

In an effort to create accountability metrics, college administrators are trying to get past inflated college course grades so as to develop more accurate measures of student learning, as well as other student outcomes (St. John, Kline & Asker, 2001; Brint, 2008). And increasingly, college budgets are being tied to accountability data and performance-based targets (Dougherty et al. 2016).

But in the rush to create accountability metrics, few asked how this process should be done so as to foster broader educational purposes, rather than narrower economic purposes. In particular, for institutions of higher education, few administrators or researchers have asked, what does student success look like and why? And how should colleges and universities measure student success so as to reinforce educational goals and student development?

For the most part, the accountability metrics that were established for colleges and universities all boiled down to money, in one way or another, not education. The purpose of college is now defined primarily in terms of human capital and labor market earnings.

Most people have come to believe three sacred truths about higher education. First, students earn human capital by learning important knowledge and skills. Second, this human capital can then used by students to barter for higher wages and benefits in the labor market. And finally, the first two steps benefit everyone by creating more jobs and more wealth in the labor market.

Thus, in creating accountability metrics, college administrators have been primarily focused on measuring knowledge or skills, or the products of knowledge, like credentials, and then correlating these products to labor market earnings. In this effort, student evaluation surveys have become the foundational assessment for almost all colleges and universities because they supposedly measure the quality of teaching, learning, and the curriculum (Johnson 2003, 140; Schneider 2017, 152).

College administrators believe that student surveys are valid accountability instruments that accurately measure the means and ends of education. Administrators also believe that teachers *produce* student learning, which means that teachers are responsible for student learning and customer satisfaction.

In some institutions, and for certain kinds of teachers, like adjunct instructors in community colleges and non-selective universities, student surveys have become the only method of assessment for employment purposes. They determined if a teacher is hired, fired, or promoted. Thus, student evaluation surveys have become high-stakes accountability instruments.

While nearly all educational administrators, and many instructors, seem to believe that student surveys offer insight into teaching and student learning (Schneider 2017, 152), researchers have overwhelmingly found that these student surveys do not measure either teaching or learning directly, or very effectively. Why? Part of the problem is that student evaluation surveys are improperly designed, calibrated, administered, and interpreted.

So, the question then becomes, if these accountability measurements aren't valid, then how can they be useful or fair assessment tools with which to evaluate either teachers or students? And further, if these instruments are not effective or fair, then what is the effect of hiring, promoting, and firing teachers based on flawed and unfair assessment tools?

The evidence is discouraging. As many researchers have documented over the past several decades, (Nichols 2017; Keeling and Hersh 2012; Rosovsky and Hartley 2002; Chen 2013), many institutions of higher education have been conducting fraud, or "academic malpractice" (Nichols 2017, 89, 87).

Students don't want to learn so many teachers are lying to students by giving them superficial knowledge, rituals, and inflated grades. This leads many students to believe that "they're actually smarter than they are," which ends up harming them in many ways when they leave school to navigate the labor market (Nichols 2017, 89, 87; see also Sperber 2000, xiv; Koretz 2017, ch. 5).

There is also another discouraging and unintended consequence with accountability metrics in higher education. Most people assume that students actually learn useful knowledge and skills in college. They also assume that these products actually drive labor market earnings. But what if this assumption is false?

By the end of the 20th century, economists were able to monetize the products of schooling for the first time by statistically connecting educational credentials to labor market outcomes. Groundbreaking research by the economist Theodore Schultz and later Gary Becker, enabled social scientists to produce elaborate cost/benefit ratios to determine a clear picture of the economic value and efficiency of various forms of schooling (Schultz 1961; Grubb and Lazerson 2004; Beach 2009; Murphy 2017, 115).

One group of social scientists documented how student knowledge and skill symbolically transforms into various forms of capital, which has been called "social capital," "cultural capital," or "human capital" (Bourdieu [1984] 2010; Swartz 1997; Schultz 1961). These differing notions of capital are proxies for the social and economic value of a student's knowledge, skill, and productive capacity in the labor market. While social and cultural capital can't be directly measured by social scientists, economists can indirectly measure human capital by using various proxy metrics, like grades, diplomas, certificates, and degrees.

Economists have studied the average economic value attached to these metrics in the labor market so as to compute a relatively precise *Return on Investment* for different types of schooling. This book will discuss this issue at length. Economists can also measure the costs of schooling and compare it to this return on investment to determine which forms of schooling are most cost effective.

A separate, more critical group of social scientists have studied the economics of schooling in a very different way. This group has been skeptical of Schultz's theory of human capital. Instead of seeing educational credentials as a measure of concrete skills or knowledge, critical social scientists have focused on the traditional relationship between schooling and the elite ideological product of "social status" (Collins 1979; Bourdieu [1984] 2010; Milner 1994).

Critics argued that the value of educational credentials has not been a reflection of anything practical, like knowledge, skills, or economic productivity. Instead, the value of academic credentials has come from possessing a scarce luxury good that gives its bearer elite social status. This elevated status was mostly due to the selective gatekeeping of expensive forms of schooling, especially private higher education and elite professional schools (Spence 1974; Collins 1979; Caplan 2018).

Many people, including many economists, still confuse credentialism with human capital. People naturally assume that academic credentials represent real knowledge or practical skills. But what few people understand, besides critical sociologists, is that credentials have traditionally been mostly a cultural currency, rather than an economic currency.

A credential gives its bearer a limited and exclusionary form of social status and power. A credential's value is determined by access to elite people or elite jobs, not any underlying knowledge or skills. A credential's value is also tied to the restricted number of existing credentials in a given labor market.

Exclusive credentials mean higher social status. A large part of the value of academic credentials has always been their scarcity. Traditionally, credentials have been luxury goods. But by the beginning of the 21st century, most academic credentials have become devalued, mass-produced commodities.

For decades, there have been two camps of social scientists battling over this issue. On the one hand, cultural critics have documented how college credentials signal mostly higher levels of schooling, which continues to exist as an exclusive luxury good. On the other hand, human capital theorists have documented how college credentials also signal higher levels of knowledge and skills, which increase the economic value of students in the labor market (Caplan 2018; Grubb and Lazerson 2004). Generally, these two academic schools do not acknowledge each other's research.

But some economists, like Bryan Caplan (2018), have tried to find a middle ground between these two warring academic camps. Caplan argued that the value of educational credentials is based on both human capital and the signaling of social status (see also Labaree 1997). In an insightful book, Caplan (2018) argued that credentials allow students to access advanced levels of education, especially higher education, which enables further investment in more advanced forms of human capital, like graduate and professional schools, which then enable higher forms of elite social status.

So, with the twin developments of mass schooling and the massification of higher education in the late 20th century, and the intensification of globalization and the creation of global labor markets in the late 20th and early 21st century, what has been the effect of increased college graduates who have earned more and more credentials? What has happened to the value of the once scarce commodity of college credentials? Looking at both human capital theory and social status theory, the outcomes have been mixed, at best. For most students, the outcomes have been negative.

To understand this riddle, it is helpful to look at East Asian history. For over a thousand years, schooling in China and Korea has been a rigged, ritualistic charade that provided only the "myth of opportunity" for most students

(Chaffee 1995, 17; Mu, Dooley and Luke 2019). The Chinese aristocracy invented schooling as an ideological façade that facilitated the maintenance of a hereditary aristocracy and the virtual enslavement of the majority of laborers in the imperial economy (Chaffee 1995).

The Chinese model of schooling was later adopted by vassal states and neighboring cultures through a mixture of hard and soft power. The Chinese system later influenced the creation of the modern bureaucratic school system in Prussia in 19th century Europe, which also sought to develop new methods of human capital formation to foster the powerful Prussian state.

Most American and Western European consumers believe that schooling, particularly postsecondary and professional schooling, creates a grand "ladder of opportunity" based on individual initiative, hard work, and "meritocracy" (Dench 2006; Markovits 2019; Sandel 2020). If you are willing to work hard enough, anyone can succeed at schooling and at life, and everyone has a chance at reaching the top through earning academic credentials.

But is this true? Or, in fact, is the opposite true? Does higher education exacerbate social and economic inequalities? Does credentialism actually limit social mobility by rewarding the rich much more than the middle class or poor? This book will examine these questions in detail. The answers may surprise you.

While many politicians and pundits have praised higher education in the U.S. and other developed democracies as a meritocratic system that enables all students to compete fairly in the labor market, the reality is much darker (Markovits 2019; Sandel 2020). Higher education is not an unqualified good, and never has been. Climbing the ladder of success through schooling has been costly and risky for students, and it has never guaranteed labor market success.

Economist Anthony Carnevale recently argued that the U.S. is "not a meritocracy, it is more and more an aristocracy posing as a meritocracy" (qtd. in Berman 2019, para. 1). Professor of law Daniel Markovits (2019) does believe that the U.S. is a meritocracy, but he argues it is a rigged, "sham" meritocracy that "blocks the middle class from opportunity. Then it blames those who lose a competition for income and status that, even when everyone plays by the rules, only the rich can win" (viii). Most people blindly believe that schools reward hard work and talent, when in fact schools unfairly enable the wealthy to solidify their power and privilege.

If institutions of higher education don't teach students useful knowledge or skills, and if college credentials have become a devalued commodity, then what is to be done? We will briefly discuss the answer to this question in the conclusion. This issue is also discussed in the companion volume, *Can We Measure What Matters Most?* There are no easy answers.

Chapter 1

Public Opinion Surveys

From Managing the Herd to Consumer Satisfaction

The oldest and most popular educational accountability metric has been student grades, which are produced by teachers in the classroom. But due to the unreliability of this metric, policy makers and school administrators have become more focused on other accountability measurements over the past several decades. This was discussed in volume one of this series, *Can We Measure What Matters Most?* Currently, one of the most widely used accountability instruments in higher education is the consumer survey, which has become a central tool for evaluating teachers.

Educational administrators first started using consumer surveys as an accountability instrument for public schools in the late 19th century. About the same time, professors began to use surveys with students in higher education in order to evaluate the quality of teachers and student learning. But it wasn't until the late 20th and early 21st centuries that student evaluation surveys would become one of the most important accountability tools for institutions of higher education in the United States.

But before we investigate the validity of this tool as an accountability instrument in higher education, which we will do in the chapters that follow, we first need to understand the history of public surveys in the late 19th and early 20th centuries. Who used these instruments, and for what purposes?

We will also investigate the theoretical assumptions researchers used to justify these instruments as management tools. In doing so, we will investigate the underlying theoretical model that supposedly validated the use of public surveys as political, economic, and educational instruments of managerial control. Finally, we will end with a discussion of how these theoretical assumptions began to change in the early 20th century with the development of the new psychology and the discovery of individual agency.

1

MANAGING THE HERD

As complex K–12 public school systems were first being developed, educational administrators wanted to establish objective and numerical "norms, standards, and scales" to quantitatively rate and compare the effectiveness of schools in the United States, especially urban schools serving the majority of students (Tyack and Hansot 1982, 160; Tyack 1974; Cremin 1961; Labaree 2005; Labaree 2011).

Over the first few decades of the 20th century, educational historians David Tyack and Elisabeth Hansot (1982) explained how the "scientific, comparative survey would sweep the nation as a kind of crusade" (161). Policy makers and school administrators believed that consumer survey data was a cheap and valid source of data that could revolutionize the management of schools.

School evaluation surveys were mostly designed and administered by university researchers who used these statistical instruments to report on various metrics of public schooling. Professors used surveys as a source of data to test their theories and publish their research. Policy makers and school administrators used survey reports as an accountability instrument to gauge the effectiveness of schools. And school administrators used these surveys as public relations campaign in order to publicize public schools as a worthy recipient of tax dollars.

George Strayer, a professor at Teachers College, Columbia University, led one of the most important university research institutes in charge of these early 20th century survey projects. He argued that evaluation surveys were not really research instruments and that they could not be used to accurately measure or evaluate schools. He explained that surveys could not address the most important problems that needed to be fixed, nor could they confirm which parts of schools were working properly.

Instead, Strayer argued, school surveys were designed more as policy and publicity instruments, which could be used to shape public opinion and rally political support around reformist initiatives, which would then supposedly increase the efficiency and effectiveness of public schools (Tyack and Hansot 1982, 163).

An early 20th century education professor at Johns Hopkins University described surveys as a way of "rating and standardizing" schools in order to "mold public opinion in its constructive attitude toward education" (qtd. in Tyack and Hansot 1982, 160). From the start, it seems, school surveys were more of an instrument of political propaganda rather than a research tool.

Up until the 1950s and '60s, most social scientists held deeply skeptical and antidemocratic beliefs about the "mass" of uneducated citizens who seemed to be destined for no other social purpose then to be manual laborers ruled over by their social and political betters. There was a widespread, pessimistic belief that most adolescents were not capable of learning much in school because those who were born to labor would never—or should never—rise above their lowly social origins.

The purpose of schools, especially public schools in urban areas, to take a phrase from Thomas Jefferson, was to enable the "best geniuses" to be "raked from the rubbish" (qtd. in Greene 1988, 28–29). Teachers did what teachers do, and only the truly capable students would naturally succeed, learning what they were told to learn, and thereby rise through the academic ranks to their predestined station in life. The "rubbish," on the other hand, were fated for lowly lives serving their betters, so they were expected to drop out of school once they learned the basics of reading, writing, and arithmetic, if they were capable of learning anything at all.

These antidemocratic views were also reflected in public opinion surveys that social scientists used for politics, business, and education. One of the first social scientists to study public opinion was Edward Bernays ([1928] 2005). He helped establish the modern field of public relations (PR) and, together with Walter Lippmann, he helped popularized the term "propaganda," which was an information technology designed in the early 20th century to manipulate public opinion and behavior.

Like many educators at the time (Gutek 1984), Bernays believed propaganda to be nearly identical to the practice of schooling: "The only difference between 'propaganda' and 'education,' really, is in the point of view. The advocacy of what we believe in is education. The advocacy of what we don't believe in is propaganda" (qtd. in Tye 1998, 97). In both cases, the fundamental belief behind both education and propaganda at the time was that people were ignorant and irrational and popular opinions could be "manufactured" by experts who knew how to "manipulate the human mind" (Goodwin 2014, 29; Hagel, Brown and Davison 2010, 35).

Only knowledgeable authorities could determine what was true and good. And these experts would decide what information was important for students, citizens, or consumers to know, whether it be truth or a noble lie (Goodwin 2014, 29–30; Hagel, Brown and Davison 2010, 35). The "mass," who were the objects of education or propaganda, would believe what they were told to believe because they were ignorant and easily manipulated sheep who could not think for themselves.

Bernays echoed the thoughts of 19th century social scientists, like sociologist Edward A. Ross, who asserted that political leaders and scientific experts were "opinion makers" who rightfully led the masses for the best interests of all (qtd. in Sklansky 2002, 203). Ross' major sociological treatise was titled, *Social Control: A Survey of the Foundations of Order*. Ross believed that "many a man thinks he makes up his mind, whereas, in truth, it is made up for him" (qtd. in Sklansky 2002, 204; see also Goodwin 2014).

For much of human history, aristocratic social conservatives have believed that the majority of human beings were herd animals who were largely determined by their biological nature and cultural traditions to think and act like timid sheep. Thus, conservatives believed that the majority of humans were in need of aristocratic shepherds to lead the flock. The ancient Greek philosopher Aristotle was one of the first to systematically codify this belief. He declared, "Some men are by nature free, and others slaves, and that for these latter slavery is both expedient and right" (qtd. in Lerner 1993, 6).

This belief sometimes took benevolent forms, but it often led to aggressive authoritarianism, and later in the 20th century it lead to fascism. The proslavery apologist and early 19th century American sociologist George Fitzhugh once proclaimed that "the rabble" was "only made to be taxed and whipped" (qtd. in Sklansky 2002, 95). Building on the myth of natural elites (Tye 1998, 94–95), 19th century social scientists and philosophers, like Fitzhugh, Herbert Spencer, and William Graham Sumner, theoretically formalized and propagated the idea of ignorant masses who needed to be led with pseudo-scientific terms and gave it the veneer of scientific legitimacy (Lears 1994, 198).

Social scientists in the 19th century argued that most human beings were part of an aggregate superorganism called "the mass" or "the masses," which made "the average man" subservient to the "group mind" (Tye 1998, 73; Sklansky 2002, 133). In 1841, Charles Mackay published one of the first books published on this topic, *Extraordinary Popular Delusions and the Madness of Crowds*, which devoted a section to the Dutch "Tulipmania" of the 1630s to help prove his point.

Nineteenth century social scientists believed that the majority of human beings were ignorant, unrefined, and uneducated (Gerzema and Lebar 2008, 5). Thus, the masses were governed by unpredictable "impulses, habits, and emotions" (Tye 1998, 73). This meant that the majority of human beings needed to be ruled by their superiors for their own protection, and the good of all. As Fitzhugh once explained,

> Men are not born physically, morally, or intellectual equal. . . . The weak in mind or body require guidance, support and protection; they must obey and work for those who protect and guide them—they have a natural right to guardians, committees, teachers or masters . . . some were born with saddles on their backs, and others booted and spurred to ride them, and the riding does them good. (qtd. in Sklansky 2002, 96)

This belief naturally advanced the interests of traditional elites, who, as a master class, benefited most from the inequitable status quo of feudal societies.

One of the most important 19th century scientists to propagate this view was the French psychologist Gustave Le Bon ([1895] 1995). He argued that the majority of human beings think and act as "crowds" (44). They are driven by a "collective mind" (44), which draws upon shared "instincts, passions, and feelings" (48).

Le Bon argued that the average individual gives into "collective halluci- nations" and becomes an "automaton," losing all individual will or identity (62). As part of a crowd, the average person becomes a "barbarian" (52), driven by "simple and extreme sentiments" (73) and making "stupid" choices (49)—just "like women" (70), who were the epitome of irrationality for 19th century male social scientists.

"The destinies of peoples," Le Bon asserted, were "determined" by their "character" and their "race," not by their creed or their government. The implications were clear: Popular sovereignty, democracy, and public educa- tion were a fool's errand because the masses were naturally inferior and thus destined to be ruled by their biological and social superiors (108–9).

During the 19th and early 20th centuries, both liberals and social conserva- tives, and even some on the radical left, held this deeply entrenched point of view. Mark Twain (1962) famously declared, "hardly a man in the world has an opinion on morals, politics, and religion that he got otherwise than through his associations and sympathies" (24).

In an early study on public opinion, which drew upon the psychology of Le Bon, Edward Bernays ([1923] 2011) explained how the average person did not make their own judgments. Bernays believed that most people just parroted "dogmatic expressions accepted on the authority of his parents, his teachers, his church, and of his social, his economic and other leaders" (88).

Bernays' contemporary, Walter Lippmann ([1922] 1997), a journalist and early neoliberal philosopher who helped develop the field of public opinion, also believed that the mass of human beings were "mentally children or bar- barians" (48). Lippmann argued that people were "absolutely illiterate," and therefore "feeble-minded" (48; see also Goodwin 2014). The average person lived in a "pseudo-environment" of cultural dogma, according to Lippmann, being pushed back and forth by traditions and cultural authorities (10).

The novelist Ann Rand shared this view. She asserted, "What is the people but millions of puny, shriveled, helpless souls, that have no thoughts of their own, no dreams of their own, no will of their own, who eat and sleep and chew helplessly the words put into their mildewed brains" (qtd. in Gray 2018, 48). In the early 20th century, the philosopher John Dewey critically sum- marized this widespread conservative belief: It reduced society to "a mere mass" and the individual citizen to "a mere minced morsel of this mass" (qtd. in Ryan 1995, 103).

Even John Stuart Mill shared these views. He was a radical liberal in the 19th century who advocated for women's rights and the enfranchisement of the working class, but Mill also believed that the average person was ideologically determined by his or her "station" in life and by "custom" (qtd. in Lebergott 1993, 16). Mill asserted that the average person was unconsciously determined by "the deep slumber of decided opinion" (qtd. in Gray 2018, 37) and therefore, "like[s] in crowds," rather than being capable of independent thought (qtd. in Lebergott 1993, 16).

This is why Mill thought that political freedom should be restricted to only "human beings in the maturity of their faculties," which excluded children and people from "backward states of society" (qtd. in Gray 2018, 91). And yet, Mill was a progressive liberal who advocated for public schooling for all as a way of elevating the faculties of traditionally marginalized and oppressed groups of people, like women, the poor, and people of color (Rosenberg forthcoming, 18).

Early social scientists, like Bernays, Lippmann and the economist Joseph Schumpeter, believed themselves to be knowledgeable authorities who could not only measure public opinion, because it was transparent and stereotypical, but they also believed they could manipulate public opinion and direct it towards more enlightened or despotic ends (Ryan 1995, 209, 216; Tye 1998, 92; Lears 1994, 206, 244; Goodwin 2014). The economist John Kenneth Galbraith called this emerging technocratic elite the "skilled engineer-managers" (qtd. in Breit and Ransom 1998, 173).

In 1915, the American Association of University Professors explained how university professors, the enlightened sages who were training the skilled engineer-managers, saw themselves as experts who could "correct the errors of popular opinion" and "retrain" the ignorant masses (Fish 2019, 86). Academic experts and policy makers thought they could mold public opinion by creating predetermined choices for citizens and consumers.

Thus, the only role that most people played in governing their own lives was saying "yes or no" to the restricted choices that the experts offered (Ryan 1995, 216; Goodwin 2014). This elitist belief laid the intellectual foundation for the modern capitalist institutions of business management (Khurana 2007; Stewart, 2009), advertising (Lears 1994; Marchand 1985) and the field of public relations (Tye 1998; Ewen 1996), as well as for modern public schooling (Tyack and Hansot 1982, 107; Cremin 1961; Labaree 2005).

As historian Jackson Lears (1994) explained, "Like other aspiring professions of the era, advertising executives participated in the regnant fantasy that 'we' (the managerial elite in question) had acquired the capacity to predict and control 'them' (the consumers) through 'social science'" (206). Many economists, like Thorstein Veblen and Alvin H. Hansen, believed that consumers didn't "act on their free will. . . . Consumer wants are no longer a matter of individual choice. They are mass-produced" (qtd. in Breit and Ransom 1998, 100).

Most educational researchers and school administrators espoused the same elitist rationale for using public opinion surveys. They wanted to not only evaluate schools and teachers but also shape and control public discourse about schooling (Tyack and Hansot 1982, 163, 166; Cremin 1961; Labaree 2005). Historian Michelle Murphy (2017) pointed out that surveys have never been objective "snapshots" (66). Instead, they have been "provocations toward modifying and scripting the behaviors or feelings they tracked" (66).

For the first half of the 20th century, social scientists preferred the objective measurement of public opinion through quantitative analysis. They naturally assumed that most people could not clearly or accurately express their beliefs. As economist Gary Becker once explained, "You can't believe what people *say*" (emphasis in original; qtd. in Caplan 2007, 117).

When early social scientists conducted qualitative research, and spoke to actual human beings to understand their beliefs, they tended to aggregate responses into stereotypical typologies, rather than actually strive to understand the idiosyncratic meaning of any individual's words. Social scientists believed that most individuals were unthinking automatons who operated as part of a hive mind. Therefore, most people did what they were told to do, either by the cultural authorities that ruled their lives, or through emotionally driven mob activities, which often led to violence and destruction.

Up until the mid-20th century, most social scientists did not listen too closely or dig too deeply into the meaning of words when common people were interviewed for a research study (Rosenberg 1988). Many social scientists still don't. Modern qualitative methodology was pioneered by 19th century historians and philologists (Turner 2014), but it wasn't fully developed until the emergence of cultural anthropology and the professionalized practice of ethnography in the mid-20th century (Kuper 1999; Hammersley and Atkinson 1995).

Instead of listening to and interpreting the nuanced meanings of respondents' words, most social scientists treated survey responses as transparent, stereotypical data that easily fit into a researcher's preestablished and "essentialist" theoretical categories. Rather than test theories by what people did or said, researchers usually assumed their theories were valid constructs that explained human thought and behavior. Thus, most qualitative data was interpreted to fit the theory, rather than trying to adjust the theory to fit the data (Engelke 2018, 49).

While all social scientists believed that public opinion could be easily manipulated, many scientists balked at proposals for outright propaganda and coercion. Such crass measures of control seemed to cross the line between impartial science into authoritarian politics. And yet, many scientists and journalists, like Bernays and Lippmann, readily used their skills to serve manipulative political causes or business initiatives (Goodwin 2014).

Despite a pretense of objectivity, social scientists gradually discovered that opinion surveys were not neutral data collection tools. They also discovered that the validity of these instruments was questionable from the start (Igo 2007; Weissberg 2002; Lears 1994, 244; Rosenberg 1988, 33; Pollan 2008, 74). While early social surveys were cloaked in the aura of science, pollsters' calculations and conclusions were "crude" and "idiosyncratic" (Weissberg 2002, 2; see also Pollan 2008, 74).

Historian Sarah E. Igo (2007) explained how "pollsters were in the business not simply of querying but of creating and constantly remaking 'the people'" they were questioning (149). Historian Jackson Lears (1994) elucidated how business leaders and government officials used public opinion surveys to help "set the boundaries of public discourse" by "rendering public debate more manageable and predictable" (244–45).

Psychologist Jerome Bruner (1983) conducted one of the first scientific studies of public surveys, and he argued that "whatever public opinion is, it is not a sum of the opinions of individuals" (45). This is partly due to the fact that most people express "unreliable" opinions because they don't really know what they believe or how best to express their beliefs into words (Rosenberg 1988, 4).

When social scientists construct survey questionnaires, they are always engaging in a "political act," according to political scientist Robert Weissberg (2002, viii). Every survey question either implicitly or explicitly takes a side in a "political struggle" over cultural legitimacy in terms of who would control the description of social reality (5–6). For example, how survey questions are phrased, and in what order, can have an effect on the responses given. One study found that simply rearranging the questions on a survey can "significantly affect the attitudes expressed" (Rosenberg 1988, 4).

Over the course of the 20th century, social scientists began to understand that surveys were always biased in two fundamental ways. However, many social scientists weren't really concerned with understanding the implications of this bias until the end of the 20th century.

First, the creators of the survey instrument were biased not only by their research objectives, but also by their social, economic, and political assumptions. Researchers' prior beliefs effected the questions asked and language used. But this wasn't a problem if you assumed you had superior knowledge and insight, as most scientists did.

Second, and perhaps more importantly, survey respondents always gave biased answers based on their subjective perception, beliefs, prejudices, and ignorance, which were shaped by cultural authorities and traditions (Banaji and Greenwald 2013; Eberhardt 2020). But this wasn't a problem if you thought you could control respondents, enlighten their thinking, or shape their responses for your own purposes.

These biases were largely glossed over by early 20th century social scientists because they thought they could control these flaws as easily as they believed that they could record and interpret public opinion. When common sense dictates the parameters of your research project, it doesn't take much theoretical sophistication or skill to measure the wetness of water.

THE NEW PSYCHOLOGY AND THE DISCOVERY OF INDIVIDUAL AGENCY AND BIAS

And yet, not all social scientists held such pessimistic beliefs about human nature. Pragmatist philosophers and social scientists in the U.S. developed a "new psychology" of human agency in the late 19th century, in particular the psychologist William James and his disciple, the philosopher John Dewey (Sklansky 2002, ch. 5; Menand 2001, 370; Ryan 1995, 75; Goodwin 2014, 31). In Germany, the gestalt psychologists Max Wertheimer, Kurt Lewin, Wolfgang Kohler, and Kurt Koffka also explored the neglected topic of human agency (Olson and Hergenhahn 2009, 255–59).

These scientists and philosophers did not see human beings as passive herd animals who reproduced groupthink and who could be easily manipulated by authorities. Instead, these researchers believed that "people are the agents of their own destinies" (Menand 2001, 371).

In 1878, William James explained, "The knower is an actor, and co-efficient of the truth . . . [humans] help to *make* the truth which they declare" (emphasis in original; qtd. in Menand 2001, 357). The new school of psychologists believed that "the brain actively transforms sensory stimulation," which meant that subjective knowledge and decision-making, the "powers of the mind," were integral to human behavior (Olson and Hergenhahn 2009, 260).

Pragmatists believed that both researcher and the researched had a stake in the game of creating knowledge and defining the social, economic, and political parameters of a culture. With this new insight in mind, the anthropologist Ruth Benedict criticized traditional social scientific methodology.

She argued that old-school scientists assumed a clear, epistemological distinction between the researcher, who was the authoritative knowledge creator, and the researched, who was the passive object to be studied and described (Engelke 2018, 41). Benedict (1934) argued that ethnographic research was not possible if researchers created "distinctions between ourselves and the primitive, ourselves and the barbarian, ourselves and the pagan" (3).

Benedict agreed with Bernays and Lippmann that people were imprinted by their culture with group beliefs, traditions, and rituals. However, she did not exempt the social scientist from cultural bias like they did. She agreed with her mentor, the anthropologist Franz Boas, that everyone wears "cultural glasses" to see and interpret the world (Engelke 2018, 31).

Benedict (1934) criticized social scientists who falsely believed they were exempt from culture, and she pointed out their biased feelings of "superiority," their "racial prejudices," and their cultural "snobbery" (8–9). She believed that *both* the researcher and the researched were biased by culture and subjectivity, and *both* were active constructors of knowledge (Hammersley and Atkinson 1995). This made creating objective knowledge problematic, if not impossible.

Thus, by the latter half of the 20th century, social scientists and psychologists began to talk less of cultural conformity, hive minds, and authoritative control. Instead, they began to attribute more personal agency to individuals and groups in their thought and action. Psychologists began breaking open the black box of human subjectivity in order to study the interrelationships between consciousness, rationality, emotions, decision-making, and goal-directed behavior (Damasio 1999; Kahneman 2011; Sapolsky 2017).

At the same time, political scientists and economists began studying the real-life choices and behavior of citizens and consumers, rather than just engaging in armchair theorizing. Slowly, the scientific consensus turned from believing in a stereotypical hive mind to believing that individuals were largely rational agents who optimized their material interests and psychological well-being, which through the hidden-hand of the market or the visible hand of government, created stable and predictable social, economic, and political patterns that could be elucidated through statistical analysis (Salsburg 2001).

But while most scientists began to assume that human beings were rational agents, a smaller group of psychologists decided to focus on the perceptual and cognitive biases in human decision-making, which caused irrational and self-defeating behavior (Lewis 2017; Kahneman 2011; Banaji and Greenwald 2013; Eberhardt 2020). Other psychologists focused on how "choices are a function of context," which means that "preferences are not fixed, global, and stable, but are instead adaptive to a wide range of factors" (Sunstein 1997, 6,14).

These psychologists discovered, as Jerome Bruner (1983) explained, that "we can only sample lightly from the biased input that our senses permit us to apprehend" (66). Rather than knowing the world objectively, we know the world through a subjective process, whereby we filter, sort, and construct our own personal and cultural realities that are more or less accurate descriptions of the objective world (66).

This led cognitive scientists, political scientists, and behavioral economists to declare that "the logical, rational, and reasonable capacities of individuals are grossly overstated or simply wrong . . . people are likely to be illogical, irrational, and unreasonable in ways that limit their capacities for autonomous self-direction and effective collaboration with others" (Rosenberg 2017, 2–3; Rosenberg forthcoming).

Psychologists paradoxically found (Mercier and Sperber 2017, 4) that while human beings do have the ability to assert individual agency and make rational decisions, most people also display "systematic" biases that lead to poor decisions and irrational behavior (Ariely 2008; Lodge and Taber 2013; Hibbing, Smith and Alford 2014; Banaji and Greenwald 2013; Eberhardt 2020). Economist Bryan Caplan (2007) reviewed the psychological research and found that "bias is the rule, not the exception" in human perception and decision-making (29).

We all have a self-centered "my side" bias and a group-centered tribal bias, which interferes with our ability to perceive and understand objective reality. Our biases also interfere with our ability to make rational decisions (Stanovich 2009, ch. 8; Mercier and Sperber 2017; Banaji and Greenwald 2013; Eberhardt 2020). As psychologists Daniel Kahneman and Amos Tversky sardonically explained: "Our comforting conviction that the world makes sense rests on a secure foundation: Our almost unlimited ability to ignore our ignorance" (Kahneman 2011, 201).

Chapter 2

The Premise of Student Evaluation Surveys

Measuring Teacher Effectiveness

As psychologists discovered more about human agency and bias, educational psychologists began to question the commonsense theory of teaching and learning, especially the widespread belief that students were the passive recipients of learning. Traditionally, most people have assumed that teachers drive the learning process through instruction, and that students simply learn whatever they are told to learn.

But by the late 20th century, psychologists wanted to understand the process of learning in more detail. They wanted to discover what was actually happening in students' brains. Rather than assume students were learning, psychologists wanted to see *how* and *if* students actually learned in schools.

At the same time, educational psychologists also began to question the traditional theory of teacher effectiveness because this theory had ignored student agency and subjectivity by overstating the control that teachers supposedly had in the learning process. Psychologists discovered that teachers were not in control of student learning.

Students' subjective beliefs, motivations, and feelings, in conjunction with their behavior and their social and physical environment, mattered much more in the learning process than anything the teacher did. Perhaps most importantly, researchers discovered that other elements in a students' culture, especially their interactions with peers and parents (Rogoff 1990; Rogoff 2003), were much more important in shaping human development and academic success than the influence of teachers and schools.

But while the complex determinants of student learning were being uncovered and documented by researchers by the late 20th century, the administrative control of teachers through accountability measurements was being intensified, and teachers were losing some control over their classrooms. In higher education, for example, once the importance of student agency and subjectivity became widely acknowledged in the 1980s and 1990s, student evaluation surveys became one of the primary methods of assessments for colleges and universities, although surveys had been in limited use for over a century (Johnson 2003, 140; Schneider 2017, 152).

In some institutions and for certain kinds of teachers, like adjunct instructors in community colleges and nonselective universities, student surveys became the only method of assessment. These high-stakes instruments largely determined if a teacher was hired, fired, or promoted. While nearly all educational administrators and many teachers seem to believe that student surveys offer insight into student learning and instructor teaching (Schneider 2017, 152), researchers have overwhelmingly found that these surveys do not measure either variable directly or very effectively.

There are two basic types of student evaluation surveys that are now in use. Most institutions of higher education use both. The first type is a standard questionnaire where students rate each item on a five-or six-point scale. Students record their scores on a paper form or through an internet portal, usually at the end of a term or semester.

Standard survey questions ask students to rate various aspects of the course, such as course format, accuracy or usefulness of exams, course goals, and challenging nature or difficulty of the course. Other questions ask students to rate various aspects of the instructor, such as encouraging questions, encouraging critical thinking, and grading stringency, as well as more personal qualities, like instructor communication, concern, knowledge, organization, enthusiasm, and availability to meet in person.

Finally, students are asked to rate various aspects of themselves and their learning, such as prior interest in material, relevance of the subjectto student, class attendance, completion of coursework, prior knowledge, how much was learned, and their expected grade. Once completed, survey scores are then aggregated and statically analyzed, usually by computing averages or weighted averages and comparing a teacher's mean scores with department and institutional means.

The second type of survey is qualitative. This type of survey either asks students open-ended questions or provides a blank space so that students can write down whatever comments they want. Many students choose not to complete the qualitative survey component because this type of instrument requires more effort. When students do write a comment, usually they do not write complete thoughts in sentences. Instead, they list fractured comments, some of which are only a few words in length, like "good class" or "hated readings".

Most administrators seem to give more weight to the quantitative student surveys because the average score is expressed as an exact number with two decimal points. This makes the rating seems more objective. It is also easier to use this number to make evaluative comparisons between teachers, classes, and departments. The qualitative survey data is selectively used, if at all, because it takes more time for administrators to read and process, and because of the messy, indeterminant, and nonsensical nature of many student comments.

Both types of student evaluation surveys provide interesting data on many important aspects of teaching, learning, and the curriculum. In particular, these surveys enable students to share subjective opinions about their educational experience and their emotions, which can be very useful data, especially for teachers. Taken as a whole, these instruments help open up both the black box of the classroom and also the smaller black box of the student's brain in terms of their learning experience.

Student evaluation surveys have become one of the most important accountability tools to assess instructors in higher education for the purposes of employment, retention, and promotion, especially for nontenure track lecturers and adjuncts. These instruments are popular with educational administrators because they provide an easy and cost-effective way to gather data on teaching and learning.

The quantitative type of survey also has the veneer of objectivity, which enables administrators to easily make evaluative comparisons and assessments between instructors, classes, and departments. Given their low cost in terms of financial resources and time, it is likely that more kinds of schools, especially high schools, will start using student surveys as accountability tools in the near future.

Besides the two types of formal surveys designed by school administrators, there are also other types of informal student evaluation surveys that can be found on the internet, like *ratemyprofessors.com*. Researchers have largely ignored this type of assessment tool because internet student surveys are highly unreliable, as are all web-based surveys. There is no transparency in terms of who uses these websites and why. Plus, these websites are for-profit businesses, some based on advertisement and others on subscription fees, so they should not be considered a legitimate source of data.

Most of the time, website reviews are unreliable and dishonest (Maheshwari 2019). One of the most popular websites for customer reviews is Yelp. This rating company has been widely criticized by many businesses for running an extortion racket, like the Mafia, manipulating reviews based on how much businesses pay for Yelp's services ("How One Restaurant" 2014). It's unclear how many other consumer-rating websites may be manipulating data or presenting falsified reviews (Maheshwari 2019).

Like other forms of web-based polling, *ratemyprofssors.com* has a high selection bias because only certain types of students will use these websites for very biased reasons, which makes the data generated very skewed and nonrepresentative. When it comes to rating professors online, it seems only the most enthusiastic or the most irritated students are motivated to air their opinions, which are often expressed with extreme language. Only a small fraction of students from any given class seem to leave web reviews because there is no real incentive to do so, other than to praise or vent.

There is also no quality control. Who knows if reviewers are actually students? Or if users were actually enrolled in the course of the professor they are rating? Of if reviewers were being compensated with quid pro quo incentives (see for example Maheshwari 2019)?

And yet, despite these many failings, some incompetent administrators still use these unreliable websites to make important employment decisions. Take for example Howard Grimes, Dean of the College of Sciences at the University of Texas at San Antonio. He used *ratemyprofessors.com* when he made a highly public decision about the possible firing of a teacher at this university because of student complaints (Grimes 2018). In a formal announcement broadcast to every member of the University of Texas at San Antonio, Dean Grimes naively declared that his supposed due diligence was nothing more than googling this untrustworthy website. And this was a Dean of the College of Sciences at a research university. We will discuss the incompetence of school administrators more below, and this topic is also fully explored in the companion volume, *Can We Measure What Matters Most?*

Student surveys are popular with administrators because they are quick and cheap accountability instruments. Students like them as well because they reinforce a broader social and economic trend, whereby citizens and consumers have been taking a more active public role in sharing their opinions about the products and services that affect their lives (Kellerman 2012, 38).

Since the 1990s, consumer-rating systems have become a widespread method for businesses to engage consumers and better meet their demands ("Barely" 2018, 65; Maheshwari 2019). With the development of the internet, and later social media, consumer-rating systems have become an important marketing and consumer satisfaction tool. As business management professor Barbara Kellerman (2012) points out, there are now "countless, relentless surveys that ask people everywhere for their opinions about everything and everyone" (39).

Every business, nonprofit organization, and many government agencies now take the traditional doctrine of consumer sovereignty as gospel (Breit and Ransom 1998, 10): The *sovereign Customer (with a capital C)* is always right. Thus, businesses are exhorted to listen closely to consumer opinions, no matter how nonsensical or contradictory. Because of the convenience of social media and web peer-to-peer reviews, there are now consumer ratings for every kind of product and service. Value has been reduced to a numberof the average "likes" or stars bestowed by satisfied or dissatisfied consumers.

Many people have become empowered by businesses and social-media marketers to think of themselves as "tastemakers" because they can publicly judge products and services through the internet (Anderson 2008, 99). But as many social scientists have pointed out, consumers "have no incentive to do their job well" ("Barely" 2018, 65). Thus, consumer ratings are not often fair or accurate.

Some consumer comments are irrational, nonsensical, or just plain lies (Maheshwari 2019). Consumer feedback is often full of emotion, cognitive biases, and omissions. Plus, many consumers complain about "factors beyond a service provider's control" ("Barely" 2018, 65).

The pressure of consumer-rating systems has been especially hard on small businesses, the self-employed, and contract workers, who are "at the mercy of the assessment system," which can seriously harm their employment prospects ("I Am Number" 2020, 55). This has created "a host of personal, social and economic anxieties" for workers, especially for self-employed contractors in the new "gig" economy (55).

Since the early 21st century, administrators in higher education have joined the educational accountability movement by collecting data on teaching and learning, then using this data to evaluate teachers for employment purposes. One of the most important accountability instruments in higher education has been student surveys. But in using these assessment tools, college administrators have largely ignored the serious problems of these data collection tools, such as validity and fairness.

While student evaluation surveys do collect interesting and important information that can be useful to educators and educational administrators, these tools have a lot of validity problems. Student evaluation surveys, like all consumer-rating systems, are dangerous tools because they often are improperly designed, calibrated, administered, and interpreted. When improperly used, evaluation surveys are unfair and demoralizing to teachers.

When it comes to education, consumer satisfaction surveys can punish effective teachers, reward the incompetent, bias institutional assessment metrics, reduce the quality of teaching, and hinder student learning—all of which leads to the corruption of education.

THE TRADITIONAL TEACHER EFFECTIVENESS THEORY

Educational psychologist Hermann Henry Remmers (1928) conducted one of the first scholarly studies of student evaluation surveys used to evaluate the effectiveness of teachers. His research article "The Relationship between Students' Marks and Student Attitude toward Instructions" was groundbreaking. This study later became part of his book, *The College Professor as the Student Sees Him*, which was published one year later in 1929.

In his early work, Remmers (1928) established a clear relationship between the ratings that college students give their instructors and the grades that students earn. In a follow-up study, Remmers (1930) found the same correlation between teacher ratings and student course grades. Remmers also demonstrated this same correlation again in another follow-up study published two decades later (Remmers, Martin and Elliot 1949).

Over the last century, since Remmers original research was published, there have been hundreds of scientific studies of student evaluation surveys. Almost all of them have affirmed his same basic conclusion. Overall, there is a positive correlation between the ratings students give instructors and the expected course grades or actual course grades that students receive (Johnson 2003, 51).

While few educational researchers doubt this positive correlation, there has been a longstanding debate over two issues. The first is the theoretical mechanism that causes this correlation. The second is what this correlation means for the assessment of teaching and student learning.

The oldest theory to explain the causal link between student evaluation surveys and course grades has been called by some scholars the "teacher-effectiveness theory" (Johnson 2003, 48). This early scientific theory was a natural extension of the traditional faith that schooling simply worked as common sense dictated it should. Teachers teach, which leads students to learn whatever the teacher tells them to learn. This assumption was based on the behaviorist research of psychologists like Edward L. Thorndike, Ivan Petrovich Pavlov, John B. Watson, and B. F. Skinner (Olson and Hergenhahn 2009; Domjan 2010).

Behaviorist psychologists focused, in the words of John B. Watson, on the "prediction and control of behavior" (qtd. in Olson and Hergenhahn 2009, 45). These psychologists had faith in "the omnipotent scientific method," as Ivan Petrovich Pavlov characterized it. They believed that science would enable complete knowledge of the objective world, which in turn would enable scientists to control the world and human behavior (qtd. in Olson and Hergenhahn 2009, 166).

These psychologists demonstrated the "simple facts," as Edward L. Thorndike pointed out, that controlled subjects will produce "gross bodily responses" to a stimulus. These responses could be produced either by a lab rat controlled by a scientist or by a student controlled by a teacher (qtd. in Olson and Hergenhahn 2009, 56). Thorndike demonstrated the "positive evidence of the absence of any general function of reasoning" (55). Rats, monkeys, or students did not think or reason. These controlled subjects merely reacted obediently to a stimulus applied by the proper authority.

Remmers' theory of teaching and learning rested on the simple, traditional faith that schooling works in the way everyone has always assumed it does. Early 20th century behaviorist psychology theoretically and empirically reinforced this traditional faith. Good teachers naturally and effectively produce student learning, which can be transparently and objectively measured by grades that are administered by teachers.

Therefore, highly successful students who have learned a lot will earn high grades. These students will also be able to recognize their own learning and the effectiveness of their teacher by seeing their grade. Thereby, successful students would then rate their good teachers with high marks on evaluation surveys.

The converse would also be true. Bad teachers produce little student learning, which results in low grades. Students who do not learn express their dissatisfaction with bad teaching by assigning lower teacher and course ratings on evaluation surveys. Simple, right?

Remmers' teacher-effectiveness theory is built on four traditional beliefs about schooling. First, teachers naturally and effectively transfer knowledge to students via a curriculum that automatically produces student learning. Second, student grades validly and objectively measure this learning. Third, students can transparently recognize their own learning and the effectiveness of their teacher. And finally, evaluation surveys validly and objectively measure the effectiveness of teaching, the curriculum, and student learning.

Over the past half-century, researchers have discovered that all of these traditional beliefs are false. But most school administrators and many teachers don't seem to know this. While some advocates of the teacher-effectiveness theory have been willing to admit that schooling is not as simple as tradition dictates, they have never strayed far from conventional wisdom.

For example, even Remmers admitted that student evaluation surveys do not produce uniformly accurate ratings. In one of his last studies, he found that student learning and course evaluation survey ratings were affected by students' perceptions and their prior academic ability. Remmers, Martin, and Elliot (1949) found that an instructor's communication style and the difficulty of the course material created a divergent effect on different kinds of students.

Specifically, the researchers found that a good teacher who taught difficult material with advanced technical terminology could be "held in high regard by his better students," while going "over the heads" of weaker students (25). Conversely, if a good teacher watered down the material, used basic language, and spent "an unlimited time in explaining relatively simple matters," then this teacher would be more "popular" with the weaker students, while alienating more advanced students (25).

Remmers and his colleagues concluded that good teachers could not be effective with both weak and strong students. Thus, good teachers routinely received both high and low student evaluation ratings. This data seemed to contradict Remmers' whole theory.

Remmers and his colleagues stumbled upon an inconvenient truth that they did not fully understand or deal with. They discovered that student evaluation ratings were determined more by the abilities and subjective bias of students rather than the quality of the teacher or the curriculum. Instead of conducting more research and changing their simplistic theory of teaching, Remmers and his colleagues decided to ignore these findings.

Remmers was a traditionalist. He continued to believe that his theory was largely correct and that this inconvenient data was an anomaly. He was not overly concerned with real-world complications because his theory had to be right—tradition dictates that it be right. Remmers still believed that student evaluation surveys were accurate measurements of teaching and learning, despite any discrepant scoring caused by different kinds of students.

Thus, for most of the 20th century, researchers, administrators, and teachers have all propagated the traditional belief in the efficiency of schooling, all the while believing that student evaluation surveys are a transparent method to record the natural, common sense phenomenon of student learning. Until the 1970s, almost all educational researchers have believed that measuring the effectiveness of teachers was like measuring the wetness of water: Simple, straightforward, and easy.

It was common sense that most students would do what they were told to do by their authoritative teachers, and that teachers would do what they were told to do by their authoritative school administrators. Educational researchers believed that those students who were innately capable would naturally become educated through schooling, and those students who failed should never have been in school in the first place.

ATTRIBUTION THEORY

Over the latter half of the 20th century, educational researchers discovered that the behaviorist assumptions (Olson and Hergenhahn 2009; Domjan 2010) behind the traditional teacher-effectiveness theory were only partially true, at best. A new generation of psychologists rediscovered the philosophical insights of the "new psychology" of human agency (Sklansky 2002, ch. 5; Menand 2001, 370), which was first developed in the late 19th century but largely forgotten by behaviorists.

Gestalt psychologists, like Kurt Lewin, Wolfgang Kohler, and Kurt Koffka, and early cognitive psychologists, like Jean Piaget, gradually realized that there was a lot more to student learning than reactionary behavioral responses to the commands of a teacher. By the 1950s and '60s, some psychologists had "rediscovered" the power of the human mind and this transformed scientists understanding of teaching and learning (Bruner 1983, 60; Gardner [1995] 2011b, 33).

The chemist and philosopher of science Michael Polanyi (1962) called this rediscovery of human subjectivity, "personal knowledge," which was different from the behaviorists search for objective knowledge. Polanyi argued that "into every act of knowing there enters a passionate contribution of the person knowing what is known, and this coefficient is no imperfection but a vital component in his knowledge" (vii–viii).

From the 1960s onward, psychologists and social scientists began to take subjective mental processes seriously. This rediscovery of human cognition was also accompanied by a "broader and deeper cultural movement to change the image of [human beings] from a passive receiver and responder to an active selector and constructor of experience" (Bruner 1983, 103; see also Rosenberg 1988, 9).

Gradually educational psychologists turned their focus away from the supposedly objective measures of intelligence scores on standardized tests and conditioned behavior. Instead, educational psychologists began to study student agency and identity in the learning process.

In particular, psychologists were especially interested in students' construction of self in relation to learning and schooling, and the construction of self through students' interactions with teachers, peers, and parents. Rather than focus on objective behavior, researchers turned their focus on the subjective perception and biased reasoning of students as these learners tried to make sense of their identity, their own behavior, and their environment.

One of the most important lines of research was focused on "attribution theory" (Gigliotti and Buchtel 1990). This field of study, as Bruner (1983) explained, focused on "what powers and traits people attributed to each other and under what conditions" (114). Attribution theory focused on how people "construct" their own individual and social worlds (114). Psychologists began to study "how people *saw* the world and themselves rather than how they or their world *were*, according to some objective criterion" (author's emphasis; 68).

The psychologist Martin Seligman upturned a half-century of behaviorism by proving that controlled subjects didn't primarily learn useful knowledge through conditioning—subjects learned helplessness. Subjects realized they were powerless to control their own life, which was being dictated by the authoritarian researcher (Olson and Hergenhahn 2009, 187), or in the case of students, the autocratic teacher.

Many teachers have assumed that high grades represent student learning when these marks are actually measuring hopelessness, despair, and depression. Many students are simply passive parrots playing school to please their teacher and their parents. Many students mindlessly demonstrate whatever the teacher wants to see or hear so that the pain or boredom of useless academic drills will stop.

One of the most important insights that psychologists discovered in the latter half of the 20th century was that all human beings perceive and judge the world with a "self-serving bias," which is tied to our evolutionary instincts for survival (Pinker 2011, 490). Psychologist Steven Pinker (2011) has explained how all people use "positive illusions" in order to "present the self in a positive light" (490, 511). Pinker (2011) summarized how

> hundreds of studies have shown that people overrate their health, leadership ability, intelligence, professional competence, sporting prowess, and managerial skills. People also hold the nonsensical belief that they are inherently lucky. Most people think they are more likely than the average person to attain a good first job, to have gifted children, and to live to a ripe old age. They also think that they are *less* likely than the average person to be the victim of an accident, crime, disease, depression, unwanted pregnancy, or earthquake. Why should people be so deluded? Positive illusions make people happier, more confident, and mentally healthier. (511–12)

In the context of schooling, educational psychologists found that many adolescents use their self-serving bias to construct a "good student" identity that can be at odds with actual learning and personal development. Psychologists have found that many students want to merely "look smart" and play school rather than to actually do the hard work of learning and growing (Dweck 2002, 24). Why? Because it is psychologically safe, and all humans want to feel safe (Edmondson 2012, 155; Edmondson 2019).

Most people want to maintain a positive self-image and high self-esteem, and rightly so. Life would be bleak if we all thought the worst of ourselves. But maintaining this optimistic outlook often requires believing in "positive illusions" about ourselves, rather than acknowledge the truth.

Most people have "unrealistically positive views" of their knowledge and abilities (Edmondson 2012, 155), which causes problems. For one, maintaining positive illusions keeps a lot of people from taking risks. Also, more troubling, our illusions keep us from "honestly acknowledging" our failures (155).

Professor of management and education Chris Argyris (1993) explained how these defensive behaviors are used in an effort to reduce the "causes of embarrassment or threat," but ultimately such behaviors don't work (15).

Why? Because these avoidance behaviors are "antilearning" techniques that "overprotect individuals" and "inhibit them from learning new actions" and growing as an individual (15, 19–20).

In schools, many students construct a positive identity as a "good student," and teachers reinforce this identity by enacting "anti-learning" rituals that do not challenge students in any way. This means teaching students how to play school rather than actually learning or growing as a person. Students build their self-esteem by getting high grades and praise from teachers and peers, rather than building knowledge or skill.

Thus, many students focus on the external learning product or outcome of an activity, which is often graded by the teacher. Students evaluate their grade by how it affects their self-esteem, rather than focusing on the learning process. Many students don't want to work hard to succeed and they dread critical feedback from the teacher and peers.

Like all of us, most students take shortcuts to quickly reach their desired end. Most students want to *feel* successful by conforming to the expectations of others, rather than work for the end that will actually make them successful in terms of gaining real knowledge or skills.

Many students put in the minimum amount of effort to preserve their good student identity, rather than learning. Students memorize whatever a teacher says, rather than critically thinking and growing as a person. Some students cheat on a test to receive a good grade without having to study. Both methods deliver the same end result as real learning with a fraction of the work.

In order to protect their positive identity, students actively seek to discount or ignore negative information or assessments that might damage their good student image. Psychologists call this process "dissonance theory" (Bruner 1983, 114) or the "confirmation bias" (Kahneman 2011). Researchers have documented how people focus on information that confirms their positive sense of self and prior beliefs, while distorting or discounting critical information that might be challenging. In order to protect their identity and enhance their self-esteem, many students embrace academic success and praise, while conversely, they distance themselves from negative criticism and academic failure.

For many students, this leads to self-limiting behavior. Psychologists call this "self-handicapping" (Pfeffer 2010, 13). Fearful students will usually maintain the status quo by focusing on what they already know or what they can already do because these learning activities are easier, more fun, and confirm their positive sense of self.

Conversely, fearful students will shy away from more difficult, challenging, or novel activities. These kinds of activities are difficult and they can lead to failure, which would damage students' self-esteem. Any "experience of failure" will put a fearful student's self-esteem "at risk" (13). So it's best to avoid trying.

Interestingly, researchers have found that student's self-esteem has dramatically increased since the 1960s (Twenge and Campbell 2009, 13). While at the same time, actual student learning and academic success has stalled, if not declined. Over the past several decades, students have become very concerned with creating a positive self-image and enhancing self-esteem, even to the point of narcissism and "grandiose fantasy" (4).

Psychologists have found a 30 percent increase in students' self-admiration since the early 1980s, with about 25 percent of adolescents scoring as narcissists (Twenge and Campbell 2009, 30). This rise in self-esteem and self-admiration has been caused in part by permissive parents who spoil their kids, constantly praise them, and call them "special," while demanding little in return (Kindlon 2001; Young-Eisendrath 2008). Many parents refuse to criticize their children, which leads to "self-absorbed" and "fragile" students who do not know how to work hard, and who break-down when given negative feedback by a teacher or a peer (Twenge and Campbell 2009, 83–84; Young-Eisendrath 2008).

This tangled relationship between student learning and positive self-esteem also affects teachers. Researchers have found that when students receive high grades in school, they are more likely to attribute those grades to their personal knowledge and skill because this reinforces their identity as a good student, which is tied to their positive self-image and high self-esteem.

Feeling good about themselves because of their achievement, many students tend to assign higher ratings to their teachers on evaluation surveys because the teacher validated their self-perception as a good student and enhanced their self-esteem. When a teacher's job depends on student satisfaction expressed on evaluation surveys, teachers are incentivized to keep the class easy and entertaining, assign less work, never challenge students, and keep grades high.

If teachers actually try to teach and challenge their students, this can cause problems. While education, especially higher education, is supposed to be built around a "culture of truth-telling," creating and maintaining this cultural norm is very difficult because truth can often be "unpleasant" to hear or deal with (Pfeffer 2015, 108). When students receive low grades, their identity as a student is challenged, they feel bad about themselves for not being smart, and their self-esteem falls.

Feeling ashamed and embarrassed, these students are more likely to psychologically distance themselves from failure by blaming external factors, such as the teacher, the content of the class, difficult assignments, or their peers. Thus, poorly performing students are much more likely to rate their teachers with low scores on evaluation surveys in an effort to push the blame away from themselves.

According to Steven Pinker (2011), "acknowledging a compromising truth about ourselves is among our most painful experiences" (490). Thus, when we judge other people's behavior, we filter their actions through our "self-serving bias" so that we preserve our positive sense of self at all costs, even if it means lying to ourselves or lying to others.

This self-serving bias can also be magnified in groups (Sunstein 2019; Banaji and Greenwald 2013; Eberhardt 2020). In one experiment, researchers set up a false wine tasting study to study how personal judgments can be biased by other people (Willer, Kuwabara and Macy 2009; Pinker 2011, 564–65). Participants were poured three glasses of wine from the same bottle, and one was spiked with vinegar to make it taste really bad. How would they react?

First, participants judged the wine on their own. Most said the vinegar wine tasted bad. Then they participated in a group discussion with some undercover research assistants who pretended to be consumers. These duplicitous agents falsely praised the vinegary wine. Interestingly, rather than stick to their own initial judgments, around half of the participants changed their private opinions and praised the vinegary wine because most of the group said it tasted great.

In another study, a group of undergraduates participated in a simulated academic discussion group that was supposedly for promising young scholars (Willer, Kuwabara and Macy 2009; Pinker 2011, 564–65). The group read a deliberately fake academic article that was filled with nonsense ideas and bogus jargon, adapted from Alan Sokal's famous text (Sokal and Bricmont 1998), which he had once used to hoax and discredit illegitimate academic journals.

Like the first experiment, participants judged the fake article on their own first. Most thought it sounded fishy. Then they participated in a group discussion with some undercover research assistants who falsely praised the article. Just like the previous experiment, most participants changed their private opinions about the article because the majority said it was great.

These experiments and many others have shown how "groupthink" can further bias our already biased opinions (Sunstein 2019; Banaji and Greenwald 2013; Eberhardt 2020). Even when we have the ability to make relatively objective judgments, like tasting vinegary wine, groupthink can lead people to discount their own knowledge or perceptions in order to conform to group expectations and enhance their positive self-image.

In a school setting, a group of dissatisfied or disgruntled students can easily turn the opinions of the whole class against a disliked assignment or teacher. Conversely, a group of hardworking and diligent students who appreciate a teacher's rigor can lift the opinions of the whole class. If a teacher's job depends on student evaluation surveys, then a group of disgruntled students can punish an unpopular teacher with low survey scores, which could put that teacher's employment in jeopardy.

While proponents of attribution theory have documented how student subjectivity and bias can distort teacher evaluation scores, some of these researchers have used these conclusions to reinforce elements of the older teacher effectiveness theory. Some psychologists believe that attribution research supports the traditional notion that student learning is reflected in both grades and evaluation surveys.

Specifically, some psychologists argue that research on attribution theory confirms that teachers get higher ratings from students who successfully learn and lower rating from students who do not learn. This view seems to confirm the traditional assumption that teachers are largely responsible for student learning, which remains a comforting belief for many researchers and educators.

However, most of the research on attribution theory has reached the opposite conclusion. Most researchers have demonstrated that student evaluation survey scores of teachers are not valid because students' subjective and self-serving opinions aren't connected to the quality of the teacher or the rigor of the class.

In particular, studies have shown that student bias drives lower survey ratings because student scores are caused by students' grade expectations and self-esteem rather the quality of teaching or learning, which we will investigate in the next couple chapters. In addition, psychologists now have a better understanding about how people lie to themselves and others to protect their self-identity and self-esteem (Ariely 2012, 158, 165; Tavris and Aronson 2015). Thus, it isn't a stretch to assume that some students who received low grades would lie on student evaluation surveys in order to blame the teacher in an effort to protect their own ego.

Chapter 3

Pressured to Please

The Negotiated Compromise of Playing School

In the 1970s and '80s, psychologists and educational researchers continued to study student subjectivity and agency in relation to teacher survey scores. This research began to challenge the traditional teacher-effectiveness theory. Over the past half century, while research has confirmed the same correlation between student evaluation survey ratings and student grades that Remmers first found, many researchers since the 1970s have developed a different theoretical explanation for why it happens.

The traditional teacher effectiveness theory does not fit the data. Instead of measuring student learning or teacher effectiveness, many researchers have now argued that student evaluation surveys are only measuring student bias, especially biased beliefs about grades, which students hope to receive or do receive. While student evaluations are linked to student grades, this correlation does not mean that most students are learning anything of value. In fact, the opposite is true.

GRADE-SATISFACTION THEORY

Over the 20th century, researchers turned away from the traditional theory of teacher effectiveness and formulated a new, more controversial theory that has been called the "grade-satisfaction theory" (Johnson 2003, 49). This theory expands upon the groundbreaking insights of Willard Waller (1932), who wrote one of the first sociological treatises on schooling.

Waller (1932) focused on how political conflict is central to formal schooling, especially in the classroom, where relatively powerless students struggle with "determined resistance" against their more powerful teachers (339).

27

Like Waller, proponents of the grade-satisfaction theory argue that teachers are caught in a political bind.

On the one hand, teachers try to create a challenging curriculum that meets professional academic standards in order to effectively teach students to learn. But teachers are also trying to satisfy the political priorities of educational administrators, the cultural priorities of the general public, and the various individual and social priorities of students—all of whom have agendas that conflict with the teacher's focus on student learning. Waller was one of the first social scientists to document how some students simply do not want to learn, and how this creates a precarious position for the teacher.

Waller (1932) discovered that teachers are often prevented from achieving their educational goals, especially fostering and developing student learning. Many students come to school unprepared to learn and some are unmotivated to be academically successful. Waller was not alone in documenting this predicament. Other researchers and practitioners had come to the same conclusion.

Several decades before Waller published his groundbreaking book, William T. Foster (1911), the President of Reed College, explained that "there will always be students who are more interested in getting through their courses than in getting profit from them" (408). These students "seek the courses which give the larger proportion of high grades," rather than choosing the best teacher who would enable them to learn the most (408). This predicament created a paradox for schools. How do you educate someone who does not want to be educated?

As sociologist Murray Milner Jr. (2006) and many other scientists have documented over the past century, students are not "raw material" that teachers can bend to their will in order to force them to learn (18). Instead, students have "a mind of their own," and they often "resist being transformed" by teachers and schools (18).

Many students see formal schooling as forced upon them by the adult world. For many students, the cultural norms and practices of schooling violate the more powerful norms and practices of parents or peer cultures. Thus, many students don't want to come to school and they don't want to learn, so they deliberately choose not to learn—or at least, they choose not to learn what the teacher wants them to learn.

Most teenagers get their information about the world from other young people, "who largely express their personal opinions and are barely any better informed than themselves," which leads to a closed, self-reinforcing epistemological loop that cuts teenagers off from the adult world ("Seize the Memes" 2019, 87). Students often care more about the opinions of their peers rather than the knowledge of their teachers or parents.

Many students are forced to go to school against their will by parents, school officials, police, and by the labor market. In one study, only 30 percent of high-income and 38 percent of low-income students viewed school positively, with the majority having mixed or negative feelings (Brantlinger 1993, 71).

Tellingly, high-income students reported that 91 percent of their parents viewed school positively, but low-income parents were actually less positive about schooling than their children (71). But these self-reported views are probably high because students also reported that they view school more positively than their friends. While 25 percent of low-income students viewed school negatively, these students reported that 43 percent of their friends had negative feelings. Likewise, 18 percent of high-income students reported negative feelings, but said that 24 percent of their friends viewed school negatively.

According to psychologist Laurence D. Steinberg (1996), when these reluctant students come to school, they resist learning and do their best to subvert the official pretext of instruction and academic success. Instead of seeing school as an academic environment, most students treat school as a social environment, as "a place to congregate with friends" (72). Steinberg argued, "Within the context of this marvelous party, classes are annoyances to be endured, just so many interruptions in the course of a busy day socializing" (72; see also Milner 2006).

Thus, to negotiate the divergent motivations and skill levels of different kinds of students, some of whom don't want to be at school or to learn, teachers often turn schooling into a behavioral ritual to make life easier on everyone. Rather than forcing students to learn, teachers set low standards, allow students to outwardly conform to ritualistic responses, and grade assignments leniently.

These formalities allow teachers to look like they are educating students in order to meet administrative expectations. Students look like they are learning by earning high grades. Administrators are happy. Parents are happy. Teachers stay employed.

Sociologists of education, like Waller (1932), came up with the grade satisfaction theory to poke holes in the naive beliefs of most educators in order to explain what really happens in schools. First, teachers ritualize the schooling process, water down the curriculum, and inflate grades in order to please administrators, parents, and students. Rather than educate students, teachers lead students through ritual exercises that try to make students feel subjectively successful, even though many students learn little, if anything through these rituals.

In exchange for low standards, less learning, and high grades, students show enough motivation to come to class, comply with instructor requests, complete course assignments, and reward the teacher with high ratings on evaluation surveys. Rather than assume that schools produce student learning and human capital, sociologists of education have documented how schools produce little more than rituals and symbolic tokens of success.

Proponents of the grade satisfaction theory argue that there is an underlying quid pro quo relationship between teachers and students in most schools. Both groups are active agents with divergent, if not conflicting, motivations and interests. While the grade-satisfaction theory hypothesizes a direct exchange of grades for ratings, no academic researcher has ever suggested that this exchange is an explicitly verbalized contract.

Instead, sociologists of education have described the cynical relationship between teachers and students as more of an implicit "compromise" (Sizer 1992), which is subtly and continually negotiated over a period of time. Likewise, there is also a compromise between teachers and administrators. Teachers outwardly conform to the ritualistic policies of administrators, including accountability assessments, in return for being left alone by administrators to run their own classrooms, and in return for raises and promotions.

THE NEGOTIATED COMPROMISE
OF PLAYING SCHOOL

Sociologists of education often call the ritualistic *quid pro quo* relationship between students, teachers, and administrators "playing school." Social scientists have documented this phenomenon for almost a century (Waller 1932; Illich 1970; Labaree 2010; Labaree 1997a; Pope 2001; Gardner [1995] 2011b).

Former university president Richard H. Hersh and education reporter John Merrow (2005) boiled this relationship down to a simple mantra: "If you don't bother us, we won't bother you" (9). English professor Murray Sperber (2005) calls this stalemate a "nonaggression pact" (138). Playing school is the opposite of real teaching and learning, and this practice corrupts the educational integrity that schools are supposed to uphold.

Social scientists have criticized the fraudulent phenomenon of playing school for almost a century (Waller 1932). Philosopher Ivan Illich (1970) argued that playing school degrades the educational process by reducing it to "a ritual game of graded promotions" (63). Psychologist Jerome Bruner (1983) quipped, "schools, teachers, subjects, grades" are merely empty "routines" of mindless conformity (178). Historian and sociologist David F. Labaree (1997a, 2010) called playing school a "game of how to succeed in school without really learning" (2010, 139).

Economist Brian Caplan (2018) recently explained it as a game of lies, adapting an old Soviet joke: "we pretend to teach; they pretend to learn" (83; see also Koretz 2017, 44; Banerjee and Duflo 2019, 29). And developmental psychologist and philosopher Alison Gopnik (2016) joked, "What schools do best is teach children how to go to school," not how to learn new knowledge or skills (190).

In his large 10-year study of adolescents in the 1980s and '90s, psychologist Laurence Steinberg (1996) found that over one-third of high school students spent most of the school day "goofing off with friends" and that 60 percent to 90 percent of students cheated on classwork in one form or another (19). Steinberg (1996) estimated that about 40 percent of students were "alienated and disengaged" from the academic practice of learning, and that these students were "just going through the motions" of playing school (62, 67).

Steinberg (1996) also estimated that less than 5 percent of adolescents were "high-achieving" students who valued learning and "academic excellence" (145–46). And perhaps even worse, the academically serious 5 percent paid a heavy social cost for learning, as the majority of students ostracized the academically-oriented minority because these good students were seen as "sell outs" who had betrayed adolescent cultural norms (160). Based on his research, Steinberg (1996) argued that "adolescent peer culture in contemporary America demeans academic success and scorns students who try to do well in school" (19).

While playing school is a negotiated compromise between teachers, students, and administrators, most proponents of the grade-satisfaction theory put the locus of control in the hands of the students rather than the adults, upending traditional beliefs about the power of teachers and administrators. Many students simply do not want to learn, and most students get what they want.

Instead of an education, which produces real knowledge and skills, many students want to engage in rituals that lead to a magic piece of paper called a degree. This fancy paper signals social distinction (Labaree 2010, 74–75; Labaree 2017, 56, 93) and employability for the labor market (Caplan 2018).

As economist Arnold Kling (2017) argues, education is "the only product where the consumer tries to get as little out of it as possible" (para. 1). Most students want to do little if any learning, and without their cooperation schools would collapse, and teachers and administrators would be out of a job. Thus, the new educational mantra: "The consumer is always right."

That is why most teachers play school with their students, as opposed to actually trying to teach. It is also the reason why a whole "cheating economy" has developed, especially in high school and in higher education. These days, students can buy everything they need to earn good grades in school, which means that many don't have to do any real leaning if they don't want to.

You can pay people to do all of your assignments and take all of your tests (Wolverton 2016). Students can also buy tailor-written essays. Prices start at $13 a page (Peterson 2019). In higher education, you can even hire people to take a course for you so you don't even have to go to class. The cheating economy is the corrupt apotheosis of the grade satisfaction theory.

For teachers and administrators, even if they are honest educators who want to develop student learning, there is not much they can do to promote the ethos of education for students who don't want to learn. This is especially true for older children in middle school or beyond who develop their own personalities and become attached to peer groups.

However, there is still much that can be done during the early childhood years, which is the most important time to develop the cognitive and noncognitive skills that students will need for success in school and the labor market (Mitchell 2018, 166; Heckman 2013; Heckman et al. 2006; Markovits 2019, 119–23). Thus, school reform initiatives, if they want to be really effective long-term, must focus on the early years of development from prenatal to early childhood, which includes teaching parents how to be parents (Tough 2008; Markovits 2019, 119–23).

Since the early 20th century, transforming children through schooling carries not only the power of tradition, but also the compulsion of law. Most students are unwilling "conscripts" who are forced to go to school (Labaree 2010, 137). Psychologists have found that when you force people to do activities that they do not want to do and have no control over them they lose all motivation to do anything productive (Deci and Flaste 1995, 58–59).

Students have been in this position for over a century in the U.S. Willard Waller (1932) was one of the first social scientists to point out that most students are "forced" to learn "many things that they do not wish to learn," which creates a situation where "students and teachers are at cross purposes" (355).

David Labaree (2010) has also focused on how students are "involuntary" subjects forced to go to school "under duress" because they are compelled to attend school by adults (153, 137). This duress can come through the force of law, in the case of K–12 schooling, or in the case of college, the social and economic pressure to climb the ladder of success in order to get a good job (Labaree 2017, 167; Collins 2002, 25).

Thus, students are often "more an object of teaching," rather than "a client" freely "requesting professional help" (Labaree 2010, 153). This makes practices of teaching, learning, and schooling very fragile and highly contingent on the willingness of any given student to go along with the program.

It doesn't help that most curriculums have no practical interest or value to teenagers and young adults. Students of all ages are subjected to "artificial, made-up subjects" that are "tedious and irrelevant" to their actual lives (Richardson 1999, 205). Many students see school as a useless academic ritual of "pretend learning" that leads to "pretend achievement" (Richardson 1999, 205).

Most students find school boring. It can be mentally and emotionally taxing to play school and pretend to achieve. But students are powerless to do anything about it. This unfortunate situation destroys students' intrinsic motivation to learn (Deci and Flaste 1995; Cialdini 2007, 94; Baker 2020, 61). Many students participate just enough in school to engage in the forced ritual and earn passing grades in order to get promoted through each grade, and finally, to graduate with their magic piece of paper (Milton, Pollio and Eison 1986).

Many students resent their powerlessness in having to learn things they do not want to learn in a place they don't want to be. It's not surprising that some students get angry. Many students channel their frustration at their teacher in an act of fruitless rebellion. This emotionally fraught situation creates a "perilous equilibrium" (Waller 1932, 10).

In most high school and college classrooms there is an "uneasy truce," or an "uneasy kind of détente" between teachers and students (Gardner [1995] 2011b, 152, 162). Most teachers struggle to maintain control over students and keep them participating in the ritual of schooling, let alone getting students to learn. So many teachers adopt "defensive teaching" strategies that require "minimal standards and minimum effort" for both students and the teacher (Gardner [1995] 2011b, 153).

If education were "unforced," as Waller (1932) once sardonically explained, life would be easy for teachers. Waller (1932) continued,

> If this process were unforced, if students could be allowed to learn only what interested them, to learn in their own way, and to learn no more and no better than it pleased them to do, if good order were not considered a necessary condition of learning, if teachers did not have to be taskmasters, but merely helpers and friends, then life would be sweet in the school room (355; see also Gardner [1995] 2011b, 162).

All young children begin their academic careers with a natural love of learning, which makes working with children in preschool through 5th grade a pleasure for most teachers. But as kids grow older and as peer cultures develop, and as more adult pressure is thrust on students, gradually schooling becomes more formal and ritualistic, and students lose their "natural curiosity and excitement about learning" (Deci and Flaste 1995, 19; Gardner [1995] 2011b).

Thus, from middle school through the undergraduate years in college, life is rarely "sweet" for teachers. The developmental psychologist Howard Gardner ([1995] 2011) noted the harsh reality of most classrooms: "Most schools are burdened with large classes, onerous rules and regulations, disruptive demands for accountability, and students who have many personal problems" (162).

Labaree (2010) has pointed out that for most students, educational success in K–12 schools has been traditionally measured by "time served rather than subjects mastered" (79), much like a prison sentence. Peter Drucker (1969) argued that "there is no reason to believe that the diploma certifies too much more than that the holder has sat a long time" (331). Thus, when such students graduate from high school and get to college, they feel like they are finally free. And what do they want?

Most undergraduate college students want a party. And they want a magic piece of paper that will give them access to a good job. Arthur Levine (2005), former president of Teachers College, Columbia, explained,

> The new majority is bringing to higher education exactly the same consumer demands they have for every other commercial enterprise with which they do business. They believe that since they are paying for college, their schools and their professors should give them what they want. And what they want is a stripped-down version of higher education. (158)

Psychologist Jean M. Twenge (2017) has documented how the adolescent generations of the past couple decades have become more "disengaged" with school and academic success. Compared with previous generations, fewer adolescents now find education "interesting, enjoyable, or meaningful" (169-70).

Researchers have also documented how "fragile" adolescents have become in terms of their mental health and their general immaturity (Lukianoff and Haidt 2018, 9; Twenge 2017). Many students do not want to be exposed to activities, people, or ideas that might challenge them or make them feel uncomfortable. These immature adolescents live in "bubbles of intellectual 'safety'" (Lukianoff and Haidt 2018, 9).

Immature and fragile students "don't want to learn anything," humanities professor Stanley Fish (2019, 77) argues, because they don't want to be exposed to any activity they haven't already experienced or any belief they don't already hold. Immature students actually find a measure of safety and comfort in the empty rituals of schooling, and they are fearful of real learning experiences.

Many adolescents these days feel that they need to be sheltered and protected from the world. They react defensively when anything or anyone threatens to pop their safety bubble or challenge their self-esteem, including being exposed to new ideas from teachers at school.

Many helicopter parents are also reinforcing this fragile attitude by trying to project their children from any perceived threat, real or imagined. This only increases the fragility of children and makes them less prepared to deal with the real-life challenges, conflicts, and stressors of adulthood. This is especially true for many adolescents who transition into the grown-up world through their college experiences (19–24).

When unwilling conscripts go from playing school and pretending to achieve in high school and then transition to college, as Keeling and Hersh (2012) point out, students who have engaged in rituals their whole life are "*less* capable of taking advantage of a true college education—less emotionally ready, less prepared to read, write, and think critically, and with less of the resilience required to persevere in the face of challenges" (115; see also Melguizo and Ngo 2020).

Every year, new cadres of unmotivated, directionless, and immature college students throw away thousands of dollars, so they can skip class, not read textbooks, not do assignments, and cheat on tests. Illogically, many college students try to "get as little as possible for their money" (Matthews 1998, 109, 205).

Even when they go to class, most undergraduates are not really paying attention to their professors, let alone learning anything. A recent study found that college students are "digitally distracted" in their classes, spending between 12 percent to 25 percent of their class time looking at their digital devices for "nonclass purposes" (Supiano 2019, para. 3).

In a recent scandal in the U.S., some rich parents bribed university officials so they could get their children in elite universities (Sandel 2020, 7). One family spent hundreds of thousands of dollars in bribes, on top of paying over $50,000 a year for tuition at the University of Southern California. Why?

As their infamous daughter explained, she went to college for "game days, partying. . . . I don't really care about school" (Langlois 2019, para. 2). This student spent more time making YouTube videos in her dorm room than going to class. She probably didn't learn much from her professors because she simply did not want to learn. While the bribery was exceptional, this young woman's attitude toward learning is pretty typical of most undergraduates these days: Why bother?

How are college instructors supposed to teach basic skills, let alone enable higher learning with students such as these? David F. Labaree (2010) explains how teachers "risk their relationship with their students in the pursuit of student learning" because real learning is difficult and it takes a lot of time (147).

Thus, most teachers fall back on playing school because it is the safer and easier strategy, for both students and teachers. Howard Gardner ([1995] 2011) explains how teachers refuse to "pose challenging problems that will force their students to stretch in new ways that will risk failures that might make both students and teacher look bad" (162). Often, neither students nor teachers are "willing to undertake risks" for real learning or effective teaching (162).

To encourage real learning, teachers must engage in uncomfortable and emotionally taxing criticism of students' work, students' motivation, and students' effort (Brackett 2019, 29). Many students resent the work involved in authentic learning. These students also resent the negative feedback, which can lower their inflated self-esteem.

As discussed in more detail in *Can We Measure What Matters Most?* effective learning requires long hours of deliberate practice, which is "significantly more effortful, and significantly less enjoyable" than playing school (Duckworth 2016, 127). Labaree (2010) describes how teachers must "use the leverage of being liked to push for a level of student performance that may result in being disliked" (147), which contributes to the "perilous equilibrium" that Waller (1932) documented in the classroom.

Thus, most teachers try to make it easy on themselves and their students. Teachers who are liked by their students get high ratings on student evaluation surveys. These likable teachers also tend to be the easiest because they just play school, rather than challenging their students to actually learn. As statistician Valen E. Johnson (2003) has explained, "Instructors who grade leniently are more likely to gain approval of their students, have better rapport in the classroom, and be reviewed positively on course evaluation forms" (48).

Thus, student evaluation surveys are not valid accountability instruments. Instead, they are a part of the fraudulent ritualization of schooling. Student surveys tell us more about the biased psychology of students who want to play school, than about the quality of teaching or the quality of the curriculum.

School administrators ignore the actual function of these accountability instruments. They treat surveys as objective measures of teaching and learning. Most school administrators avoid the hard work of actually understanding the process of education and encouraging their teachers to teach, let alone the more rigorous study of the validity of accountability metrics. Administrators play their own version of school by pretending that they are keeping schools accountable with ritualized assessments that do not really work.

As Waller (1932) pointed out a hundred years ago, "The teacher must do something in the classroom, and routine teaching is the easiest thing to do" (443). This is why schools usually reward "docile assimilation and glib repetition" rather than actual learning (Waller 1932, 24). Most accountability metrics have always rewarded playing school, not real teaching or learning, which is harder to see and often impossible to measure.

Developmental psychologist Howard Gardner ([1995] 2011) argued that "even when school appears to be successful, even when it elicits the performances for which it has apparently been designed, it typically fails to achieve its most important missions," like teaching students how to learn, helping them to develop emotional intelligence (3), or preparing them for the labor market.

Many students, including the highest achieving A-level students, according to historian and Vice Provost for Instruction Ken Bain (2004), have merely been schooled with simple tricks, rather than actually educated. These schooled students can only "plug and chug" useless, abstract information, "memorizing formulae, sticking numbers in the right equation, or turning the right vocabulary into a paper . . . understanding little. When the class is over, they quickly forget much of what they have 'learned'" (24; see also Deci and Flaste 1995, 49).

Looking back on his own experience as a student, business professor Charles Handy (1990) explained, "I came to realize that I had learned nothing at school which I now remember except this—that all problems had already been solved, by someone, and that the answer was around, in the back of the book or the teacher's head" (57).

Howard Gardner ([1995] 2011) explained that an "overwhelming body of educational research" has shown that "even those students who have been well trained and who exhibit all the overt signs of success—faithful attendance at good schools, high grades and high test scores, accolades from their teachers—typically do not display an adequate understanding of the materials and concepts" they were supposed to learn in school (3; see for example Milton, Pollio and Eison 1986).

Most students have grown up with schooling. They have become accustomed to playing school. So, when students are challenged and pushed to learn the material so they can become competent, many resent the violation of the nonaggression pact of playing school. The status quo is broken and this disturbs many students.

When teachers push students to demonstrate real learning, students almost always complain about the work and difficulty involved. Some students go farther. Some students look for ways to punish teachers who set high standards. Students engage in passive resistance in the classroom, make vocal complaints, or give low survey evaluation scores. Sometimes, students go so far as to file grievances with the administration.

In rare instances, some students will get aggressive in the classroom. In these extreme cases, which are sadly becoming much more common, students use verbal threats and physical violence against teachers (Mercedes 2019). Some teachers feel not only "harassed and bullied," but also "scared in school" (Mercedes 2019, para. 1).

Take for example, some elementary school teachers in Houston, Texas. These teachers complained about students spitting in their face, pulling their hair, punching them, and throwing desks and science equipment at them (Mercedes 2019, para. 6–10). And these are elementary school teachers! Just imagine what some middle school and high school teachers go through in the same district.

Any teacher who pushes students beyond the traditional confines of "playing school" (Pope 2001; Labaree 1997a) will often suffer for it, in one form or another. Pushing students to really learn "violates an unwritten agreement" that both students and administrators rely on (Gardner [1995] 2011b, 6). Pushing students to learn upsets the status quo of schooling.

So, when it comes to asking students to evaluate teachers who actually teach and demand that students learn, how can this process work objectively? How can anyone expect disgruntled students to accurately evaluate an undesirable activity that they are forced to do? How can anyone expect an immature student to accurately evaluate a demanding teacher who has required them to do unpleasant tasks? Under such circumstances, objectivity is impossible. Thus, the validity of many student survey scores is fatally flawed.

PRESSURED TO PLEASE: DEMORALIZATION AND ACADEMIC MALPRACTICE

Some proponents of the grade satisfaction theory take it one step further. These critics point out how both fraud and extortion can easily arise in schools. When a strict teacher tries to enforce learning, students and administrators can react by pressuring the teacher to lower standards and play school, or else suffer the consequences. In the 1970s, professor of communication Jerry L. Winsor (1977) argued,

If giving relatively high evaluations is seen as a means to further a career as an educator, and if these evaluations are viewed partly as a popularity contest where relevant demands of academic rigor are negatively valued by students, the psychological pressures to lesson requirements and to escalate rewards appears on obvious result. (83)

More recently an anonymous professor explained, "students strive to 'work the system,' using university procedures to get the grades they desire, rather than those they have earned, and if necessary, to punish faculty who refuse to accede to those demands" (Anonymous 2019, para. 6).

Thus, on the one hand, unscrupulous instructors can cynically play school, grade leniently, and gain popularity with students in order to receive high student evaluation marks, which would result in promotion, higher pay, and higher institutional status. On the other hand, an instructor with high standards and objective grading criteria who cares about student learning might feel psychologically pressured, if not extorted, by students, administrators, and other instructors to get with the game and play school like everyone else.

Many school administrators and public policy makers have adopted a naïve understanding of teachers. They falsely believe that teachers are solely responsible for student learning. They also have an equally naïve understanding of student evaluations. They believe that these accountability instruments provide direct evidence of both teacher effectiveness and student learning.

Thus, teachers are caught in a bind, especially nontenure tract lecturers at community colleges and nonselective universities. Teachers feel pressured to please students as consumers, and they feel pressured to please administrators as supervisors.

In order to keep a job and get promoted, teachers have to minimize consumer complaints. How can this be accomplished? The easiest and quickest way for teachers is to inflate institutional effectiveness metrics: higher grade-distributions, higher student evaluation marks, more positive student comments, higher retention rates, and higher graduation rates (Schneider 2017, 54; Koretz 2017, 62).

But this pressure to inflate accountability metrics comes with great professional and moral cost for teachers. To explore this issue, it is helpful to turn to the experiences of K–12 teachers who have had to deal with oppressive accountability metrics for several decades. Professor of education Doris A. Santoro (2018) has documented K–12 teachers' "high level of dissatisfaction" with their jobs in the United States due to widespread "demoralization," which she defines as the "inability to enact the values that motivate and sustain their work" as teachers (3, 43; see also Payne 2008, 39).

Many teachers passionately care about being a teacher and "the integrity of the profession" (88, 43). But so many teachers "cannot do what they believe a good teacher should do" because there is "dissonance between educators' moral centers and the conditions in which they teach" (88, 43). For many educators in the U.S. and around the world, it is simply impossible to be an effective teacher.

Santoro (2018) documented the travails of a teacher named Reggie who had to resign after 10 years because, "You play ball or leave with your ethics" (1). Santoro (2018) analyzed the "isolation" that many educators feel as "conscientious objectors" (8, 4). Some teachers stand up "in the name of professional ethics" in order to demarcate the line between the "good work" of proper teaching from the bad work that violates professional standards, like playing school (8, 4).

Many professional teachers have a "craft conscience" (91). These teachers take pride in their identity as teachers. They have special knowledge and skills, which they have acquired through dedicated practice. So, when administrators dictate new accountability practices that violate professional standards, some teachers feel that "they are degrading their profession" by following along. When administrators force teachers to violate their professional standards of practice, they endure what Santoro calls "moral violence" (91, 138).

One issue that many teachers complain about is administrative pressure to pass students who do not meet educational standards by demonstrating adequate learning and/or effort. As Santoro documented, some teachers lament that they "damaged the integrity of my work when I passed that student" (Santoro 2018, 32).

Other teachers explain how they are sometimes pressured by administrators with what Santoro calls "moral blackmail" (136). Some administrators criticize or shame teachers in an effort to change student grades. Sometimes administrators threaten official reprimands if teachers don't do what they are told, which could include a fine or dismissal (136, 97).

Some administrators are in a similar situation to teachers. Sometimes, school administrators feel pressured by students and parents, or by more senior administrative officials and policy makers (96). These administrators push their teachers because they themselves are being pushed by authorities higher up the bureaucratic hierarchy. Schooling is sometimes a naked expression of political power.

Some teachers are disgusted by the degraded situation of playing school or conforming to school politics. So many teachers want to quit their jobs every year, but can't. These unfortunate teachers do not "have the financial or personal means to take a stand" (70). These teachers can't afford to live up to their principles.

Thus, many teachers are "trapped in the system," as William Deresiewicz (2014, 49) explained. They are stuck in a cycle of moral violence and have to endure endless amounts of moral blackmail. Trapped teachers become demoralized by their working conditions. And to make matters worse, demoralized teachers increase the dysfunctional school environment, which reinforces a negative cycle that often makes educational reform impossible (Payne 2008, ch. 2).

This has led political scientist Tom Nichols (2017, 89, 87), and many other researchers (Keeling and Hersh 2012; Rosovsky and Hartley 2002; Chen 2013), to claim that schools have been conducting "academic malpractice" or outright fraud. Nichols argues that teachers and schools are lying to students by giving them superficial knowledge and inflated grades.

To please students and increase accountability metrics, many schools have hollowed out the academic curriculum in order to create a vast array of meaningless "gut" courses. Nichols (2017) explains a "gut" course as a class where a student "can pass by exchanging oxygen for carbon dioxide for a set number of weeks" (90). This leads many students to believe that "they're actually smarter than they are" (Nichols 2017, 89, 87; see also Sperber 2000, xiv; Koretz 2017, ch. 5).

The academic curriculum at most community colleges has devolved into whole programs of gut courses (McGrath and Spear 1991), and the same could be said about many nonselective colleges and universities, which would explain why these less prestigious institutions of higher education led to lower labor market outcomes for underprivileged students (Giani 2016). This disturbing trend continues unabated all over the U.S.

While students may benefit from this academic malpractice and fraud while they are in school, they are ultimately hurt once they graduate. That is, *if* they graduate. For example, although A and B grades currently make up over 80 percent of all grades in higher education (95; Rosovsky and Hartley 2002), around half of all college students, and a majority of community college students, fail to graduate with a degree in six years.

Many students who do graduate end up leaving school with a "meaningless degree" (Sperber 2000, xiv) because they didn't learn anything. They have no job prospects and thousands of dollars of student loan debt. And perhaps even worse, Nichols (2017) argues, "Unearned praise and hollow successes build a fragile arrogance in students that can lead them to lash out at the first teacher or employer who dispels [the] illusion" that they do not actually have any real knowledge or useful skills (84).

Many critics argue that this situation should be a "public scandal" (Sperber 2000, xiv). But sadly, this situation has been largely ignored by the public for decades. Partly because institutional fraud creates perverse incentives for administrators and teachers to buy into and perpetuate the fraud (Payne 2008, 41; Koretz 2017).

Many instructors, especially part-time adjuncts in higher education, are scared of honestly talking to their students, let alone objectively evaluating course work, because they fear that students will complain on evaluations, which will result in loss of employment (Childress 2019; see also Payne 2008, 44). The head of the National Adjunct Faculty Guild recently reported,

part-timers are terrified of being rigorous graders, terrified to deal with complaints about the course materials, terrified to deal with plagiarists. A lot of them are working as robots. . . . If you're afraid to give an honest grade or an honest opinion, you're not teaching (Gregorian, 2005, 86).

This situation happens in many high schools as well. Educational professor Charles Payne (2008) wrote about a Chicago high school that was extremely "dysfunctional" (57). Many "kids could often do pretty much what they wanted" because nobody dared to supervise or control them, let alone try to teach them anything (57).

When schools focus on accountability metrics, like grades and student evaluation surveys, administrators "forc[e] weaker or less secure teachers to become dancing bears, striving to be loved or at least liked" (Nichols 2017, 98). This leads to the erosion of academic standards by creating a "vicious circle of pandering and grade inflation" (Nichols 2017, 98; Rosovsky and Hartley 2002; Koretz 2017).

This problem has been reinforced and exacerbated since most institutions of higher education now operate like for-profit businesses. In the 21st century, most college administrators assess the quality of higher education with a "demand-side view" (Ginsberg, 2011, 170). This orientation privileges the "interests and preferences of students," who are considered customers.

Colleges must please their customers. This leads to a "presumptive distrust" of faculty, who are simply the hired help (Buckman, 2007, 33). Administrators now often assume that the consumer is always right. This means that the teacher is always wrong.

Sadly, this presumption has corrosive effects. Rather than trying to enlighten the minds of students, according the Murray Sperber (2000), many K–12 schools and institutions of higher education have "stopped trying to give their students a meaningful" education (xiv).

Instead, colleges offer empty rituals, comfortable accommodations, and football games. Perhaps the perfect symbol of this degradation in higher education can be seen at Louisiana State University. In 2019, the football team enjoyed a cutting edge 21st century sports stadium with every imaginable luxury, including luxury leather chairs in the locker room. At the other end of campus, the "decrepit" university and flood-damaged library crumbled to dust (Jarvis 2019).

Chapter 4

A Question of Validity

Student Surveys Don't Measure Teaching or Learning

Some researchers have called the focus on bias in student evaluation surveys a "witch hunt" (Marsh 1984, 730). However, Valen E. Johnson (2003) and many others have argued that the existence of student bias, and the general invalidity of survey scores, is "almost beyond question" (50).

Speaking from his personal experience as an instructor, Johnson (2003) argued that every college teacher knows that students "often do complain loudly and vigorously about grades that they feel are undeservedly low," and that these same students "frequently register their dissatisfaction with their grades by denigrating teacher effectiveness" on student evaluation surveys (50).

But more important than mere anecdotal evidence, Johnson (2003) surveyed almost a century of scientific research on education and demonstrated how student bias systematically distorts evaluation surveys. His findings corroborate the conclusions of psychologists and social scientists in other disciplines, especially in political science, who have demonstrated for almost a half-century that subjective bias distorts the results of all public opinion surveys (Rosenberg 1988; Lodge and Taber 2013). As psychologist and political scientist John R. Hibbing explained,

> Give people the same visual stimulus and they will respond differently. They see different things and pay attention to different things, and the pieces of information sieved out by these contrary perceptual screens are processed into different conclusions and beliefs. (Hibbing, Smith and Alford 2014, 118; see also Banaji and Greenwald 2013; Eberhardt 2020)

Johnson (2003) and many other educational scholars have shown that most research on student evaluation surveys contradicts the teacher effectiveness theory and clearly corroborates the grade-satisfaction theory. In fact, a lot of data substantiates the more extreme theory of student blackmail.

If you study the literature on this topic, it is clear that student evaluation surveys are not valid instruments for evaluating teaching, student learning, or the curriculum. That's why the American Sociological Association, the American Historical Association, the American Political Science Association, the National Communication Association, the American Educational Research Association, and 13 other scholarly associations have all stated that student surveys should not be relied upon "as a measure of teaching quality" (Supiano 2019, para. 2). And yet, these invalid tools have proliferated.

STUDENT SURVEYS DON'T MEASURE TEACHING OR LEARNING

One of the first studies to investigate the validity of student evaluation surveys was conducted by Mirum Rodin, a professor of psychology, and her husband Burton Rodin, a professor of Mathematics. They designed one of the most important, and controversial, experimental studies that contradicted the teacher effectiveness theory and supported the grade-satisfaction theory.

In the early 1970s, they published a widely cited article in the highly regarded academic journal *Science*. Rodin and Rodin (1972) focused on a single introductory physics class, which was taught by Burton Rodin with the help of 11 teaching assistants who taught 12 recitation sections that were structured identically. The only difference between these sections was the teaching assistant.

Rodin and Rodin (1972) analyzed the relationship between student evaluations of these teaching assistants and the grades students received in order to see if course evaluation scores were correlated to student learning. They also controlled for students' academic ability by using grades received in the previous quarter. They found a correlation of −.746 to −.754 between surveys and grades. This meant that students who received the highest course grades also assigned the lowest ratings to the teaching assistants, and vice versa.

This study not only clearly demonstrated that student evaluation ratings are invalid measures of teaching quality, but also that these surveys are unfair and discriminatory. Each teaching assistant used the exact same pedagogical methods and curriculum, and yet they received divergent student evaluation scores due to the subjective bias of students. Rodin and Rodin (1972) concluded, "good teaching is not validly measured by student evaluations in their current form" (1166).

Psychologist David S. Holmes (1972) conducted another interesting experimental study at about the same time. His research also disconfirmed the teacher effectiveness theory and supported the grade-satisfaction theory. He specifically analyzed the relationship between students' grade expectations and student evaluation ratings by collecting data on students' expected course grade in addition to their test grades, final grades, and student evaluation surveys.

Holmes selected students who earned A or B grades on early assignments, and he surveyed them to see if their expected grades matched the actual grades they received. He then randomly sorted these students into either an experimental group or control group. For the experimental group, Holmes gave students an artificially low grade on the final exam, which would cause students final course grade to drop by a full letter. For the control group there was no change of grade. He then administered the student evaluation surveys to see how an unexpectedly lower final exam grade and course grade would affect the course evaluation surveys.

Holmes (1972) found that students who received the unexpectedly lower grade gave lower ratings on 10 out of 19 items on the survey. The correlation on five of those 10 items was statistically significant at the .05 level, while the other five came in at a .10 level. Thus, Holmes conclusively demonstrated that student evaluation ratings are strongly biased by grade expectations and do not validly represent the quality of teaching, learning, or the curriculum.

Johnson (2003) later analyzed five other experimental studies that replicated Holmes basic design. and all of them demonstrated the same conclusion. High student evaluation ratings where strongly correlated with high grades, not the quality of teaching, learning, or the curriculum (77–80; Greenwald and Gillmore 1997).

After reviewing most of the evidence on the subject, Johnson (2003) designed his own experimental study at Duke University in order to explicitly test the relationship between student evaluation surveys, expected and received grades, mean course grades, and prior interest in the subject matter. Johnson (2003) found that course grades were the most important predictor of a student's response to items about the quality of teaching on the evaluation survey, even more important than a student's prior interest in the course subject (92).

Johnson demonstrated that course grades explained 36 percent of the course evaluation rating, while prior student interest explained 30 percent. Thus, 66 percent of an instructors' evaluation rating had nothing to do with the teacher or the curriculum.

Johnson also found that higher mean course grades were correlated with "decreases in the level of course difficulty, the extent to which students were challenged, and the time students spent on course material" (94). Johnson (2003) concluded that the evidence clearly supported the grade-satisfaction theory:

Students' responses to the survey were significantly affected by the grades that the students either expected to receive or already had received. For most items, the influence that students' grades had on their responses to the survey ranged from about one-fourth to one-half of the importance of the consensus rating . . . grades do, in fact, represent a serious bias to student evaluations of teaching. . . . It seems that students measure their success in a course, and implicitly the quality of instruction, by the grade they receive or expect to receive. Poor grades are thus associated with poor teaching; students who receive low grades tend to denigrate instruction when they complete teacher-course evaluation forms. (100)

While subjective bias is the main problem with student evaluation surveys, this qualitative bias gets hidden and compounded when survey results are expressed in numbers and analyzed with statistics (Labaree 2011). Philip B. Stark and Richard Freishtat (2014), professors of statistics and education at the University of California, Berkeley, conducted a comprehensive study of student survey evaluation scores. They focused on the mathematical validity of the statistical analyses of these scores (Stark and Freishtat 2014; see also Kamenetz 2014; Berrett 2014).

Stark and Freishtat (2014) found that the concrete quantitative measurements produced by student surveys were misleading, at best. They concluded, "Averages of numerical student ratings have an air of objectivity simply because they are numerical," but the actual quantitative measurements and statistical analyses were meaningless from a mathematical point of view (Stark and Freishtat 2014, 3, 5; see also Labaree 2011).

In particular, student evaluation surveys have low and selective response rates, which make the validity of the averaged numbers problematic. Evaluation surveys are not usually mandatory, so only certain kinds of students will complete them, which means that average survey scores do not represent the whole class.

To make matters worse, often very satisfied or very unsatisfied students respond to surveys, so the results can be polarized. Thus, when numeric measures of polarized student opinions are averaged, Stark and Freishtat (2014) argue, "Such averages and comparisons make no sense, as a matter of statistics" (5–6).

Political scientist Robert Weissberg (2002) addressed this same problem with political polling. He concluded, "amalgamating individual choices into singular, indisputable collective outcomes is nearly impossible" (30). Any claim based on such statistical averaging always comes with a wide margin of error (Rothschild and Goel 2016).

Furthermore, many of the questions asked on student surveys lead to nonsensical answers from a mathematical point of view. For example, one student who rates the teacher highly added together with another student who rates the teacher poorly does not balance out to the conclusion that the instructor's teaching was mediocre. There is no valid way of mathematically averaging out these distinct claims.

Student evaluation surveys produce very specific numbers, which appear to rate survey items precisely and objectively, such as 2.78 out of 5 for "the instructor was available during office hours." However, these numbers are invalid and completely meaningless from a mathematical and logical point of view. Either the instructor held office hours or she didn't. A 2.78 out of 5 does not make any sense because such a score violates the mathematical Law of the Excluded Middle, which states that there is "no middle ground between true and false" (Sigmund 2017, 211).

To make matters worse, all student evaluation survey scores are averaged down into a single index number, which is then used to rate and compare individuals, departments, and schools. However, as the Nobel Prize winning economist Paul A. Samuelson mathematically demonstrated, all index numbers are flawed in practice because "there will always be some bias which will make even the most ideal index number subject to some ambiguity" (Breit and Ransom 1998, 114).

But perhaps even more important, as statistician and professor of business management W. Edwards Deming pointed out over fifty years ago, there is a lot of natural variability in all data, which makes it impossible to precisely compare individuals using any statistical model. He argued that the statistical evaluation of people with numerical ratings could be broken down into only three meaningful categories: People outside the control limits "on the bad side," people outside the control limits "on the good side," and most people who fit within the control limits (Walton 1986, 92; Aguayo 1990).

Deming argued that there was no way to accurately disaggregate the majority of people in the middle within the control limits. Everyone in this mathematically designated middle category should receive the same rating with the same rewards (Walton 1986, 92). But that is not what happens with student evaluation surveys.

Incompetent department chairs and deans incorrectly believe that 3.6 is actually statistically better than 3.5 or 3.4. The data do not support this type of conclusion. In fact, given high standard deviations and high margins of error, there is often no statistically significant difference between ratings of 3 and 4. Sometimes, with very low sample sizes, there is no statistically significant difference between ratings of 2 and 5.

But even if reliable quantitative or qualitative data was gathered and precisely expressed through accurate mathematics, this would not solve the problem of validity. Data would still need to be analyzed and interpreted with an appropriate theoretical framework to make the data valid and meaningful.

Why? Because data are not self-explanatory by themselves. Plus, data collection tools never produce neutral measurements. Mike Potter, a chief technology officer, explained, "We all think that data are so objective, but they are actually as interpretable as Shakespeare" ("The New AI-ssembly Line" 2020, 9). Potter argued that "data are never neutral and must always be questioned" because "they may be collected for political reasons or in a way that hides things" (9).

In order to make data meaningful, a researcher needs an accurate theory. Biologist and anthropologist David Slone Wilson (2002) explained, "a theory is required to see the things that are in front of our faces" (125; see also Isaacs 1999, 73). Philosopher Nelson Goodman (1978) elaborated on this same principle a bit more poetically, "Although conception without perception is merely empty, perception without conception is blind" (6).

Data doesn't mean anything without a theory. Without a theory, a researcher can't see the relevant data to validate a hypothesis. According to Wilson (2002), "We fail to see the evidence, not because it is obscure or requires sophisticated measuring devices, but because we are employing the wrong theories" (125, 132).

Having a valid theory is essential for statistics to work. And yet educational administrators are theory blind. Most administrators treat student survey data as pristine, self-evident facts. They naively regard student surveys as impartial yardsticks that produced objective data that needed no interpretation.

Administrators routinely misinterpret student survey data because they don't understand how it was generated. Nor do they understand the multiple conclusions that the data can lead to. Data can lead to false conclusions or absurdities if the wrong theory is used.

Making sense of subjective data is tricky, especially consumer opinions expressed on surveys. It's hard to understand what people really mean when they express their preference, and it is even harder to know how a person's subjective opinions are actually connected to the objective world. Political scientist Robert Weissberg (2002) explained,

> Today's polls are not akin to a yardstick that indifferently records immutable data. The very ascertainment of public sentiment, as presently executed and interpreted, almost always constitutes a political act; 'measurement' and 'meaning' are often seamlessly blended. Rather than being a yardstick, the poll more closely resembles a rigid container into which liquids can be poured. No matter what the liquid's initial form, when poured it follows the container's shape. (6; see also Rosenberg 1988)

Social scientists have known for over half a century that survey measurements are never neutral. Business professor Peter Drucker (1969) stressed that every yardstick used to measure "bespeaks a value judgment regarding the purpose" of the activity being measured or the organization doing the measuring (196). Many educational administrators seem unaware of the fact that survey questions are "political acts" that presuppose a particular theoretical understanding of teaching and learning.

But even if a valid theoretical framework is used to analyze survey data for the basis of evaluations, all theories are incomplete approximations of the reality they seek to describe, predict, or evaluate. Statistician George Box warned that "all models are wrong, but some are useful" (qtd. in Zuckerman 2019, 245).

The most successful theories get enough right that they can be used to accurately understand, predict, and evaluate the phenomena they seek to explain. But as many successful quantitative researchers have pointed out, "all formulas are fallible"; therefore, "never place too much trust" in any one particular theory or model (Zuckerman 2019, 213).

There can also be competing frameworks that can be applicable to explaining a situation, which naturally leads to uncertainly over any conclusions. For example, in education, history professor Kevin Gannon (2018) explains how student evaluation surveys can be used to reinforce multiple, competing narratives about the teaching and learning done in a particular classroom: "We need to remember that data acquires meaning only through context" (para. 20).

A teacher might be highly competent and pushing a student hard to promote excellence. However, from the student's point of view, the teacher might seem mean, overbearing, or even abusive. Whose meaning is the right meaning in this situation?

As Philip E. Tetlock, an expert on judgment and decision-making, explains: "Even if [people] looked at the same evidence—and there's likely to be some variation—it is unlikely they would all reach precisely the same conclusion" (Tetlock and Gardner 2015, 131). Thus, you can never take any data as self-evident, especially student survey data.

Let's go back to a previous example. As a matter of statistics and mathematics, as we just discussed, the average mark of 2.78 for the instructor holding office hours is clearly nonsensical and invalid. But taking an ethnographic approach, the score of 2.78 could have many competing meanings, depending on whose vantage point a researcher might take.

Maybe the instructor was inconsistent in holding office hours. Maybe some students were confused about when and where office hours were held. Maybe some students who received low grades were punishing the instructor with low marks on all survey items. Or, there could be several other logical possibilities.

But which meaning is the right meaning for this data? It's impossible to ever know for sure without a full interview of each and every student so as to explore the subjective meaning of their survey responses and the specific context they were operating within (Rosenberg 1988). Even then, there is no way to know for sure.

As political scientist Cass R. Sunstein (1997) explained, "Choices are inarticulate, and hence unhelpful predictors of behavior, without an account of what lies behind them" (15). He went on to add that "preferences are constructed, rather than elicited, by social situations" (38).

Students do not have stable or reliable understandings of their educational experiences, and their opinions are shaped by many variables, both inside and outside of the classroom.

Sunstein (1997) explained that "it is often hard to know what people would 'like' or prefer, because their judgments and desires are entangled with norms, meaning, and role, and because once one or more of these is changed, they may be better off either objectively or subjectively" (55). Student evaluation surveys never make an attempt to get "behind" student answers to try to understand what students really mean, why they really hold the opinions they do, and how this is connected to their peers, their teacher, and influences outside of the classroom and school.

And that's the important point that everyone needs to remember, especially administrators who use these survey scores to evaluate teachers' employment status. The precise-looking student evaluation scores are not only mathematically invalid, but they are also qualitatively invalid. Survey responses do not transparently represent complete and meaningful statements because no one was present in either the context of the classroom or the context of filling out the survey to know why students answered the way they did.

At best, survey scores represent highly subjective, biased, and indeterminate data. Decoding the meaning of qualitative data always requires the messy and complicated work of interpretation and judgment from an outsider reconstructing the original context of the act or utterance. This decoding process is always shaped by the theoretical, political, and personal proclivities of the ethnographer (Hammersley and Atkinson 1995; Geertz 1973; Fish 1980; Rosenberg 1988). As Weissberg (2002) explained, "There can be no such thing as a perfectly politically neutral extraction of real public sentiment" (47).

Thus, while student evaluation surveys are a popular and cost-effective way to gather data on the black box of the classroom, it is clear that these surveys are not valid accountability instruments because they do not measure teaching or learning. In fact, they do not measure anything directly.

Bob Uttl (2017) and his colleagues conducted one of the most recent meta-analysis of student evaluation surveys. Their study is perhaps the most comprehensive one ever done. They made the following conclusions: There is no correlation between survey scores and student learning; students do not learn more from teachers with high evaluation ratings; and at best, surveys explain about 1 percent of the variance in measures of student learning.

For almost a century, researchers have consistently found that not only are student evaluation surveys highly correlated with course grades, but they are also correlated with grade inflation and lower levels of student learning. Further, overreliance on student evaluation surveys can lead to fraud or extortion because instructors feel compelled to play school and inflate grades in order to keep their job and get a promotion. That's why 18 scholarly associations have all stated that student surveys should not be relied upon "as a measure of teaching quality" (Supiano 2019, para. 2).

STUDENT SURVEYS ARE NOT FAIR TO TEACHERS

Over the past 15 years since Johnson (2003) published his seminal book on the subject, there have been many more scientific studies on the questionable validity of student evaluation surveys. Almost all of these studies have reaffirmed that these instruments are highly biased because they are strongly correlated with course grades, grade inflation, lower standards, and lower levels of student learning.

Researchers have also found that these instruments are unfair to teachers because they are based on the subjective emotions and beliefs of students, which are largely beyond an instructor's control. This is especially damaging to quality teachers with high standards because they often receive the lowest evaluation scores, even though they produce the most learning.

These instruments are also discriminatory. Student ratings are correlated with a vast array of prejudices based on teacher characteristics that have nothing to do with teaching, such as race, nationality, gender, and attractiveness.

Take for example a recent study published in the *Journal of the European Economic Association*, which found that students rated women about 37 percent lower than male instructors ("Purblind Prejudice" 2017, 74). In this controlled experiment, close to 20,000 student evaluations were studied after students were randomly assigned a male or female instructor for the same course.

Persistent gender bias was documented, with both male and female students, although male students displayed more gender prejudice. Such bias was clearly demonstrated by the fact that women instructors received lower ratings for teaching materials when both male and female instructors used the exact same teaching materials and textbooks.

Another study conducted by the American Economic Association specifically focused on female professors in the field of Economics, a traditionally male-oriented field. This study found that almost 50 percent of female economists surveyed said they have "personally experienced discrimination or unfair treatment" with student teaching evaluations, while less than 10 percent of male economists said the same ("#EconomistsToo" 2019, table 2).

There have been many studies over the last couple of decades, which have clearly shown that student evaluation surveys are not just subjectively biased, but "hypersensitive," because student opinions can be "influenced by the tiniest and most irrelevant things, from the comfort of the seats to the time of day the course is offered" (Nichols 2017, 97; Pascarella and Terenzini 2005, 115).

Of course, part of the problem has always been traditional stereotypes of what a teacher is supposed to look like and how they are supposed to act. In one of the first sociological studies of education, Willard Waller (1932) explained some of the traditional variables that "determined the prestige of the teacher and his ability to control the classroom" (212). For Waller, these variables included: age, social background, physical characteristics, dress, manners, manner, attitude, voice, expression of features, and personality. The most important characteristic of a teacher, Waller asserted, was "his voice" (226).

But there seemed to be another variable that actually was more important, although Waller was not fully aware of it. Waller admitted that it was "not easy to explain how the size and the strength of the man teacher influence the attitudes which students have toward him" (219). As Waller unconsciously pointed out, it was clearly common sense at the time that all good teachers were men, and no doubt many women teachers suffered lower student evaluation scores merely because of their sex, as they still do almost a century later.

Waller also warned that there was a "natural social distance" between teachers and students, which sometimes created "mutual misunderstanding amounting to enmity," so a good teacher needed to be aware of cultural stereotypes in order to play their expected part so as to increase student compliance and achievement (212). According to Waller, all good teachers needed "a certain facility in acting" in order to be successful (233).

Perhaps the most important finding of the last decade has been the negative correlation between student evaluation surveys and student learning. Michela Braga, Marco Paccagnella, and Michele Pellizzari (2014) conducted a novel experiment to track student learning beyond the confines of a single course. They found that students gave the lowest evaluation scores to the most competent professors who enabled the most student learning.

In this study, professors of prerequisite courses were matched with the grades of students in future, advanced classes. Professors who taught their students the most and enabled them to get the best grades in the future were given on average the lowest evaluation ratings. This study confirmed the conclusions of other studies, which found that students seek out teachers who are easy and who award high grades because many students don't really care about learning. They just want high grades (Milton, Pollio and Eison 1986).

Thus, as many researchers have concluded: "If you make your students do well in their academic career, you get worse evaluations from your students" (Kamenetz 2014, para. 15; see also Stark and Freishtat 2014, 12). Braga et al. (2014) explained that students do not like to be pushed and challenged by a professor, even though this rigorous type of teaching has the greatest impact on future learning.

When you look at the international data, as psychologist Laurence Steinberg (2014) points out, "Students in countries that score highest on tests of achievement typically report enjoying school *less*. That's because their schools demand more hard work from them" (author's emphasis, 110).

Psychologists have also demonstrated that some people are naturally predisposed to focus on negative words and emotions, which can distort memories of challenging or painful experiences (Hibbing, Smith and Alford 2014, 125–29). Thus, many students can *feel* that a challenging educational experience was negative even though they learned a lot.

Dennis E. Clayson (2009) recently published a meta-analysis in 2009 and found that there was only a small association between student evaluations and student learning, although no connection with instructor teaching. However, such correlations were only applicable to some kinds of teachers and subjects. Interestingly, Clayson found that when researchers more objectively measured student learning, the less it was correlated with evaluation scores, which suggests that effective teachers with objective standards are penalized the most by students on these surveys (see also Pfeffer 2015, 28–29).

This result was probably due to the fact that higher learning is the result of harder effort and higher standards, a situation which often translates into lower grades. The hardest professors with the highest standards often enable the most student learning, which some researchers have linked to greater educational and economic success, although it must be noted, the correlations with these subsequent positive outcomes are small, and they were only for high ability students (Braga, Paccagnella and Pellizzari 2016; see also Duckworth 2016). Thus, as professor J. Scott Armstrong concluded, higher "teacher ratings are detrimental to students" (qtd. in Pfeffer 2015, 28).

It is clear that the stress and strain of authentic learning does negatively impact students, but a teacher can help mediate this stress. There is quite a bit of research on how a teacher's positive attitude and positive feedback can contribute to positive student emotions and self-efficacy, which play a role in academic achievement (Hattie and Timperley 2007; Cavanagh 2016; Oettingen 2014, 91).

However, that's not the whole story. Some might find this surprising in today's student-centered climate, but researchers have found that positive feedback from a teacher is negatively correlated with student learning, and that negative feedback is actually positively correlated with learning (Duckworth 2016; Oettingen 2014).

Furthermore, van Doorn, van Kleef, and van der Pligt (2014) specifically looked at the emotional tone of an instructor's voice to measure the effect of happy and angry emotions on student learning. These researchers found that critical feedback delivered in an angry tone was associated with higher student learning. What could be driving that finding?

First of all, psychologists know that negative emotions "help narrow and focus our attention," which can assist the learning process (Brackett 2019, 29). A teacher's negative tone can also be an emotional spark, which motivates students to work harder to address the instructor's criticism. Van Doorn, van Kleef, and van der Pligt (2014) found that students did not report any increased negative feelings in reaction to the angry tone of a teacher, which is surprising because many students do get upset by teacher criticism, especially if it is delivered with a negative tone of voice.

To better understand the role of emotions in student learning, we need to turn to biology. An instructor's emotional tone can be valuable feedback for a student because emotional states are connected to our "innate instincts," which help program our behavior, especially when we are young (Mitchell 2018, 92).

According to neuroscientist Kevin J. Mitchell (2018), our feelings "tag" our sensory perceptions so that incoming information becomes coded with "subjective, affective value" (92). Our emotions influence our behavior, especially strong emotions (Brackett 2019). Psychologist Barbara Tversky (2019) explained that emotion is prior to thinking or understanding. Her "third law of cognition" states, "feeling comes first" (42). We feel before we think.

Thus, emotion plays an important role in learning. When a teacher gives a student positive feedback this makes the student feel good. A good feeling reinforces the student's belief that he or she already has knowledge or skill so there is no instinctual drive to do anything further. The student feels good knowing that he or she already knows.

On the other hand, negative feedback points out a deficiency of knowledge or skill, which creates a problem for the student and produces a negative feeling. Being aware of this deficiency, students worry that their incompetence will negatively affect them in the near future, if it isn't already doing so in the present.

Thus, there is a natural tendency to react to negative feedback and the negative feelings that arise, especially if that feedback is delivered in a negative emotional tone. When we feel bad, we all have an instinctual need to do something to remove the undesirable stimulus. Therefore, we are highly motivated to act, which can increase learning.

An important part of good teaching is to help students understand their own incompetence through critical feedback. Students are lulled into a false sense of confidence that impedes their learning. A teacher needs to help motivate students to work harder in order to recognize their incompetence and to become competent.

Psychologist Gabriele Oettingen (2014) has found that when students fantasize about positive grades they want to receive, they develop a false sense of competence, which leads to less studying, which results in lower grades (14). In fantasizing about high grades, students "fool [their] brains into thinking [they] were already successful," which leads to less motivation and lower energy, which in turn leads to failure (50). Students need to learn not only how to develop realistic goals, but also how to "benefit from negative feedback, since it allows them to adjust their behavior and do what they need to do to acquire new skills" (112; see also Pfeffer 2010, 41).

While direct, negative feedback is an essential pedagogical tool, these days teachers often interact with students who "melt under the slightest pressure due to their extreme fragility," leading some researchers and educators to call early 21st century adolescents "Generation Snowflake" and "a nation of wimps" (Twenge 2017, 154, 166; Luckianoff and Haidt 2018). Adolescents and young adults are also extremely self-centered and preoccupied with their own subjective beliefs and feelings, which often creates a lot of miscommunication and misunderstanding between students and teachers.

Dr. Oliver Sacks (2017) explained how "speech is open, inventive, improvised; it is rich in ambiguity and meaning. There is a huge freedom in this, making spoken language almost infinitely flexible and adaptable but also vulnerable to mishearing," (127). Mishearing can often "sabotage meaning" and lead to miscommunication and disagreement (127).

Nonverbal communication is also full of ambiguity. For example, most people cannot accurately read faces for emotions (Brackett 2019). One study found that 70 percent of the time a person expressing a scowl was not angry. Scientists have found that "there are no such things as recognizable facial expressions for basic emotions which are universal across cultures" ("Face Blind" 2020, 17).

Teachers or professors almost always try to interact with students and deliver constructive criticism with the best of intentions. But many students negatively react to teacher feedback and criticism. Furthermore, rather than accept their own mistakes, students often blame the teacher. This situation makes teaching very difficult.

Most K–12 and college administrators, seeking to serve their consumers and their parents, have adopted an overprotective ethos so as not upset or displease sensitive students (Luckianoff and Haidt 2018). Psychologist Jean M. Twenge (2017) explains how many students and school administrators believe that "no one should ever say anything that makes a student feel bad, even if it might inspire him or her to do better" (157; Luckianoff and Haidt 2018).

Thus, many teachers, including instructors and professors in higher education, are afraid of giving students honest and direct negative feedback out of fear that students will complain. This puts teachers in an uncomfortable bind: Do you try to teach for authentic learning, which involves criticism and hurt feelings, or do you avoid all of this work and misunderstanding and just play school, thereby sacrificing student learning? Many teachers these days settle for the latter because it's easier.

The effectiveness of teachers depends a lot on the biased perception of students. But it's not just students who are making naive and biased judgments about teachers. Administrators are doing it too. Interestingly, recent research has shown that administrative observations of teachers in K–12 schools suffer from the same kinds of biased and discriminatory flaws as student evaluation surveys in colleges.

Many studies of K–12 schools have found that men and teachers of color receive lower observational ratings then do women or white teachers (Jacob and Walsh 2011; Campbell 2014; Jiang and Sporte 2016; Campbell and Ronfeldt 2018). These studies also found that teachers who work in schools with high concentrations of low-income students receive lower evaluations than teachers in wealthy districts because low-income students are more challenging to teach (Steinberg and Garrett 2016; Campbell and Ronfeldt 2018).

Campbell and Ronfeldt (2018) concluded that teacher evaluations "may not be equitable" (4) because of "rater bias" (22) connected to various student characteristics, which are outside the teacher's control. Thus, teachers' student evaluation scores are not caused by "instructional quality but, instead, who they teach" (29). Interestingly, researchers have also found that teachers in low-income schools have lower VAM scores as well as observational scores (Lauen and Gaddis 2013; Sanders and Rivers 1996; Sass, Hannaway, Xu, Figlio and Feng 2012).

But the data is not only biased by student attributes. It's also biased by more trivial and arbitrary issues (Koretz 2017, 149–159), like when a test is administered. Researchers have found significant differences in teachers VAM scores depending on whether data was used from student tests in the fall or the spring semesters (Atteberry and Mangan 2020). Worse, many teachers are evaluated based on the scores of students who are not even in their classroom, like art teachers being evaluated based on the scores of students in a math or English class (Koretz 2017, 149–159).

This means that even relatively objective measures, like VAM scores, can still be very biased, if not largely invalid, not only because of measurement errors, but also because of environmental and political conditions completely outside teachers' control, such as dysfunctional working conditions in schools and the socioeconomic backgrounds of students (Kraft and Papay 2014; Ronfeldt 2015; Schneider 2017, 59; Koretz 2017, 149–159).

After analyzing the major deficiencies of student evaluation surveys, Stark and Freishtat (2014) came to this conclusion, "We're confusing consumer satisfaction with product value" (Berrett 2014, para. 2). They went on to say, "there's general agreement that student evaluations of teaching don't mean what they claim to mean" (Kamenetz 2014, para. 10)

Student evaluations tell us about the biased and emotional mind of the student. They tell us very little, if anything, about the instructor, teaching, student learning, or the curriculum. It can be useful to study and understand student perceptions, but teachers and administrators need to be clear about what is actually being measured and why.

Unfortunately, no one is having this conversation. Stark and Freishtat (2014) conclude: "It's totally valuable to ask [students] about their experience, but it's not synonymous with good teaching" (Berrett 2014, para.14; see also Bunge 2018).

Chapter 5

Predictably Irrational

The Cognitive Miser and the Limits of Consumer Choice

In the 21st century, almost all adolescents in the U.S. and other developed countries have been "trained as consumers from the cradle" (Matthews 1998, 101; Sperber 2000). And like all other consumers, adolescents are poor judges of product quality. Not only do consumers lack knowledge about products and their application, but they also think illogically and make irrational decisions when it comes to choosing what to buy and when (Thaler 2015; Thaler and Sunstein 2008).

It is hard, if not impossible, for many consumers to form accurate judgments, especially when the product is complex or intangible, like health care or education. It's even harder still when the product is a person, as most voters in democratic countries show poor judgment when electing officials or voting on policies (Rosenberg, forthcoming; Lodge and Taber 2013; Hibbing, Smith and Alford 2014; Shenkman 2016; Shenkman 2008; Caplan 2007; Jacoby 2008; Popkin 1994).

CAN CONSUMERS ACCURATELY EVALUATE PRODUCTS?

In a famous study conducted in the 1970s, psychologists Richard Nisbett and Tim Wilson (1977) went to the mall to sell women's stockings. In particular, Nisbett and Wilson wanted to study the reasoning that consumers gave for making a particular purchase. Upon buying a pair of stockings, some consumers explained, "This one looks more resistant" or "I prefer the color of that one" (231–59). Unbeknownst to these consumers, the researchers were selling completely identical pairs of stockings.

Most consumers find it difficult to judge the quality of a product, especially when it is a product or service that is very complex or intangible (Kotler and Keller 2012, 357). These particular people at the mall could not tell that all of the products before them were exactly the same. They also were incapable of accurately judging the quality of the product. At the same time, these consumers were creating many biased and fictitious reasons for choosing one pair of stockings over another, all the while truly believing that they were rationally in charge of purchasing the best product on the market.

This early study of consumer choice later helped psychologists and marketers discover why branding is so important for businesses (Lindstrom 2010; Lindstrom 2011; Banerjee and Duflo 2019, 73). Most consumers have no idea how products work. They can't really tell the difference between similar products (Gerzema and Lebar 2008; Kotler and Keller 2012).

So, marketers bombard consumers with brands and advertising campaigns, which manipulate consumers into believing that well designed and expensive products in fancy packaging with memorable brands are higher quality products than cheaper products with plain labels and no ad campaign. Established brands develop a "reputation" for quality, for coolness, or for value, which "wards off competition" (Kotler and Keller 2012; Banerjee and Duflo 2019, 73–74). Most companies sell an idea, not just a product.

Over the course of the 20th century, education and schooling have become consumer products just like any other good or service, especially higher education (Rhoades 1987). Many researchers, professors, and college presidents have pointed out that higher education formally transformed from an academic institution into a business by the 1980s (Sperber 2000; Bok 2003; Washburn, 2005; Birnbaum 2000), although the political economist Thorstein Veblen perceptively noted that this economic transformation started at the beginning of the 20th century (Spindler 2002, 52–53).

Not only do colleges and universities use the logic of the market to explain and justify their operations, but most college administrators see their organizations as commercial businesses that sell branded commodities and services to customers (Birnbaum 2000, ch. 4; Twitchell 2004, 50; Lukianoff and Haidt 2018, 198–99). Higher education is big business.

Most students don't think of a college degree in terms of an education any more. Instead, students are consumers, and they see college as an investment in human capital. They also see it as a very expensive and relatively exclusive luxury product (Aronowitz 2000; Markovits 2019). A college degree has become a "value proposition" that will enhance the private wealth of the customer who is able to buy it (Khurana 2007, 343–44).

Like many other businesses, colleges sell commodities and services. Colleges and universities have become "knowledge factories" that sell credits, certificates, and degrees (Aronowitz 2000). Since the late 20th century, college has become priced according to market demand (Childress 2019, 76), and the price is high because it has been a relatively scarce commodity. For over half a century, business has been booming.

To some critics, the marketing and commodification of higher education is nothing less than a "clever scam" to deceive unsophisticated consumers who don't understand what they are buying (Sperber 2000, 53; Childress 2019; Aronowitz 2000; see also Kotler and Keller 2012, 357). Your average high school graduate knows next to nothing about how to judge the quality of a college or a degree program, so the situation is ripe for corrupt practices, as seen with the recent scandal of selling access to elite universities in the U.S. (Langlois 2019).

Herb Childress (2019) points out that it is "standard operating" procedure in higher education to "offer vastly different tiers of service to vastly different populations of privilege" (15; see also Grubb and Lazerson 2004; Markovits 2019). Lower class and first-generation college students get the worst educational experience at cheaper nonselective universities and community colleges, which offer watered-down curriculum taught by impoverished adjunct instructors who are assisted by underresourced and overwhelmed student service providers.

Upper class students, on the other hand, are much more likely to come from a home with at least one college graduate. These students tend to be more sophisticated consumers who have more resources to not only select higher quality, selective schools, which are much more expensive, but also to get accepted into these selective schools, some of which turn away over 90 percent of applicants each year.

COGNITIVE SHORTCUTS: EMOTION, PRICE, AND BRAND

Over the past several decades, social scientists have found that the average consumer is not very smart when it comes to choosing the best products and avoiding deceptive marketing practices. Most consumers incorrectly rate brand-name products much higher in quality than do experts who have more sophisticated knowledge. Why? Consumers confuse their psychological feelings about brands with the actual quality of the business' products, which most consumers don't fully understand (Sloman and Fernbach 2017, 148; Lindstrom 2010; Lindstrom 2011; Kotler and Keller 2012).

With the case of higher education, many students choose a college based upon an emotional identification with a brand (Matthews 1998, 34; Childress 2019, 73). Students often think of community pride, family connections, peer recommendations, or a great football program. One study found that 43 percent of prospective students choose a college based on their first experience visiting a college (Sodexo, 2019). That same study also found that 83 percent of students believe that the physical environment of a college campus is "more important than a university's reputation" (Sodexo, 2019, para. 8).

Some students enroll in college because of an appealing advertising campaign, which can often be seen on billboards or heard on the radio. Going to college is now advertised like any other consumer product or branded service. To maximize their revenue, most colleges now use recruiters and advertising campaigns to enroll as many students as possible.

Many college admissions offices have quotas they have to meet so admissions officers will do and say almost anything to enroll a student (Matthews 1998, 33). Some institutions sell enrollment to the highest bidder (Langlois 2019; Golden 2006). And some schools are fraudulent scams, like Trump University, which wasn't even a school, let alone a university.

Few students actually investigate the educational quality of an institution or the merits of a specific program of study before enrolling (Labaree 2017, 126). Many students enter college with no declared major or career plan. Few students know if they have actually chosen an appropriate college to give them the knowledge or skills that they will need in the labor market, or in life.

The average consumer makes many types of irrational decisions when it comes to buying a product or service. The psychology of price, which is often connected to brands, is a case in point (Kotler and Keller 2012, ch. 14). The average consumer mistakes price for quality, believing that expensive products must be of higher quality because they cost so much (Cialdini 2007, 5; Kotler and Keller 2012, 388).

Routinely, consumers rate expensive products much higher in terms of quality than do experts (Sloman and Fernbach 2017, 148). Part of the problem is that most consumers "don't know what they want"; thus, they don't know how to value goods or services until they are given some kind of contextual frame of reference to understand their choice (Ariely 2008, 3; Tversky and Kahneman 1982). When consumers see several products that all look essentially the same, the only *real* difference they can see and understand is a different price. So, consumers use their common sense and assume that a higher price must mean higher quality, and vice versa.

Recently, the discount shoe store Payless Shoe Source played an elaborate prank on unsuspecting consumers (Phillips 2018). The store falsely claimed that a fictitious Italian designer named Bruno Palessi created a new luxury brand of shoes, when in fact this designer was a play on the store's real name, Payless. The store was actually selling the same old cheap Payless shoes, just hyped up with a new brand and an advertising campaign, which was created by DCX Growth Accelerator, an advertising business that specializes in media pranks, or what the company calls "culture hacking" (Phillips 2018, para. 9).

Cheap Payless shoes were given price tags ranging from hundreds of dollars to as high as $1,800. A lot of people bought the cheap shoes at highly inflated prices. These consumers also raved about the "high quality" and "high fashion" of the cheap shoes, with some people even calling them "stunning," "elegant," and "sophisticated" (Phillips 2018, para. 21).

After consumers were duped into buying the shoes, they were led to a back room where the ruse was revealed. They grossly overpaid for cheap shoes because they were deceived by a marketing campaign. Consumers got their money back and were able to keep the shoes for free. After realizing the prank, one unsuspecting consumer explained, "We wouldn't have ever known. We were really convinced. They had us fooled, like completely" (Phillips 2018, para. 27).

Businesses know that the psychology of price can manipulate consumers with any kind of product, even one as simple as shoes. But price becomes an even more important signal with complex products or services that the average consumer can't understand. When it comes to choosing a college or university, many students erroneously believe that an expensive price tag must mean a higher quality education and a more prestigious degree (Labaree 2017, 123).

The naïve association of price and quality has been used by some expensive trade schools to swindle unsophisticated students with poor quality programs. Perhaps the most notorious example was the fraudulent scam of Trump University, which was not a university or even a school.

Sometimes this belief about price can be true. For example, Harvard University, an expensive, private liberal arts college, is considered one of the best and most exclusive schools in the world. However, many people in the education industry believe that Harvard is "the most overrated brand" in higher education because it is "one of the most timid and derivative schools" (Twitchell 2004, 55).

When you think about it, all universities offer the same basic classes. They all have the same kinds of professors who hold the same basic qualifications. They all have the same basic facilities and services. And yet one university can cost $10,000 a year while another one can cost over $50,000.

Some state universities, such as the University of California or the University of Washington, deliver high-quality education that rivals, if not exceeds, what one would get at a more expensive private school, like Harvard. And yet these state schools all cost less than half as much. But how many high school graduates actually know this?

The psychology of price acts as an irrational barrier for most first-generation college students who know little, if anything, about higher education. Most first-generation students come from low-income families and these students are fearful of the exorbitant costs of college. These students think that they cannot afford higher education. Many of these students don't know that they qualify for student aid that would greatly reduce the price of college, even in some cases making college virtually free, although the value of grants has eroded over the last couple decades (Goldrick-Rab 2016).

Most first-generation students, about 52 percent, choose to attend low-cost community colleges (Childress 2019, 34). Why? Because they don't know they can actually afford high-quality higher education with student aid. So, they choose the cheapest type of college that is close to home. However, students don't realize that community colleges provide lower quality education and offer less student services.

Students who enroll at a community college actually decrease their chance of ever earning a degree. Only 60 percent of community college freshmen will make it to their sophomore year. More importantly, only about 15–25 percent of these students will eventually go on to earn their bachelor's degree (Beach 2011a; Childress 2019, 37). Students never read about these dismal statistics in any community college brochure.

Because of their ignorance, the average consumer focuses on the easy to see variables of a product, like brand or cost, which are often only loosely correlated with actual quality, if these variables are connected at all (Gerzema and Lebar 2008). This can easily lead to manipulation, if not fraud. For instance, over the past decade or more, businesses have been reducing the quality and/or size of common consumer items, but retaining their traditional price, all in an effort to maintain corporate profits by manipulating ignorant consumers who don't notice ("Cut-price" 2019, 62).

Consumers often can't judge the quality of products or services. They usually ignore, or just don't understand, the complex variables that determine quality because these variables are unknown, difficult to see, or hard to comprehend (Kotler and Keller 2012, 357; Kahneman 2011). Even sophisticated consumers make "stupid" decisions when buying products or making important decisions (Sternberg 2002).

The main problem is more than simple ignorance. Fundamentally, the human brain is deeply flawed due to the evolutionary history of our species. Psychologist and behavioral economist Dan Ariely (2008) has documented how most people are "predictably irrational" in their behavior and decisions (53). While we believe we make reasoned and rational decisions, most of the time we actually make decisions based on nothing more than automatic biological processes and emotional "gut feelings" (53). Let's explore how this works.

THE DUAL-PROCESS BRAIN AND
THE COGNITIVE MISER

The human mind evolved from our primate ancestors in order to survive a primitive world of rudimentary decision-making, mostly focused on food, safety, sex, tribal relationships, and avoidance of predators (de Waal 2016; Shenkman 2016). We are not biologically equipped to navigate the modern world of globalized urban economies, sophisticated technology, lying politicians, deceptive advertising, and addictive products (Shenkman 2016; Pinker 2002; Wilson 1978).

A couple of decades ago, psychologists and cognitive scientists discovered the "dual-process theory" of the brain (Stanovich 2010). These researchers found that the brain has two systems of thinking. The older, more primitive part of the brain uses unconscious processes to make automatic decisions and take instinctive actions.

The newer, more sophisticated part of the brain uses conscious, critical thinking to weigh evidence and use judgment in order to form more accurate beliefs and take deliberate action. But higher-order critical thinking requires a lot of energy and effort, so it is often impractical to use for a lot of everyday decisions. Thus, our irrationality and stupidity are at root caused by "mindless" automatic decisions made by the primitive, emotional parts of our brain (Hyman 2002, 20).

Keith E. Stanovich (2009, ch. 6) and other psychologists have demonstrated how our brain is often a "cognitive miser." Our brain defaults to the primitive parts of the nervous system to make quick, energy efficient decisions. Due to its evolutionary history, our brain always seeks to expend the least amount of energy and effort in order to think as quickly and simply as possible. The cognitive miser often makes irrational decisions because it relies on instinct, rather than a critical appraisal of the objective environment (Ariely 2008; Kahneman 2011).

The cognitive miser is the oldest part of the brain in charge of "basic biological regulations" and it goes by many names (Damasio 1994, 128). Nobel Prize winner Daniel Kahneman (2011) and many other psychologists call the primitive, automatic process of the brain "system 1" or "fast thinking" (28; Haidt 2006, 14–17; Greene 2013; Stanovich 2009, ch. 3; Mercier and Sperber 2017, 46). Psychologist Walter Mischel (2014) calls it "hot" thinking, or an emotional reflex (7). Other scientists call it the "low" or "old" part of the brain (Damasio 1994, 128).

Automatic thinking reflexes, like our "fight or flight" response, may be very useful when avoiding predators or natural disasters. However, the many biases of the cognitive miser often interfere with our ability to understand the complex realities of the 21st century (Cialdini 2007). These biases also prevent us from making rational decisions or taking effective action.

Perhaps most importantly, our cognitive miser of a brain uses "heuristic" frames to process information (Stanovich 2009, 78, 91; Tversky and Kahneman 1982). Many psychologists have demonstrated how the cognitive miser "effortlessly makes quick judgments that feel right intuitively but are often dead wrong" (Cialdini 2007; Mischel 2014, 98; Tversky 2019, 46).

Automatic, reflexive thinking puts us at risk not only because we make stupid decisions, but also because others can manipulate our natural biases, such as politicians or advertisers, who present us with predetermined choices that put us at a disadvantage (Cialdini 2007; Stanovich 2009, 91; Banaji and Greenwald 2013; Eberhardt 2020).

In order to control the automatic-thinking reflexes of the cognitive miser, we have to consciously and deliberately *slow* our thinking down. We have to engage with our cognitive processes by turning on our more sophisticated, reflective mind in order to critically think and make a rational decision (Kahneman 2011; Stanovich 2009; Mercier and Sperber 2017, 46).

To engage in critical thinking, we first need to examine our thought process to become aware of the errors caused by the automatic reflexes of system 1 so that we can correct them. Then we need to analyze the relevant evidence and employ rational, system 2 critical thinking in order to evaluate whether the evidence proves a claim true or false. This process helps us make rational decisions and take effective actions.

But even when we engage in critical thinking, many psychologists have demonstrated that mistakes are still prevalent, partly because there is usually a "tug-of-war" going on in our brain between system 1 and system 2 processes (Shenkman 2016, xxvii). Our biases are hard to perceive, and harder still to correct (Kahneman 2011, 28; Banaji and Greenwald 2013; Eberhardt 2020). Psychologists like Daniel Kahneman (2011) have demonstrated empirically that our minds are naturally "gullible," "biased to believe" almost anything, and "lazy" (44–49, 81).

We have a hard time recognizing that our subjective beliefs are based on illusions, or that our cultural common sense is based on irrational traditions. Even when presented with contradictory information about the objective world, most people chose to ignore or discount this information so as to continue to justify their prior, common sense beliefs.

Philosopher and psychologist Joshua Greene demonstrated that "false beliefs, once they've become culturally entrenched—once they've become tribal badges of honor—are very difficult to change, and changing them is no longer simply a matter of educating people" (Greene 2013, 94; Banaji and Greenwald 2013; Eberhardt 2020).

The cognitive miser is especially hard to reform because our brain likes to take shortcuts whenever possible. Cognitive shortcuts can sometimes be useful because they save us time and energy. But mental shortcuts are always potentially dangerous.

According to Daniel Kahneman (2011), our brains are naturally biased to "jump to conclusions on the basis of limited evidence," creating a superficial, stereotypical form of knowledge (86). Our cognitive miser brain also looks for the easiest form of evidence available, behaving like a drunk looking for car keys in the dark. Instead of looking in the most logical places, which are dark, a drunk person starts looking in the most improbable places because there is better light (Popkin 1994, 218). So too with our brains. We look for evidence that is easy to find, not evidence that is the most logically valid.

For instance, our brain instinctively makes decisions based on short-term data stored in our working memory, which is a repository of recent experiences. But this part of the brain has a very limited capacity to store data (Evans 1989, 29). In contrast, our brain often ignores data in our long-term memory, which holds a lot more information than our working memory.

We have to consciously prompt ourselves to search our long-term memory, which takes a lot more mental effort and time. Thus, deeper thinking is often neglected for the quicker, more superficial sort. While quick thinking shortcuts, or biases, save us time and energy, they usually produce incomplete or unreliable information, which often leads to bad decisions.

Automatic thinking reflexes are not the only problem with our subjective experience. Our perceptions are constituted through emotions. Our thinking is also informed by emotions (Damasio 1999; Brackett 2019; Tversky 2019, 42). While emotions provide motivation to act, strong emotions, such as fear, sadness, happiness, or greed, can also cloud or block our decision-making processes (Damasio 1994; Brackett 2019).

We literally cannot see clearly when we have strong feelings. The emotional system of the brain receives information and acts instinctively before the rational neocortex has time to process what has happened (Goleman, 1995, 17–21). Thus, our automatic fight-or-flight response makes snap decisions before we even fully perceive the experience, let alone rationally understand it (Haidt, 2001).

Emotion also prioritizes information in our memory. Information presented in a highly emotional way will always seem more meaningful or important to us than information presented rationally without emotion (Popkin 1994, 16; Kahneman 2011). Plus, we become emotionally committed to our personal beliefs. So, it's natural for us to resist new information when it challenges what we already believe to be true (Haidt, 2001; Caplan 2007, 100–101).

While we like to equate the truth with rationality, many psychologists, political scientists, and economists have demonstrated that for most people, seeking out the truth is *irrational* because it takes too much time and effort. The truth doesn't often bring enough material or emotional rewards.

For most consumers, as Gordon Tullock argued, "It is irrational to be . . . well-informed because the low returns from data simply do not justify their cost in time and other resources" (qtd. in Caplan 2007, 94). Some economists call this predicament "rational ignorance" because, as Brian Caplan (2007) explains, many "rational, selfish individuals choose to be ignorant" (94).

Caplan (2007) argued that we all have "mixed cognitive motives" (115). Thus, prioritizing objective truth in order to make rational decisions is but one of many values, which may or may not be important to us in any particular circumstance. Many of our cultural or emotional commitments affect our judgment when we are seeking the truth, especially our material self-interest or social pressure (Caplan 2007, 115). Thus, as Caplan (2007) paradoxically argued, it can be rational for most people to be irrational because everyone else is irrational, and because it's much easier than trying to be rational. Caplan called this state of being "rational irrationality" (123, 141).

Many people do *not* care about the truth. They often "actively avoid" seeking it out. The truth can interfere with our self-image, our self-esteem, our traditions, or the maximization of our personal well-being (Caplan 2007, 123). So, people avoid the truth.

Take for example college students. The pay a lot of money to learn new knowledge and skills at school. When professors confront these students with new knowledge about the world, many students ignore it. Instead, students hold on to their mistaken beliefs. Accepting new information would challenge their old worldview and the trusted, traditional authority of parents, peers, priests, and political leaders. Many students would rather remain ignorant.

Ken Bain (2004) argued that many students defensively "perform all kinds of mental gymnastics to avoid confronting and revising the fundamental underlying principles that guide their understanding of the psychical universe" (23–24). Nobel Prize winning psychologist Daniel Kahneman famously gave a personal example from one of his classes. He told his students how their decisions "violated a fundamental rule of logic." In response, one student in the back of the room shouted, "So what! You just asked for my opinion" (qtd. in Lewis 2017, 327)!

For most people, it is too difficult and uncomfortable to question preestablished beliefs and values. It is too difficult to recognize ignorance in order to correct thinking errors. Searching out the truth is too hard or too uncomfortable.

The limitations of our biological brains make the effective practice of education very difficult, if not impossible. A teacher has two jobs. They have to instruct a student. But more importantly, a teacher has to fight against the cognitive miser in students' brains. Usually, most teachers lose this fight.

Chapter 6

Are Students Capable of Evaluating Teaching or Learning?

An Investigation of the "Fox Effect"

While all human beings make illogical, emotional, and ill-informed judgments every day, this weakness is more serious with teenagers and young adults. Due to the nature of adolescent development, as psychologist Laurence Steinberg (2014) pointed out, "poor judgment" is simply a "consequence of the way their brains work" (68). This leads teenagers to engage in "stupid" and often self-destructive behavior that adults find hard to understand (68).

Steinberg (2014) once asked his teenage son why he ran away from the police. "What were you thinking?" Steinberg asked, to which his son replied, "That's the problem. I wasn't [thinking]" (87). To put it mildly, adolescents are very unreliable sources of information and not prone to effective self-reflection. So, why have institutions of higher education designed accountability instruments, like student surveys, which assume that adolescents can honestly and objectively evaluative their own learning and the quality of their teachers?

This is an interesting question. It becomes even more problematic when we reflect on the predicament of playing school and the limitations of the biological brain, which we discussed in a previous chapter. But there is also another problem. Because many students don't care about schooling, let alone the improvement of teaching or learning through evaluation surveys, mischievous adolescents actually have an incentive to lie on surveys.

Why lie? Sometimes a lie is just unconscious. A lie can be a defense mechanism to protect a student's self-esteem, as we already discussed. But many students lie on purpose. Some students want to play games. Or they want to punish a teacher they don't like. Or perhaps they want to protest their involuntary incarceration in a school they hate. Also, when looking at high profile leaders and celebrities, there are no negative consequences for lying in our culture, and no benefits for being honest (Pfeffer 2015). So, why not lie?

For all these reasons, and more, student evaluation surveys do not tell us much, if anything, about the quality of teachers, the curriculum, or even student learning. We can't even rely on student surveys to give us honest, subjective information about the internal state of students or their preferences.

While student surveys can tell us something about the subjective perceptions of adolescent students as consumers, and their experiences in schools, especially students' expectations about their grades, this kind of data should be handled very cautiously. Researchers or school administrators can't assume that students take these surveys seriously or honestly.

Most of the time, consumer surveys are simply "happy sheets," as management professor Jeffrey Pfeffer (2015) called them (27). Survey instruments are "'smiley-face' indicators of success" (27). These instruments measure consumer satisfaction, not the actual quality of a product or service (27). So why are these unreliable instruments used for high-stakes accountability purposes in schools?

CAN WE TRUST PUBLIC OPINION SURVEYS?

Each individual lives in their own unique subjective world. While we interact with other people and the objective world every day, which helps to balance and widen our perspective, our subjectivity severely biases our understanding of reality (Beach 2018). The root cause of subjectivity is the human brain. Dr. Oliver Sacks (2017) explained, "consciousness is always active and selective—charged with feelings and meanings uniquely our own, informing our choices and interfusing our perceptions" (183).

After we subjectively experience the world, we also subjectively categorize it and associatively store our experience in memory. "The chief reason we find bias everywhere," according to political scientists Milton Lodge and Charles S. Taber (2013), "is because it is rooted in the very architecture of memory" (227). While subjectivity can make our lives meaningful and emotionally rich, our subjective bias can also lead us to misperceive and misunderstand the world, leading to a lot of bad decisions.

The phenomenon of human subjectivity makes opinion surveys highly unreliable data, *at best* (Igo 2007; Weissberg 2002; Rosenberg 1988; Pollan 2008, 74). At worst, opinion surveys produce pure fiction or just nonsense. The academic field of nutrition science is a great example of the unreliability of opinion surveys (Pollan 2008, 77–78). Politics is another. Journalist Rick Shenkman (2016) reviewed a lot of the research on voter irrationality and he argued that "if we want to get at the truth about people's motives" then "we shouldn't think we can simply ask them," xix).

Shenkman (2016) found that not only are people ignorant and unreasonable, but most people cannot fathom just how ignorant and unreasonable they actually are, especially when they try to "offer reasonable explanations" for what are fundamentally irrational and instinctual thought processes (xix; see also Lodge and Taber 2013, 21). Most people think they see the world relatively objectively, but as many psychologists and social scientists have argued, "If you think you are not biased, you are fooling yourself" (Hibbing, Smith and Alford 2014, 7; Banaji and Greenwald 2013; Eberhardt 2020).

The foundations of human subjectivity are the faculties of perception and memory, and both are deeply flawed (Beach 2018; Sacks 2017; Sacks 2012). All of our subjective beliefs and opinions rely on our personal experiences, which are imperfectly stored in either our long-term or short-term memory. Even when people want to sincerely talk about the past, their memory not only biases which information gets recalled, but also how that information gets interpreted and communicated when it is brought to our attention (Mercier and Sperber 2017, 60; Lodge and Taber 2013, 152).

In fact, as neuroscientist Antonio Damasio (1999) explained, "we have usually little direct control over the 'strength' of memories or over the ease or difficulty with which they will be retrieved in recall" (226). All memory is a combination of reflection and re-creation. While "memory isn't an outright fiction," as English professor Jonathan Gottschall (2012) pointed out, it is a "fictionalization" of past experience (168).

This means, as psychologist Frederic Bartlett explained, that memory is "an imaginative reconstruction, or construction" of a personal experience that may or may not have really happened (qtd. in Sacks 2017, 98–99; see also Damasio 1999, 227). When people fill out opinion surveys, they are relying on questionable memories of the past.

Psychologists have documented that "even the most vivid" of memories can be biased or misleading, depending on a host of factors (Gopnik 2009, 136; Tavris and Aronson, 2015; Sacks 2017). Even more troubling, people have the capacity to create detailed, but fictional, memories that are "completely false," but feel very real (Gopnik 2009, 136; Sacks 2017). Psychologists call these false memories "confabulations" (Gottschall 2012, 108–9, 161).

Confabulations are personal fictions that feel real and become an important part of a person's identity. Dr. Oliver Sacks (2017) recalled an interesting story of his own experience with this phenomenon. He explained how he "assumed that the memories I did have—especially those which were very vivid, concrete, and circumstantial—were essentially valid and reliable, and it was a shock to me when I found that some of them were not" (102).

When we personally recall information from our subjective memory, we can never know for sure if everything we remember is actually true. Often it is not. Sacks (2012) has demonstrated that it is "not always easy to discern where the boundary lies between hallucination, misperception, and illusion" because there is no "consensual validation" to verify that what we think we see or remember is actually real (ix–x).

As psychologists Carol Tavris and Eliot Aronson (2015) have explained, memory is an "unreliable, self-serving historian. . . . Memories are often pruned and shaped by an ego-enhancing bias that blurs the edges of past events, softens culpability, and distorts what really happened" (6). Management professor William Isaacs (1999) pointed out that "another word for 'not thinking' is 'memory'" because "human beings live out of their memories, insulated from direct experience" with reality (5).

While memory exists on a gray line between fact and fiction, so to do lies, at least some of them. While we can consciously and deliberately lie, we can also unconsciously lie to both others and ourselves. While most people think of themselves as generally honest, it may be surprising to learn that we all lie, often a lot (Ariely 2012; McLaughlin and Rorty 1988).

Psychologist Dan Ariely (2012) explains how "human beings are torn by a fundamental conflict—our deeply ingrained propensity to lie to ourselves and to others, and the desire to think of ourselves as good and honest people" (165). Researchers have found that dishonesty comes in two basic forms.

First, people can be dishonest because they are deliberately lying to others, for various reasons, but often for personal gain or to make themselves look good. One research report randomly sampled one thousand Americans and found that 40.1 percent of surveyed respondents "admitted to telling a lie in the previous twenty-four hours" (Pfeffer 2015, 117). Another report found that the average American lies 1.65 times a day (117). Everybody lies, and many people do it quite often.

Second, and perhaps more importantly, people can unconsciously lie to themselves due to the brain's natural tendency for motivated thinking (Lodge and Taber 2013, 24; Pfeffer 2015). We often perceive ourselves and others in way that promotes a "positive self-image" (Ariely 2012, 158; Stephens-Davidowitz 2017, 105–8; Tavris and Aronson, 2015; Pinker 2011, 490; "Don't Even Ask" 2018; Pollan 2008, 74). We want to protect our self-esteem, and preserve our preestablished beliefs.

One of the most important discoveries in modern psychology is the practice of self-deception (Mele 2001; Shenkman 2016, ch. 6; McLaughlin and Rorty 1988). We believe many things about others and ourselves because we *want* our beliefs to be true, not because they are true (Mele 2001, 11; Pinker 2011, 491; Pfeffer 2015, 39; Shenkman 2016, ch. 6). We seem to be biologically programmed to lie to ourselves and to others in order to make ourselves seem "wiser, abler, and nobler" than we really are, although there can be many motives for lying, especially to ourselves (Pinker 2002, 265; Pinker 2011, 491).

One of the most interesting cases of self-deception was Binjamin Wilkomirski, who published a well-received book in 1995 about being a Polish Jew in a German concentration camp during World War II. A few years later, however, the facts came to light. Wilkomirski was Swiss, not Polish. He was also not a Jew. And much worse, he had never been to a concentration camp.

While some people called him a fraud, Dr. Oliver Sacks (2017) argued that Wilkomirski suffered from an "extended fabulation" (116). His "primary intention was to deceive himself" because when he was confronted by the facts, "his reaction was one of bewilderment and confusion. He was totally lost, by this point, in his own fiction" (116–117). Sacks explained that "once such a story or memory is constructed, accompanied by vivid sensory imagery and strong emotion, there may be no inner psychological way of distinguishing true from false, nor any outer, neurological way" (120).

As economists always point out, incentives matter. If consumers have no personal incentive to take a survey seriously, then they are more likely to lie, either accidentally or on purpose (Weissberg 2002; Stephens-Davidowitz 2017, 108; Pollan 2008, 74). In nutrition science, researchers have found that people lie a lot about what they eat and how much. Journalist Michael Pollan (2008) argued that "the entire field of nutritional science rests on a foundation of ignorance and lies" (76). Scientists have found that "people on average eat between a fifth and a third more than they say they do on questionnaires" (Pollan 2008, 74).

An enterprising social scientist has recently studied big data sets on the web. He estimated that about one third of all people lie in everyday conversations when they are gossiping with friends, family, and co-workers. Using this as a baseline estimate, at least 30 percent of survey responses could be false or unreliable (Stephens-Davidowitz 2017, 107).

However, it is important to note that there is a gray area between unconscious lying and shifting, uncommitted preferences. When we consider the quick, anonymous, one-off nature of most consumer surveys, as opposed to face-to-face conversations with people we will have to see again, the amount of lying or unreliably expressed preferences on surveys could be much higher (Lodge and Taber 2013).

And when it comes to dishonesty, social scientists know that teenagers are the worst offenders. Researchers who work with children know that immature teens often deliberately "mess with surveys" (Stephens-Davidowitz 2017, 108). In one study of adopted teenagers, around 19 percent of the participating teens lied about being adopted, the very first and most important question of the survey, which fatally compromised the results of the whole study, wasting a lot of time and money (Stephens-Davidowitz 2017, 108). These teens were most likely pranking the gullible researcher, but there could be other interpretations as well (Tavris and Aronson 2015).

Considering all of this, while consumer surveys are plagued by dishonesty, the rate of lying could be much higher for student evaluation surveys in schools because adolescents are particularly unreliable respondents. Not only do immature teens have no incentive to be honest, some of them will be deliberately lying for fun, out of revenge, or because of peer pressure.

Both the unreliability of human memory and the propensity of humans to lie raise important questions about the validity of not only opinion surveys, but also eyewitness testimony in courts of law. Dr. Oliver Sacks (2017) explained that "the testimony of eyewitnesses is notoriously subject to suggestion and to error, frequently with dire results for the wrongfully accused" (118; see also Loftus 1996).

The unreliability of biased, subjective opinions can also be compounded and camouflaged with statistics. Survey data is often presented mathematically, often with statistics. But there can be large margins of error with such statistics, especially when the sample population is small and not randomly chosen. Statistical analysis of opinion surveys can only be taken seriously if the data comes from a large, randomly selected sample, preferably a sample with at least hundreds of respondents, if not thousands. That is rarely the case with student evaluation surveys. Most classes are very small, with less than 30 students.

However, even with a large, random sample of survey data, statistical analysis does not guarantee useful or meaningful information. As we discussed, Stark and Freishtat (2014) have shown how the concrete statistical measurements produced by opinion surveys can often be misleading, if not completely meaningless (5).

Most consumers don't know if statistics are accurate, and many don't care. Pollsters use the statistical analysis of opinion surveys to project a veneer of objectivity in order to better manipulate ignorant consumers, which is an old, established tactic of public relations firms and advertisers. Critics have called this deceitful practice, "lying with statistics" (Huff 1954), or what professor of journalism Charles Seife (2010) called, the deception of "proofiness." The popular website Yelp seems to have turned this kind of deception into a business model ("How One Restaurant" 2014).

Any survey that does not follow rigorous qualitative procedures can be methodologically compromised, especially if researchers ask biased or leading questions. "What is the answer?" Alice B. Toklas asked Gertrude Stein on her deathbed, to which Stein responded, "What is the question" (qtd. in Weissberg 2002, 10)? Survey questionnaires either implicitly or explicitly frame particular issues based on particular theoretical assumptions, which may be wrong or at least debatable.

These frames of reference help determine not only the answers respondents give, but also the very thinking and decision-making that respondents use to come up with their answer (Ariely 2008; Tversky and Kahneman 1982). As statistician and journalist Nate Silver (2012) pointed out, "numbers have no way of speaking for themselves. We speak for them. We imbue them with meaning" (9).

Thus, investigators have to be careful about distinguishing the "signal" from the "noise" in statistical research. This includes not only designing valid studies, but also *not* "selectively picking out the parts we like and ignoring the remainder" (4–5). Rarely do pollsters take such care with surveys. Pollsters usually pander to a target audiences for material or political gain, often to manipulate that audience to sell a product or recommend a candidate for office, as recent complaints about the website Yelp have alleged ("How One Restaurant" 2014).

In the late 19th century, British philosopher and political activist John Stuart Mill argued, "In politics it is almost a triviality to say that public opinion now rules the world" (qtd. in Shenkman 2016, 9). But up until the mid-20th century in most democratic countries, public opinion was important only in the domain of politics, and nowhere else. But since the 1960s, the narrow domain opinion polling in politics broke loose.

This trend has intensified since the 1990s, with the development of the world wide web and social media. Consumer satisfaction surveys and user rating systems have now expanded into almost every domain ("Barely" 2018, 65). Most businesses and nonprofit organizations now use these tools to seek out personal connections with voters and consumers. But as consumer surveys have proliferated, especially on the web, there has been little, if any, attention to methodological quality in terms of how these surveys are constructed, administered, and interpreted (Silver 2012; Weissberg 2002; Rosenberg 1988). This problem has become particularly acute with political polls.

Take for example recent political polling on the former U.S. president, Donald Trump. Trump was uniquely unpopular, but it had been hard to figure out his exact approval ratings, which ranged from 39 percent to 55 percent at the beginning of 2017. Nate Silver (2017) found that survey measures of Trump's popularity depended a lot on who was polled and how.

In particular, Silver found that Trump's approval ratings were "systematically higher" in polls of likely or registered voters, versus polls of all adult Americans (para. 3). Trump's popularity also varied systematically by how people were surveyed. When Americans were called live on the telephone and interviewed, Trump's approval ratings were lower than if people were called by an automatic telephone service, or if they were polled online.

To make matters worse, not only have opinion polls on Trump been highly varied and unreliable, but Trump and his supporters have often "cherry-picked" the polls with the most favorable results that made him look good. While no surprise, his detractors picked the polls that made him look worse (para. 15). No wonder the average American voter has been hopelessly confused about politics (Popkin 1994; Jacoby 2009; Shenkman 2008; Weissberg 2002).

The previous example points out an important flaw with all public opinion surveys. Most people are unaware of how and why they make decisions (Shenkman 2016; Lodge and Taber 2013). The method of polling has a definite effect on voters' preferences, which shows how irrational and instinctual decision-making is for most people.

Take for example the research of political scientists Larry Bartels and Christopher Achen. They discovered that the United States presidential election of 2000 between George W. Bush and Al Gore was decided by 2.8 million voters across the country who voted against the incumbent, Al Gore, who was previously Vice President under Bill Clinton. Why did they vote against Gore? Because the weather in their state was either "too dry or too wet" (qtd. in Shenkman 2016, xxiv).

You read that right. Bartels and Achen concluded that bad weather produces a clear trend in American politics. They found that "adverse weather conditions cost the incumbent 1.5 percentage points" on average in most elections (qtd. in Shenkman 2016, xxv).

And it's not just the weather. Political scientists have also found "clear evidence that the success and failures of the local college football team before Election Day significantly influence the electoral prospects of the incumbent party" (qtd. in Shenkman 2016, xxvi). Every year, millions of American voters irrationally blame incumbent politicians for weather and sporting events. And we expect these same people to give us useful survey data on products and services?

User-rating systems make consumers feel important and empowered. Businesses want people to think that they are catering their products and services around consumer opinion. And some businesses certainly do take consumer comments seriously (Anderson 2008, 99). But the rise of user rating systems, as political scientist Tom Nichols (2017) argues, has given ignorant consumers a dangerous sense of pseudo-knowledge and overconfidence.

Consumer satisfaction surveys "create a habit of mind in which the layperson becomes accustomed to judging the expert, despite being in an obvious position of having inferior knowledge of the subject material" (Nichols 2017, 97). As political scientist Robert Weissberg (2002) pointed out, opinion polls implicitly "assume that the public can play a useful role" in deciding public policy, designing consumer products, or delivering services (7). However,

Weissberg argued, this is actually a "highly debatable" proposition that hasn't been proven by researchers (7).

In fact, most research suggests that consumers and the public at large are highly irrational decision makers. As amply documented by political scientists, the most damning evidence is that most people can't even reliably and consistently state their own beliefs, attitudes, and preferences (Lodge and Taber 2013, 22). Most people don't actually know what their own opinions are. The danger of consumer ignorance is most pronounced with services in general (Kotler and Keller 2012, 357), especially highly technical services, like healthcare, engineering, and education, but it is also a serious problem in politics (Nichols 2017). It is hard to see and understand the quality of a service, as opposed to a product that we can hold in our hand.

Most consumers do not have the ability to judge the quality of a doctor or pharmacist, so why would we expect them to be able to judge a teacher? Virologist Roberto Burioni sardonically explained, "Does an aircraft engineer take a vote among the passengers as to how many wheels to put on an airplane? No—the engineer is the expert, he's trained for this job, and it's his job to decide" (qtd. in Starr 2020, 17).

Matthew Stewart (2009), a philosopher and former business consultant, attacked the very idea of students evaluating teachers as absurd: "Customer satisfaction is a good way to sell shoes; but it is a bad way to relieve ignorance. It is fundamentally stupid to base the content of an education on what the as-yet uneducated person decides as best" (295; see also Nichols 2017).

THE FOX EFFECT: CAN STUDENTS ACTUALLY EVALUATE TEACHERS?

Do any professional organizations seek out feedback from uneducated consumers in order to hire or fire trained experts on the basis of satisfaction surveys? For the most part, the answer is clearly, no. Not doctors or dentists. Not lawyers or engineers. Not mechanics or electricians. But schools do. Teachers are perhaps the only professionals, especially adjunct instructors in higher education, whose employment contract and promotion eligibility are largely dependent upon consumer satisfaction surveys.

And what do student consumers want? In a recent study of student evaluation surveys in higher education, economist Mindy S. Marks demonstrated that most students responded to the evaluation survey in terms of a single issue: Popularity (Berrett 2014). Most students read every survey question as, "Did I like the professor?"

Likability is a biased and largely unconscious commonsense categorization based on emotions and cultural identification. Political scientists have called this decision-making shortcut the "likability heuristic" (Lodge and Taber 2013, 4; Sniderman, Brody and Tetlock 1991, ch. 6). It is highly correlated with a person's cultural background and race (Banaji and Greenwald 2013; Eberhardt 2020).

Psychologists have shown how human emotions can be "readily divided into positive or negative" categories, as well as high energy and low energy categories (Brackett 2019). Thus, we all have an automatic need to "like" or "dislike" the people we encounter (Cialdini 2007, ch. 5; Brackett 2019; Tversky 2019, 42).

So, instead of reading survey questions objectively and trying to form accurate and fair judgments about teacher performance and course quality, students usually make instant and reactive judgments of "like" or "dislike." These judgments are formed during the first contacts between student and teacher, usually within minutes after meeting, sometimes within seconds. After this "like/dislike" judgment has been formed, it prevents you from seeing what's clearly before your face; all you're seeing now is a label" such as "I like this person so I will interpret everything they do in a positive way" (Brafman and Brafman 2008, 75; see also Cialdini 2007, ch. 5; Pfeffer 2010, 9).

The converse is also true. For example, as Brafman and Brafman (2008) point out, "Once a professor is described as cold, his personality and teaching ability cease to matter: his students dislike him anyway. The diagnosis bias causes us to distort or even ignore objective data" (75). Everything that a disliked professor does will be interpreted in a negative way.

But first impressions and likeability are not accurate measures of teaching ability. These "rapid social judgments" turn out to have "no validity" in terms of actual teacher competence (Tversky 2019, 46). Plus, just because you don't like someone, it doesn't mean you can't learn from them. Many researchers have pointed out that it's important to be able to learn from all experiences, even from people who are different from you, or from people you don't like or don't respect (Pfeffer 2010, 8–9).

Research shows that rather than caring about a teacher's competence, many students care more about a teacher's attractiveness, personality, or personal beliefs (Berrett 2014, para. 18; see also Cialdini 2007, ch. 5; Lodge and Taber 2013, 8; Pfeffer 2015, 25). And as we have already demonstrated, students care most about the grades they will receive, and whether or not a teacher will easily give out high grades (Johnson 2003). If a teacher gives a student a good grade and makes a class easy, then they are liked. If a teacher gives low grades and makes a class hard then they are disliked. It's often as simple as that.

The likability heuristic is yet another example of consumer irrationality (Cialdini 2007, ch. 5). Consumers often confuse popularity for competency, or as a marker for quality, especially immature adolescent consumers who prize being accepted and admired by their peers above all else (Steinberg 2014, 95). Thus, in consumer-driven schools, teaching and the curriculum are tailored to what students subjectively "like" and feel is fun or cool, not what students actually need to become educated and professional adults.

The whole point of life for adolescents, as psychologist Laurence Steinberg (2014) pointed out, is the maximization of pleasure (74) and enhanced peer group status (95), not the development of knowledge or skills, or planning for the future. Thus, in consumer-driven schools, teachers are hired and fired because of their popularity and coolness, or their easiness and leniency as graders, not because of their teaching ability or the learning they enable.

Education is a complex and difficult "product" to understand, let alone evaluate. While everyone has a simple, common sense belief about what teaching entails, most people, including educational administrators and some teachers, cannot explain the proper practice of teaching or the science of learning. Professor of education Theodore R. Sizer (1992) explained, most students are not "apt at self-diagnosis nor much given to intellectual self-consciousness" (3). So why would educational administrators ask immature consumers with limited knowledge or experience to effectively evaluate a complex product like teaching, especially since students only directly experience a fraction of what an effective teacher does? As Matthew Stewart (2009) pointed out, having students judge the quality of teachers is "fundamentally stupid" (295).

This line of reasoning raises another important question. We've been asking if students *should* rate their teachers because of the natural biases of the human brain. We have demonstrated that human subjectivity leads to irrational and unfair decisions. But perhaps there is an even better question. Are students even capable of understanding and recognizing the qualities of good teaching? Is evaluating a teacher even *possible*?

Some researchers actually set up experimental studies to test this very question. In what has been called "the Fox affect," clever researchers have shown that no matter the age or sophistication of the student, whether they are adolescents or even highly educated, adult professionals, most students cannot accurately recognize, let alone judge, the important qualities of a good teacher.

Even worse, most students cannot actually distinguish between a real teacher and a paid actor delivering a deliberately fake lecture with false information. Why is this? Because most students simply want to play school. Most students prefer entertainment over education. Thus, most students are easily seduced by people who *act* like teachers but who do not teach, or cannot teach (Sperber 2000, 87).

As Willard Waller (1932) pointed out almost a hundred years ago, in the eyes of a student, a good teacher is a good actor (233). Most people want schooling to be fun. They want "edutainment," rather than an actual education (Pfeffer 2015, 25, 29). Students want to feel like they are learning, but not actually do the hard, painful work of learning.

The first and most famous study to empirically investigate the ability of students to evaluate teachers was conducted in the early 1970s. It was published in the *Journal of Medical Education*. Naftulin, Ware, and Donnelly (1973) invited eleven professionals who had degrees in psychology and social work to attend a lecture called "Mathematical Game Theory as Applied to Physical Education."

The lecture was presented by Dr. Myron L. Fox, who was introduced as an expert on mathematics and human behavior. The attendees enjoyed a lively and witty lecture. Then they were asked to fill out a student evaluation survey at the end. All of the attendees agreed that Dr. Fox had increased their interest in the topic. Ninety percent agreed that Dr. Fox was enthusiastic, well organized, and interesting.

Dr. Fox was also videotaped. This tape was shown to two other audiences. On one occasion, a group of professionals trained in psychology saw the tape. Like the first class, a majority of this second group rated Dr. Fox highly as a teacher.

On another occasion, this videotape was presented to 33 students who were enrolled in a graduate-level university course on educational philosophy. These students were also highly educated, with 21 having already earned a master's degree and 8 having a bachelor's degree. This group of students was given a survey evaluation after watching the video. They rated Dr. Fox very highly as a teacher.

About 97 percent agreed that Dr. Fox was interested in his subject. About 91 percent said he used adequate examples. About 87 percent said he had aroused their interest in the topic. About 81 percent said his teaching was interesting. And finally, about 70 thought he was well organized (Naftulin, Ware and Donnelly 1973, 632–33). So, what was the purpose of this study?

It turns out that Dr. Fox was not a doctor or a university professor. He wasn't even a teacher. In fact, he was a professional actor who had been paid to impersonate a university lecturer.

And to make matters worse, the researchers had deliberately written a false and nonsensical lecture filled with "double talk, neologisms, nonsequiturs, and contradictory statements" (631). None of the professionals or students in any of the three audiences seemed aware of the fact that they received a lecture filled with nonsense.

This study really calls into question the whole legitimacy of secondary schools, institutions of higher education, and even employee training seminars. What do students really learn in school, if anything? The students in this study obviously don't understand real teaching from acting, or even legitimate information from nonsense. They also couldn't tell if they were learning or not. And yet most students left this experience *feeling* more competent and educated, even though there were not. These are disturbing results.

Naftulin, Ware & Donnelly (1973) wanted to prove that students, even highly educated students, were in no position to evaluate the quality of the teacher, the curriculum, or even their own learning. Further, these researchers wanted to demonstrate that not only are students poor judges of teacher quality, but that they could be easily deceived and manipulated "into feeling satisfied that they had learned despite irrelevant, conflicting, and meaningless content" (630).

As Valen E. Johnson (2003) pointed out about this study, most students cannot seem tell the difference between flashy entertainment vs. real education. Perhaps even worse, most students seem to prefer entertainment from an actor, rather than the hard work of authentic thinking and learning that comes from a teacher (135).

Ware and Williams (1975) replicated the Fox study with the same actor, although the second time they designed a more complex study with 200 undergraduate students who were given a more elaborate 18-item questionnaire. These students were also given a 26-item exam to test their learning.

The students were randomly assigned to one of six lecture groups, which were organized around two measured criteria. The first variable was lecture content quality, which was broken into low, medium, and high. The second variable was seduction, which was broken into low and high. The seduction variable represented entertaining qualities, such as "enthusiasm, humor, friendliness, expressiveness, charisma, and personality" (151).

Ware and Williams (1975) found that the content criteria affected student test scores, but it did not affect the teacher evaluation scores when the instructor was highly seductive. Thus, when students encountered the highly seductive teacher, they rated the actor very highly on teaching ability in the low, medium, and high content classes, despite the fact that students in the low and medium lectures were exposed to significantly less information and did worse on the exam.

While the quality of lecture content predicted student achievement on the exam, it was not a predictor of student satisfaction with the teacher in the medium- and high-seduction classes, only the low-seduction classes. Thus, these researchers proved that teacher evaluation scores were not correlated with the quality of student learning. Ware and Williams (1976, 1977) conducted two more replication studies and found the same basic effect.

Over two decades later, a psychology professor designed a naturalistic experiment to test the effect of seductive, expressionist speaking techniques

on student survey evaluation scores (Williams and Ceci 1997). These seductive techniques had been taught by a professional media consultant who had
been invited by university administrators to conduct teacher-training workshops for professors on a college campus.

The psychology professor had taught the same course for almost 20 years.
He wanted to see if these seductive techniques could manipulate student
evaluation scores. For the experiment, he collected his student evaluation
scores after the fall semester. Then in the spring, he taught the same identical
course in the same way, except for introducing some of the seduction techniques taught by the media consultant.

The professor found no improvement in student learning as measured by
exam scores. However, he was awarded higher student evaluation scores on
every survey item, especially on the instructor enthusiasm question, which
rose from a mean rating of 2.14 in the fall all the way up to 4.21 in the spring.
His overall course rating went from 2.50 up to 3.91.

Interestingly, while student achievement was flat, students rated their own
self-perceived achievement much higher, from a mean of 2.93 in the fall up to
4.05 in the spring. They also rated instructor knowledge higher, from 3.61 up
to 4.05. Students even rated the quality of the exact same textbook much
higher, from 2.06 up to 2.98. Clearly, students have no objective understanding of teaching, the curriculum, or even their own learning. But students are
highly influenced by seductive communication techniques.

Since the first paper was published in the early 1970s, many other Fox
effect studies have been conducted. All of these studies substantiated the
same basic conclusions. Student survey evaluation scores are not correlated
to either learning or the quality of teaching. Students are also highly influenced by a teacher's physical appearance and seductive acting techniques
(Johnson 2003, 136–38).

In one study (Ambady and Rosenthal 1993), researchers wanted to see how
much instructor attractiveness and nonverbal communication contributed to
student survey evaluation scores. A control group of students were shown
only three ten-second video bits of a lecture that was muted with no sound.
A second group of students took a whole semester class. Both groups were
exposed to the same teacher.

Interestingly, the evaluation ratings of the control group closely matched
the ratings of the students who took the whole course. This suggests that
most students hastily formed their opinions in seconds about the quality of
the teacher based on unconscious judgments of physical appearance and
non-verbal communication. Most of these students were oblivious to actual
teaching skill or their own learning.

These experiments have been replicated and confirmed in other domains
outside of education, especially with political decision-making (Shenkman

2016, ch 5; Lodge and Taber 2013, 8) and organizational leadership (Pfeffer 2015). Most people expect "leaders," which includes teachers, to act out a stereotypical script of what leaders should look like and what they should act like. In short, people expect leaders "to act like a leader, to act in a way that inspires confidence and garners support" (Pfeffer 2015, 98–99).

Attractiveness is a particularly influential bias in most people's reasoning about effective leadership. Researchers have found that "physical appearance exerts a strong influence on character perception" (Lodge and Taber 2013, 8; Pfeffer 2015, 25). This phenomenon is often called the "beautiful-is-good halo effect" (Lodge and Taber 2013, 8; Pfeffer 2015, 25).

In one influential study, researchers found that it takes most people only "a tenth of a second to draw an inference about someone's traits" (Shenkman 2016, 62). And when researchers gave people more time to make thoughtful judgments, "they simply use it to grow more confident in the accuracy of their inference," not to critically think about the person in order to be more precise and truthful (62).

Another study found that most people form favorable opinions about others who look similar to themselves. This shows that many people make biased judgments based on stereotypes drawn from their personal and cultural experiences (63; Banaji and Greenwald 2013; Eberhardt 2020).

In a literature review on the Fox Effect, Abrami, Leventhal, and Perry (1982) argued that there were two basic conclusions to be gleaned from this line of research:

> First, instructor expressiveness had a substantial impact on summary and global ratings but much less on student achievement. Second, lecture content had a substantial impact on student achievement but much less on student ratings. (454)

Several studies (Cohen 1987; Koon and Murray 1995) have also shown that student evaluations of teaching account for less than 20 percent of the variance in student achievement between different sections of the same class.

Marsh and Dunkin (1992) found that "most variance in achievement scores at all levels of education is attributable to student presage variables" (170). They also found that teachers, teacher methods, and school practices have very little effect on student achievement (170). Even elite private schools have little to no effect on student achievement (Pianta and Ansari 2018), as student socioeconomic variables account for almost all variance in school performance (Schneider 2017, 81).

Thus, the evidence seems to prove that teachers don't have much of an impact on student learning, although the curriculum and school resources do. More importantly, students can't recognize their own learning or explain why it happens. Nor can they recognize or appreciate quality teaching.

Most students mistakenly confuse seductive entertainment for education. Most students prefer the former rather than the hard work of actually learning. As one Ohio State University undergraduate explained: "A good prof in a lecture course is an entertainer . . . a bad prof is a prison guard" (qtd. in Sperber 2000, 87).

Most students want to do as little learning as possible. Thus, a good teacher is an easy and entertaining teacher who makes few demands on students, especially by not being a "prison guard," which presumably means an instructor who actually requires students to come to class prepared to learn. With this in mind, Johnson (2003) argued,

> The use of student evaluations of teaching for administrative purposes and as measures of overall teaching effectiveness has been an unqualified failure. Not only has their use for these purposes had the unintended consequence of altering the dynamics of student-instructor interactions in ways that are not yet fully understood, but current teacher-course evaluation forms are, at best, only modestly correlated with actual student achievement. (151)

In his own statistical analysis of student achievement in higher education, Johnson (2003, 159–60) found that the biggest predictors of student success were (from highest to lowest): student GPA (+3.82), student grades in prerequisite classes (+1.52), relevance of class (+1.51), challenging assignments (+1.10), grading stringency of instructor (+0.79), instructor enthusiasm (+0.65), and class attendance by student (+0.62).

Johnson also found that student survey course ratings were negatively associated with student achievement and instructor knowledge. In particular Johnson found negative correlations with course difficulty (–1.15), the challenging nature of a class (-0.89), instructor knowledge (–0.61), and encouraging questions (–0.47).

Further, Johnson (2003, ch. 6) found that when it came to taking optional elective classes, students were twice as likely to choose courses with inflated grade averages of A, than they were with courses graded at a B average. This demonstrates a clear student bias against more rigorous science and mathematics classes because those classes demand real learning which is harder work.

SHOULD PROFESSIONALS GIVE CONSUMERS WHAT THEY WANT?

In reviewing studies on student evaluation surveys and academic achievement in institutions of higher education, it is clear that students prefer easier classes where they will not be challenged so that they can earn higher grades, even though this will result in less learning or no learning. Students want "edu-tainment," not an education (Pfeffer 2015, 25, 29).

This situation creates a difficult paradox for teachers and educational administrators. As consumers, students prefer less studying, less difficulty, and less learning. As educators, teachers prefer more studying, more difficulty, and more learning. Whose preferences should school administrators be following?

Over the last few decades, it is clear that school administrators believe that their primary duty is to serve student consumers, especially in higher education where students pay for a significant portion of tuition. This shift toward "consumer-driven" organizations can be seen in almost all institutions and organizations, not just schools (Starr 2017, 468).

While it might seem intuitive to most people that organizations should give consumers what they want, this can actually be a dangerous strategy because consumers don't usually know what they want, or what they need (Kotler and Keller 2012). Take health care, for example.

Over the past couple decades in the U.S., the government has been figuring out how to increase the quality control of health care through accountability metrics, which mirrors in many ways the accountability movement in U.S. schooling (Cuban 2013, 112). Health care public policy has been more and more focused on consumer "choice" and consumer "empowerment" (Starr 2017, 466). Just like schooling, there is a hidden underlying assumption, as educational historian Larry Cuban (2013) pointed out, "Doctors are totally responsible for what happens to patients and patients, perversely, play no part in healing" (117).

One of the biggest changes in healthcare has been to measure and rate the quality of care that patients receive. The Centers for Medicare and Medicaid Services mandated certain evaluation measures from hospitals and care providers, which included patient-satisfaction surveys. Collecting survey data sounds reasonable, right?

Not really. Patient surveys have had a perverse, unintended consequence (Gregory 2016; Cohen 2018). A 2012 study published in the *Archives of Internal Medicine* concluded that highly satisfied patients were spending more money on prescription drugs and dying at higher rates (Gregory 2016). In a follow-up study in 2014 published in *Patient Preference and Adherence*, 48 percent of doctors surveyed said that they were overprescribing pain medication, sometimes inappropriately, because patients asked for it and the doctors were worried about patient evaluation surveys.

Another study found that doctors were overprescribing antibiotics because of the same reason (Cohen 2018). After analyzing 8,437 patient satisfaction surveys, researchers found that antibiotic prescriptions were the most important factor driving high ratings on surveys (Gregory 2016). One of the surveyed doctors explained how some patients were "well aware of the patient satisfaction scores and how they can use these threats and complaints to obtain narcotics" (qtd. in Gregory 2016, 19–20). Another doctor warned, "It is very problematic because it creates an incentive for physicians to do things that are not medically necessary in order to drive up their satisfaction ratings" (qtd. in Cohen 2018, para. 6).

The U.S. spends more on health care than most other countries in the world. A big part of this expense is unnecessary and expensive medical tests, which lead to the overtreatment of patients. Some people have blamed hospitals and doctors for being greedy in boosting the bottom line, but there is a simpler and more troubling explanation: patient preference (Freedman 2019).

Too many people want their doctors to perform a bunch of unnecessary tests and procedures. Many patients complain, and they rate doctors lower on surveys when they don't get what they ask for. Doctors are also fearful of malpractice lawsuits so they conduct extra tests to protect themselves (Freedman 2019, 29).

Take for example back pain, which is one of the most prevalent injuries that most people face at some point in their lives. Only 15 percent of back pain has a specific cause that can be treated medically, and only about 1–5 percent of people suffering from back pain require urgent medical treatment ("Backs to the Future" 2020, 18). In America in 2013 about $88 billion was spent on back and neck pain, almost as much as the $115 billion spent on cancer.

But unlike cancer treatments, most procedures for back pain are unnecessary and ineffective ("Backs to the Future" 2020, 17). The most effective procedures to treat back pain are nonmedical. They include getting more regular exercise, stretching more, adjusting diet, and reducing stress. But many patients don't want to hear about these remedies because they require too much work.

Like teachers and other professionals, doctors have been increasingly feeling pressured by consumer surveys and the dogma that consumers are always right. Traditionally, doctors have struggled to uphold professional ethics and resist the "sovereignty of consumer choice" (Starr 2017, 23). But lately, many doctors have been giving in to consumer choice and committing malpractice. Like other professionals, doctors are increasingly scared of how negative patient comments can now affect their reputation, their business, and their ability to attract new clients.

The predicament of doctors is very similar to the predicament of K–12 teachers, adjunct college instructors, and even some tenured college professors. To avoid the consequences of negative student evaluations, teachers at every level are giving students what they want, even if doing so violates professional codes of conduct and defeats the official purpose of schooling.

Like doctors, many teachers with high standards and professional ethics feel pressured, if not extorted, by students, parents, administrators, and even other teachers.

Everyone seems to be saying: Give consumers what they want. In the case of education, this means giving students high grades without demanding much work or learning in return. When teachers and administrators align the institutional mission of schooling with customer satisfaction, they begin to neglect, if not betray, the very purpose of education. This is like consumer-oriented doctors, who are often called "quacks" (Starr 2017, 23). These kinds of doctors are more likely to betray their oath to promote the overall health of their patients.

The "consumer is always right" mantra, expressed most directly with the proliferation of consumer satisfaction surveys, also puts too much emphasis on the role of service providers. It creates passive consumers who expect their every need to be satisfied without doing much, if anything, for themselves. This can be inefficient and self-defeating when it comes to life-changing services, like healthcare and education, where doctors and teachers can only do so much for consumers who are largely responsible for their own health and learning.

A recent study found that 74 percent of the variation in life expectancy around the world was due to consumer lifestyle choices, especially activity levels, smoking, and diet (Freedman 2019, 28). Medical researchers have found that only 10 to 25 percent of life-expectancy improvements can be attributed to services provided by doctors and other medical staff (29). This is similar to what educational researchers have found. Teachers and schools account for only 10–15 percent of the variance in student achievement (Kelly 2012a, 10; Marsh and Dunkin 1992, 170), while professional coaches account for around 20–30 percent of a team's success (Berry and Fowler 2019).

Service providers need to rethink the "customer is always right" mantra, especially in complex life-enhancing services, like health-care and education, where consumers don't usually know what is best for themselves. When it comes to education, most students do not know what they want, let alone what they need in order to be successful in the fast-changing global labor market of the 21st century.

It is the job of the experienced and knowledgeable teacher, as it is with parents and other responsible adults, to make some important decisions for the immature student in order to guide him or her toward knowledge, skills, and goals that will help develop the neophyte into a fully functioning and successful adult (Steinberg 2014). While children have "natural learning capacities," the difficulty for parents and teachers is how to develop these capacities, while also shifting them toward the "unnatural" (Gopnik 2016,

188) academic knowledge and specialized skills that students need to learn in order to be successful professionals in a globalized economy.

Teachers and schools are not often successful at this task. As psychologist Alison Gopnik (2016) argues, rather than teach students how to learn and develop as individuals, schools often "teach children how to go to school" and play school, a useless set of skills (190).

But while human beings have natural learning capacities, we also have equally powerful capacities for ignorance, laziness, peer pressure, and cultural conformity, as we have already discussed in detail (Cialdini 2007, ch. 4; Kahneman 2011; Sunstein 2019; Sapolsky 2017, 469–74). Teachers are always fighting against the widely documented "Dunning-Kruger Effect" (Nichols 2017, 43–44).

The more a person is ignorant and incompetent, the less likely they will acknowledge their ignorance and incompetence. Incompetent people are much less likely to want new knowledge. Incompetent students are more likely to believe that they are already knowledgeable and competent. Thus, many students resist new learning to fix a problem they cannot acknowledge.

As human beings, we all have a natural "confirmation bias," which leads us to automatically discount or reject all information that goes against our preestablished beliefs and cultural point of view. This bias leads us to automatically accept information that confirms our prior beliefs (Evans 1989, ch. 3). Thus, incompetent people are often "ignorant but happy," so they don't want to change, explained journalist Ian Leslie (2014, 40).

Most people are "confident that they have the answers," so they "become blithely incurious about alternatives" (40). Nobel Prize winning psychologist Daniel Kahneman and his colleague Amos Tversky were among the first researchers to empirically demonstrate this paradoxical predicament (Lewis 2017). Kahneman (2011) later summarized their stark conclusion, "Our comforting conviction the world makes sense rests on a secure foundation: Our almost unlimited ability to ignore our own ignorance" (201).

In acknowledging and trying to overcome the Dunning-Kruger Effect, teachers are caught in a double bind. Acknowledging one's ignorance is the first step toward knowledge. But many students rest comfortable in their traditions, beliefs, and common sense. Therefore, most students refuse to admit their ignorance or do anything about it. They don't want to learn.

The act of exposing students' ignorance and engaging them in real learning is a difficult, laborious, and often painful process (Sizer 1992, 150). As Keeling and Hersh (2012) pointed out, real student learning "requires harder work" from both teacher and student (55). This creates a disincentive for both parties. True learning demands a significant "investment of time, focus, and intensity of effort," which most students and many teachers would rather avoid (55).

Education is a mysterious activity. Most consumers cannot really fathom the value of their education until many years later. Stanley Fish (2010), a professor of law and English, has argued that student evaluation surveys are "all wrong as a way of assessing teaching performance: they measure present satisfaction in relation to a set of expectations that may have little to do with the deep efficacy of learning" (para. 5). Fish went on to explain,

> But when, as a student, I exit from a class or even from an entire course, it may be years before I know whether I got my money's worth, and that goes both ways. A course I absolutely loved may turn out be worthless because the instructor substituted wit and showmanship for an explanation of basic concepts. And a course that left me feeling confused and convinced I had learned very little might turn out to have planted seeds that later grew into mighty trees of understanding. (para. 3)

Chapter 7

Signaling or Human Capital?

Credentialism, Degree Inflation, and Socioeconomic Inequality

Prior to the 20th century, higher education was centered on moral and civic instruction with a specific focus on training elites for sociopolitical leadership (Lucas 1994; Thelin 2004). These traditional purposes were gradually replaced during the 20th century with a new end: training consumers for skilled work. Some economists have called this trend the "vocationalization" of schooling (Grubb and Lazerson 2004).

Higher education in the United States, and most other advanced industrial nations, is now closely linked to economic development and the global labor market. College has become a diverse training ground preparing students for both occupational and professional careers, offering a vast system of vocational programs and labor market credentials (Aronowitz 2000; Brint and Karabel 1989; Grubb 1985; Grubb and Lazerson 2004; Kantor 1988; Kliebard 1999).

Because postsecondary schooling has been largely reduced to job training, institutions of higher education are now judged by the "logic of the all-encompassing market," according to Harvard Business School professor Rakesh Khurana (2007, 334). College is an investment, not an education.

Thus, since the early 20th century, schools have been producing new accountability metrics focused on labor market credentials, such as diplomas, degrees, and short-term certificates (Levin, Beach and Kisker 2009). This particular accountability initiative has been called "credentialism" by social scientists (Freidson 1986, 63; Graeber 2015, 22; Levin, Beach and Kisker 2009).

Most American and Western European consumers believe that schooling, particularly postsecondary and professional schooling, creates a grand "ladder of opportunity" based on individual initiative, hard work, and rewarding merit (Dench 2006; Markovits 2019; Sandel 2020). Policy makers and school administrators have ideologically linked credentialism to the principle of meritocracy: The most talented and hardest working students earn the highest rewards in the labor market (Markovits 2019; Sandel 2020).

We are told that if you are willing to work hard enough, anyone can succeed at schooling and at life. Everyone has a chance at reaching the top through schooling and earning academic credentials (Sandel, 2020). Most people believe that college degrees produce high financial returns and upward social mobility, especially for the social and economically disadvantaged (Aronowitz 2000; Beach 2011a; Brint and Karabel 1989; Grubb 1985; Grubb and Lazerson 2004).

But is this true? Or, in fact, is the opposite true? Does higher education exacerbate social and economic inequalities? Does credentialism actually limit social mobility by rewarding the rich much more than the middle class or poor? Let's investigate.

The development of human capital theory in the 20th century allowed economists and government officials to formally recognize and measure the value of schooling and human labor for the first time. Economists focused on the accountability metric of credentials, which became a proxy for human capital. Credentials were linked to average earnings in the labor market for different segments of the population in order to put a dollar value on the economic returns of schooling.

Many policy makers and pundits have turned the economics of credentialism into a political myth, which some critics have called a new "secular faith" (Wolf 2002, xi; Grubb and Lazerson 2004; Sandel 2020). Most people seem to believe that higher levels of education and more credentials will not only bring higher levels of economic earnings for all workers, but also higher levels of national and global economic development for all countries (Wolf 2002, xi). Doubting this new "secular faith," according to economist Alison Wolf (2002), "places one somewhere between an animal-hater and an imbecile" (xi).

The basic premise of this new faith is based on fact. Earning a high school diploma, a bachelor's degree, or an advanced professional degree in the U.S. and other developed industrial economies has marked economic benefits, which have been widely documented since the mid-20th century.

For example, in the U.S. from 1964 to 2012, the average man with some college has gained almost 20 percent more real income, while men with a bachelor's degree have gained 40 percent, and men with graduate or professional degrees have gained almost 100 percent. High school dropouts now earn less real income than comparable men in 1964, and high school graduates are not doing much better (Clausing 2019, 29).

But these highly publicized statistics have always been calculated "on average" by economists and government officials (Grubb and Lazerson 2004, 162), which masks stark inequality based on gender and race. Also, the high outlying wages of a small number of top earners often skews the whole distribution making the average seem much higher than it really is for most Americans.

For example, while the "average" graduate from Yale University in the 1950s earned more than the average American at the time, one study found that 80 percent of the alumni during this timeframe actually earned below the national average because the highest earning alumni skewed the distribution so much (Salsburg 2001, 245).

As professor of education Kern Alexander ([1996] 1976) once explained, there is no such thing as an "average" financial return to a college degree: "The economic value of education is distorted by factors such as intelligence, parent's education, race, sex, urban versus rural, north versus south, health, education quality, and other [variables] too numerous to explore" (89; Paulsen 2001, 60, 74; Grubb and Lazerson 2004; Hertz 2006; Mishel et al. 2007; Wolf 2002).

Thus, the actual value of a college credential is highly variable and inequitably allocated based on many individual and social factors, most of which are beyond the control of either students, teachers, or schools.

While more and more students in the U.S. and around the world have been graduating from high school, going off to college, and earning advanced degrees, this situation has not been an unqualified good for either individual students or society at large. While more people have earned a college degree than ever before, increased levels of education around the world have also been connected with increased levels of social, economic, and political inequality (Grubb and Lazerson 2004, 164; Jacobs and Skocpol 2005; Hochschild and Scrovronick 2003; Putnam 2015).

Take for example the United States. Economist Kimberly Clausing (2019) has shown that while almost 90 percent of "children born in the 1940s out-earned their parents" in the U.S., only half of those born in the 1980s were able to do so, and the earning potential of millennials has become even worse (17).

From 1980 to 2014 there has been almost no income growth for the bottom 50 percent of Americans, while the top 1 percent has seen over 200 percent income growth (Clausing 2019, 18). Many students around the world are finding out the hard way that earning a college degree does not automatically lead to a job, let alone a stable, high-paying job with good benefits. Further, most college graduates eventually discover that a college degree does not raise you anywhere close to the top of the socioeconomic ladder of success.

Nowhere is this issue more concretely demonstrated than in sub-baccalaureate schooling, especially the community college, which was engineered by administrators and policy makers in the early 20th century as an educational halfway house between high school and college. Over the last half-century, about half of all college students in the U.S. have entered higher education through a sub-baccalaureate institution. For economically underprivileged students, the vast majority begin and end their college career in these institutions.

Few community college students ever attain more than a couple of years of postsecondary schooling, with over 70 percent never completing a two-year degree, certificate, or transferring to traditional college or university (Dougherty 2001; Beach 2011a; Brint and Karabel 1989). Despite attending a so-called "college," community college students do not experience anything that deserves to be called *higher* education. Sub-baccalaureate institutions tend to offer an anemic repackaging of high school academics and mid-skilled vocational training, if they offer anything of value at all (Beach 2011a; McGrath and Spear 1991; Eaton 1994).

In the 21st century, while schooling can confer economic benefits and increased social status through the earning of credentials, such benefits are more uncertain and conditional than they were in the 20th century. In the U.S., as in many other advanced industrial democracies around the world, schooling is not a meritocratic ladder to success promoting upward economic mobility for all (Markovits 2019; Sandel 2020). Instead, schooling has often reinforced and exacerbated inequality, especially higher education.

Economist Anthony Carnevale recently argued that the U.S. is "not a meritocracy, it is more and more an aristocracy posing as a meritocracy" (qtd. in Berman 2019, para. 1). Professor of law Daniel Markovits (2019) does believe that the U.S. is a meritocracy, but he argues it is a rigged, "sham" meritocracy that "blocks the middle class from opportunity. Then it blames those who lose a competition for income and status that, even when everyone plays by the rules, only the rich can win" (viii).

Most people blindly believe that schools reward hard work and talent, when in fact schools have always unfairly enabled the wealthy to solidify their power and privilege (Carnevale, Fasules, Quinn and Campbell, 2019b; Markovits 2019; Sandel 2020). We will discuss this in more detail in the next chapter. Most likely this predicament will only get worse as the 21st century unfolds. Let's find out why.

HUMAN CAPITAL THEORY: MEASURING
THE ECONOMIC VALUE OF EDUCATION

From the mid-19th until the 21st century, the net national product of the United States has grown on average by 3.4 percent per year (Atack and Passell 1994). While the development of land and the investment of capital have been significant contributing factors in this significant rate of growth, one of the most important factors behind the economic growth of the United States has been human labor, including the development of intangible forms of intellectual labor, which became increasingly important over the 20th century.

Economists estimate that between 41–49 percent of the growth of the net national product from 1840 to 1990 was due to the development of human labor supplies and laborer skills (Atack and Passell 1994, 19). Prior to the 19th century, most laborers did not barter for a job in a labor market looking for the highest wages they could find. The invention of wage labor was largely resisted up until the 19th century, as many workers believed that "capital commands labor, as the master does the slave" (qtd. in Sandel 1996, 175).

Up until the 19th century a significant portion of the labor force around the world was enslaved or in a state of debt peonage. As labor markets were invented, drawing from the historical practice of slavery, workers faced many forms of "wage discrimination" based on race, ethnicity, and gender, and also based on race- and gender-segmented occupations, which also tended to be geographically segregated (Atack and Passell 1994, 533; Goldin 1990; Roediger 2003).

For example, in 1860 black slaves constituted about 21 percent of the labor force in the United States (Atack and Passell 1994, 522). Most of these enslaved men and women, once they were officially "freed," still continued to be economically enslaved by debt peonage in the agricultural economy of the South (Ransom and Sutch, 2001). In fact, white, black, and brown agricultural workers in the South were not actually economically "free" because the value of their cash crops and labor was determined by the wealthy merchants in charge of regional markets, many of whom also owned the land that workers labored on (Ransom and Sutch 2001, 165).

Much the same could be said about agricultural and industrial laborers in the North and West (Atack and Passell 1994, 539; Edwards 1979; Painter 1987). Women were also highly active yet largely invisible participants in the labor force for centuries in the "hidden market" of the home. Women's contribution to the net national product was long neglected by government officials and economists, and the domestic economy of the home is still officially under-measured and under-appreciated (Boydston 1990; Goldin 1990).

Historically, labor markets have not only been discriminatory, based on race, gender, and class, they have also been regionally "segregated," which has limited the mobility of laborers to move to new locations in order to find better economic opportunities (Atack and Passell 1994, 529, 543).

For most of human history laborers were largely, but never completely, neglected by political rulers. Later, professional economists didn't treat them much better, despite the economic importance of labor. Up until the 19th century, most laborers were classified as property owned by nobles, just another part of aristocratic estates, like trees or cattle. Laborers were classified as commodities to be bought and sold by capitalists in the labor market (Sandel 1996, 196).

Interestingly, up until the 19th century, manual laborers were often valued less than livestock. When employed, a laborer became another form of "raw material" to be "controlled" by managers, like a horse or a piece of pig iron (Edwards 1979, 26; Kliebard, 1999, 52). One 19th century intellectual explained, "You, with the command over labor which your capital gives you, are a slave owner—a master, without the obligations of a master. They who work for you, who create your income, are slaves, without the rights of slaves" (qtd. in Sandel 1996, 175).

Artisans and skilled craftsmen, on the other hand, have always been able to retain some control over their labor and working conditions due to their special skills and relative scarcity in many labor markets. Skilled craftsmen have also historically relied upon the collective power of guilds and craft unions to protect their earnings (Edwards 1979, 31), although this power began to weaken in the late 19th and early 20th centuries, as labor was deskilled due to industrialization and automation.

In the late 18th and 19th centuries, English political economists, like Adam Smith and David Ricardo, and European socialists, like Karl Marx, argued for a labor theory of value to highlight the important role of the working classes for the global capitalist economy. For young democracies, like the United States, some critics also pointed out that "there is an inevitable and irresistible conflict between the wage-system of labor and the republican system of government" (qtd. in Sandel 1996, 185).

Some politicians agreed with this analysis and worked to strengthen labor protections. In 1861 President Abraham Lincoln, who corresponded with Karl Marx, declared, "Labor is prior to and independent of capital. Capital is only the fruit of labor, and could never have existed if labor had not first existed. Labor is the superior of capital, and deserves much the higher consideration" qtd. in Graeber 2018, 230).

However, the full economic value of labor was not realized by most politicians and economists in the U.S. until the middle of the 20th century. This change was caused the widespread development of three important social institutions: labor unions, secondary and postsecondary public schooling, and formal legal equality.

Labor unions allowed for a growing body of legal rights for laborers, better working conditions, and some measure of free time to develop nonoccupational pursuits, like education (Dawley 1991; Edwards 1979; Lichtenstein 2002). The development of free public secondary schooling and growing access to post-secondary schooling allowed unskilled and skilled laborers alike to increasingly send their children to school to earn academic credentials that would increase their value as laborers in the marketplace (Brint and Karabel 1989; Kliebard 1999; Lucas 1994; Peterson 1985; Thelin 2004; Tyack 1974; Banerjee and Duflo 2019, 147).

And finally, the development of formal legal equality for all American citizens allowed black, brown, and immigrant laborers to more freely unionize, educate themselves and their children, and negotiate their labor in less discriminatory labor markets—although into the 21st century, formal legal equality has not always translated into full social or economic equality for many people in the U.S. and other advanced industrial countries (Gerstle 2001; Jillson 2004; Patterson 2001).

In the 1960s, psychologist and management professor Douglas McGregor (1960) and economist Theodore W. Schultz (1961), then the president of the American Economic Association, broke with classical economic theory and repositioned the laborer as the foundational element of modern economies and national economic growth.

Both McGregor and Schultz thought that laborers in the U.S. were becoming more economically valuable because they were becoming more educated. Therefore, they assumed, workers were becoming more knowledgeable and skilled. These economists broke with the 19th century belief that "the hiring of a laborer by a capitalist should simply mean the sale of a commodity in open market by one free agent to another" (qtd. in Sandel 1996, 190).

Schultz (1961), in particular, saw schooling as an economic service that transformed the laborer by producing skills and knowledge, which he believed created a new "form of capital" (2). Schultz called it *human* capital (see also Hirsch 1976, 45; Bills 2003). Human capital transformed the laborer from a mere "commodity" into a newly empowered capitalist who had command over a limited and highly coveted form of wealth: knowledge.

Knowledge became the primary currency for the late 20th century "knowledge economy" (Drucker 1969, ch. 12). The theory of human capital transformed education into an economic transaction and schooling into an economic institution. Schools were now conceived as factories that produced knowledge and human capital. Social and economic resources could be "embedded" in students as knowledge and skills by schools in order to make students more valuable by increasing their productivity as workers (Murphy

2017, 115; Banerjee and Duflo 2019, 147). Students were re-conceived as investors in themselves who expected a handsome ROI, or return on investment, for their schooling.

Elaborating on an idea first put forth by English political economists in the late 18th and 19th centuries (Graeber 2018, 230), Schultz (1961) argued that human capital was turning out to be the most valuable capital of all: "The productive capacity of human beings in now vastly larger than all other forms of wealth taken together" (2).

Schultz (1961) positioned his theory away from classical accounts of laborers as "something akin to property" (2–3). Instead, Schultz believed that human capital was actually a form of productivity that was mutually beneficial for both the individual and society.

He argued that human capital ultimately led to increased freedom for the individual, enabling a greater variety of opportunity and choice. This correspondingly increased the general welfare of each individual. And because everyone was more productive, and personal utility was maximized, this would also develop and expand both national and global economies (Schultz 1961, 2–3; see also Inglehart and Welzel 2005, 24).

There was also a moral component to human capital theory. Beginning in the 1950s, sociologists and policy makers began talking about how postindustrial democracies were creating a new "meritocracy," an enlightened and equitable social order that valued hard work and individual merit through schooling as the rightful basis of success, rather than traditional forms of social distinction based on family, class, gender, race, and religious affiliation (Horowitz 2006; Sandel 2020).

The English sociologist Michael Young coined the word meritocracy in 1958 as an ironic critique of the moral implications of human capital theory (Dench 2006), but the American sociologist Daniel Bell (1973) popularized the concept and transformed it into a serious intellectual and political idea in the 1970s.

Bell (1973) argued that "technical skill" learned in college, or "what the economists call 'human capital,'" was becoming the rightful "gatekeeper" that would "determine the future stratification" (410) of a new world order. Business professor Peter Drucker (1969) famously called this postindustrial new world order a "knowledge economy" (ch. 12).

Drucker (1969) argued that knowledge was becoming "the central capital" and "the crucial resource" of the late 20th century economy (xi, 152). Drucker (1969) and Bell believed that "knowledge creates productivity" and drives economic growth (150). The rising importance of human capital was creating "a new technical elite," according to Bell (1973, 410) who would manage not only the economy but also politics and social institutions.

But Bell (1973) also worried that the meritocratic ideal of "equality of opportunity" through schooling would not produce an "equality of result" in the economy, society, or in politics. Bell feared that entrenched forms of discrimination, such as race, sex, and class, would corrupt meritocratic institutions, reinforce traditional privilege, and end up exacerbating socio-economic inequality (414). Few policy makers or educational administrators took his worries very seriously (Sandel 2020).

By the 1970s, policy makers, professors, school administrators, and even many teachers began to propagate the idea that education was primarily an investment in human capital. This notion was fast becoming the reigning theoretical paradigm for justifying the social and economic value of schooling, especially for institutions of higher education.

In the 1970s education professor Kern Alexander ([1996] 1976) explained how the idea of human capital represented a new form of prosperity. Human "resources," Alexander argued, were now "the true basis for the wealth of nations" (85–86).

But combined with this new economic celebration of labor came an economically reconceptualized notion of education, which Alexander and others now defined as

anything which (a) increases production through income in the capacity of the labor force, (b) increases efficiency by reducing unnecessary costs, thereby reserving resources for the enhancement of human productivity . . . and (c) increases the social consciousness of the community so that living conditions are enhanced. (86)

Gone were the idealistic days when education was once defined in terms of morality, character formation, personal development, or intellectual discovery. Now education was "a commodity that can be manufactured, packaged, bought, and sold" (Twitchell 2004, 50).

Unlike John Dewey's ([1916] 1966) idealistic and popular theory of education, Kern Alexander offered an instrumentalist conception of schooling, which promised increased knowledge production, increased economic efficiency, and increased material living conditions for all. But this economic conception of education reduced a complex epistemological and developmental activity into a mere productivity equation. Education was reduced to schooling.

Somehow increased educational production through efficient schooling naturally and inevitably lead to "enhanced" individuals and a growing economy (Alexander [1996] 1976, 86; see also Wolf 2002; Grubb and Lazerson 2004). This was the very idea that sociologist Michael Young derided in his satirical book on meritocracy where he coined the term (Dench 2006; Markovits 2019, 258).

Alexander ([1996] 1976) admitted that some people would find his definition of education unappealing or insulting, as many do not educate themselves merely to "maximize income" (88). But the human capital conception of education was irresistible for many policy makers and administrators in democratic countries who wanted to promise a better life to their constituents and clients.

While the economic paradigm of human capital did bring increased respect for human labor in the 20th century, it also reduced the value of education and schooling to an "overly simplistic" and "naïve" economic transaction. Schools became knowledge factories that produced uniform products: labor market credentials. This conception of education had a corrupting influence on schooling and and the practice of education, which was discussed the companion volume, *Can We Measure What Matters Most?* (see also Grubb and Lazerson 2004, 164).

Human capital theory also masked inequitable social structures, like discrimination, social segregation, and economic inequality, which complicate the simplistic equation that education automatically increases earnings and economic development for all people in all places at all times. As economist Alison Wolf (2002) pointed out, "qualifications pay: but not equally" (15).

While some economists have used human capital theory *expansively* to investigate how education, schooling, and economic development can *sometimes* be correlated to individual achievement and socio-political equality (Grubb and Lazerson 2004; Sen 1999), most economists have used this theory rather *narrowly* to empirically explain the correlation between schooling and average individual earnings in the labor market (Breneman 2001; Dale and Krueger 1999; Leslie and Brinkman 1988; Paulsen 2001).

Most economists of higher education now routinely use human capital theory to refer to the "outputs" of higher education in terms of "individual rates of return" (Breneman 2001) to a college degree. Since the 1960s, economists have typically used human capital theory to study the financial returns of an "investment" in a baccalaureate degree, as compared to the returns of a high school diploma or dropping out of high school (Bell 1973; Grubb 1992; Grubb and Lazerson 2004; Paulsen 2001; Rosenbaum 2001).

Professor of education Michael B. Paulsen (2001) demonstrated that the long-term earnings differential between workers with a high school diploma and workers with baccalaureate degrees or higher in the U.S. has been substantial. This earnings differential started to increase in the 1980s. In the 1960s and '70s, students with a college degree earned about 47 percent more than those who had only a high school diploma. By the 1980s this earnings differential had grown to 67 percent, and it would later rise to 77 percent by

1997 (Paulsen 2001, 64–65), although by the 21st century this growth has since leveled out and stalled for most people.

Paulsen (2001) calculated that the average private rate of return for a baccalaureate degree was somewhere between 9 percent and 15 percent a year (65; see also Markovits 2019, 183). But this rate of return could vary substantially for any given individual for many reasons. One of the most important factors effecting earnings is choosing a profession (Grubb 1992, 1999). The labor market does not value all college degrees the same.

Degrees from fields like business, health sciences, and engineering have shown strong economic returns over the last few decades, while fields like agriculture, education, and the arts have shown marginal economic returns. Wolf (2002) found that a bachelor's degree in science, engineering, or social science created an 18 percent to 25 percent wage premium for men between 1984 and 1991, while a degree in the arts delivered only a 2 percent to 4 percent gain, which means the ROI for an art degree did not even keep up with inflation (33).

The value of a degree also varies a lot by geography. This is due to the differential economic needs of local labor markets. For example, most degrees, no matter what the field, are worth much more in cities than rural areas, although some cities pay more of a premium than others (Moretti 2015; Moretti 2012).

Various types of workers continue to face many forms of discrimination in the labor market, based on race, gender, sexual orientation, and age, which causes "inequalities in the marginal benefits accruing to individuals who invest in higher education" (Paulsen 2001, 74–76; Grubb 1992; Grubb and Lazerson 2004).

Thus, the high "average" rates of return that politicians and economists often focus on have been skewed by privileged groups of workers who make above average wages, such as those with high skills, natural abilities, or those who belong to privileged social groups based on gender, race, and class (Breneman 2001, 8; Dale and Krueger 1999, 30; Dey and Hill 2007; Grubb 1992; Grubb and Lazerson 2004, 158; Mishel et al. 2007; Rosenbaum 2001, 68–81).

In the U.S. and Western Europe, white men with college degrees still capture most of the economic gains of higher education because they get the best jobs with the highest pay (Carnevale et al. 2019b). Women and people of color still earn considerably less. The variable of race is correlated to discrimination, but it also serves as a proxy for parental wealth. Parental income is still highly correlated with a student's ability to earn a degree and the wages they will eventually earn once they leave college.

Social class still plays a big role in not only who goes to college, but also who succeeds in the labor market. While around 32 percent of students by age

29 have earned a BA degree or higher in the U.S., there is a dramatic difference between the degree attainment rates of rich and poor. In 2016 about 58
percent of students in the top income quartile had earned a BA by 24 years of
age, compared with only 20 percent in the second to lowest quartile, and only
11 percent in the bottom quartile (Markovits 2019, 134–35; Sandel 2020).

One study found that 71 percent of privileged students who came from
the top SES quartile would end up with above-median SES by age 25, even
though their academic performance was at the lowest level in kindergarten
(Carnevale et al. 2019b, v). The same study found that the highest achieving
kindergartners who happened to be born in the lowest SES quartile would
struggle to succeed. Only 31 percent of these bright yet poor students would
end up with above-median SES by age 25.

Even in the 21st century, the benefits of schooling are inequitably dis-
tributed, largely because of the residual effects of longstanding racial and
economic inequality, especially in the U.S. (Kozol 1991; Putnam 2015;
Markovits 2019). While all students have access to schooling, not all schools
are equally resourced, especially with qualified teachers. The poorest students
in the U.S. still have low odds of being successful in terms of graduating with
a college degree, getting a good job, and building wealth.

THE PURPOSE OF SCHOOLING: HUMAN CAPITAL OR SIGNALING SOCIAL STATUS?

While there has been a clear positive correlation between schooling and
earnings since the 1960s in the U.S. and other developed countries, some
economists have questioned the validity of human capital theory in terms of
explaining the cause of this relationship.

While economists agree on the economic value that schooling generates,
some doubt the validity of human capital theory, which is based on a rational
choice framework that assumes that schooling produces valuable knowledge
and productive skills for all students. What if this assumption is wrong?

What if students are just playing school, as we pointed out earlier? What
if most students don't actually learn any real knowledge or useful skills, but
still earn an academic credential? If students don't have productive knowledge or skill,then why is schooling being rewarded in the marketplace? That
wouldn't be rational.

If schooling doesn't really create human capital then gaining higher and
higher levels of schooling wouldn't be a prudent investment, for either students or society. Spending a lot of money on useless credentials might actually
be harmful. As Alison Wolf (2002) pointed out: "It is no more self-evident

that, since some education makes some of us rich, more would make more of us richer than it is that 'two aspirin good' means 'five aspirin better'" (28).

Nobel prize winning economist Michael Spence (1974) and award-winning sociologist Pierre Bourdieu (Swartz 1997) were two of the first social scientists to argue that instead of producing productive forms of human capital, schooling actually produced nonproductive symbolic capital through educational credentials, which can be seen as a special form of currency that generates and transmits elite social status.

According to Pierre Bourdieu ([1984] 2010), a person's social status is a form of social and cultural capital that brings power, freedom, and economic resources (see also Keltner 2016). Humans have an innate need for social status, which is part of our evolutionary heritage, a trait we share with our closet biological relative, the chimpanzee (Wrangham and Peterson 1996, 191; Tomasello 2014; Keltner 2016).

Our species evolved within an environment of "competitive social interactions" wherein we competed with others for food, dominance, mates, and territory (Tomasello 2014, 20). While social and cultural capital are connected to economic capital, these are distinct forms of privilege that go beyond financial resources (Swartz 1997, 78). However, Bourdieu argued that economic capital is the most important "root" from which all other forms of social and cultural capital grow (qtd. in Swartz 1997, 79–80).

And while social status is a good that people covet, it is not an absolute good, like food or water. It is, as economists Fred Hirsch (1976, 11, 20) and Robert H. Frank (1985, 7–8) pointed out, a "positional good." Social status only makes sense in reference to other people whom we are symbolically competing against in a battle over limited social resources.

As Frank (1985) explained, "The outcome of the struggle to survive depends much less on one's strength in any absolute or global sense than on how strong one is relative to the others with whom one must compete directly for important resources" (32; see also Wrangham and Peterson 1996).

Our struggle for survival depends, as psychologist Michael Tomasello (2014) pointed out, on social evaluation. We instinctively judge our peers. And we are aware of how they judge us. Everyone jostles over their relative status in the various social groups that we live within and depend upon for survival (47; see also Keltner 2016).

Thus, in the race for economic gain and social status, we are all contestants running on a "positional treadmill" (Frank 1985, 136; see also Hirsch 1976; Markovits 2019, 152–53; Grove 2015, xix). Manager and business professor Andy Grove (2015) explained, "You must compete with millions of individuals every day, and every day you must enhance your value, hone your competitive advantage, learn, adapt, get out of the way" (xix; see also Edmondson 2012, 22).

None of us are trying to be fast in any absolute sense, so much as faster than those around us who we are competing against in our local environment. To survive and thrive as top dog in our neighborhood, we only have to outrun our neighbors, not everyone else in the world. As the old joke goes: You don't have to outrun the bear that is metaphorically chasing you in the woods. You just have to outrun the other campers you are with (Frank 1985, 189).

However, if one aspires to greater social status at the highest levels, say CEO of a multinational corporation or President of the United States of America, then one is competing with a larger pool of the most powerful and ambitious contestants. And only a few can win the spoils—and avoid getting eaten by the bear.

Educational credentials, like high school diplomas or college degrees, can sometimes represent real knowledge or practical skills (Wolf 2002; Caplan 2018). However, certifying knowledge or skill has never been the primary purpose of academic credentials, as we will discuss in the next chapter when we talk about ancient China, where the academic degree was invented. Academic credentials have always been used in most societies as a "signal" about the social status of an individual, not the knowledge or skills that person is supposed to possess (Spence 1974; Sunstein 1997, 155; Caplan 2018).

An academic credential has been a badge of honor that set a special individual apart from most others in a competitive society or labor market (Spence 1974; Labaree 1997a; Swartz 1997, 83; Caplan 2018; Freidson 1986, 34; Bills 2003). Credentials create "stereotypes" about the value of employees, and the value of a specific credential is based partly on the human capital it is supposed to represent, and partly on the positional good of social status it creates (Sunstein 1997, 155).

As political scientist Cass R. Sunstein (1997) explained, signaling stereotypes are not "very accurate," but they are "economically rational" because they are "cheaper to use" than "more fine-grained approaches" that would require detailed analysis of an individual person's background knowledge, skills, and experience, as well as detailed knowledge of all the groups, organizations, and institutions that influenced that person(155).

Take, for example, doctors. For most of human history, physicians were more of a "status profession," rather than a skilled, "occupational profession" (Starr 2017, 38). Doctors were certified as special people who had the proper schooling, "social graces," and "connections" (Starr 2017, 38). But most doctors had no idea how the human body worked or how to cure diseases or treat injuries.

A medical degree was a badge of distinction, but a middle-level badge. It did not allow doctors entry into the aristocracy, nor did this credential enable most doctors to accumulate any wealth (Starr 2017). A medical degree, like all other academic credentials, was more about individual social status than any objective measure of human capital. There were few practical dividends for patients or society.

In the late 19th century, a young Hungarian physician described the degraded predicament of doctors in the emerging democracy of the United States:

> Abroad, the medical degree per se invested the physician with a social standing and authority unknown in America, where in 1874, the meager educational requirements made it easy to secure a diploma after "two sessions of so many weeks a year." With some exceptions, the rank and file of the profession were— as far as general education went—little, if any, above the level of their clientele. And the clientele not only felt this, but knew it. (qtd. in Starr 2017, 81)

This is why the economist Fred Hirsch (1976) called the academic credential a positional good: "The value to me of my education depends not only on how much I have but also on how much the man ahead of me in the job line has" (3), or how much education my client or customer may have.

For most of human history, academic credentials and human capital have been two very different things. Up until the mid-20th century, talented craftspeople with specialized knowledge and skills rarely, if ever, had an academic credential, and they never had much social prestige. At the same time, most college graduates possessed little if any real knowledge or practical skills, but they were elevated above almost everyone else because they had superior social status.

The most powerful and wealthy people in every society have been the aristocrats, who rarely if ever possessed knowledge, practical skills, or academic credentials. Most aristocrats historically prided themselves on their uselessness. Aristocrats did nothing of use or value, but they possessed exclusive social status by virtue of their heredity, custom, and their traditional monopoly on violence, usually in terms of control over the military.

By the end of the 20th century, with the massification of higher education, academic credentials began to act as multifaceted signals representing *both* social status and human capital, but this was a new development in human history. Schooling has always been a relatively exclusive commodity, so earning an academic degree was traditionally enough to make one stand out from the crowd as a privileged person.

Economist Robert Frank (1985) explained how "many of the most important decisions ever made about us depend on how strangers see our talents, abilities, and other characteristics" (148). But in a large, diverse, urban society, it is very hard and expensive to get reliable information about strangers. This is partly why schools were invented. Schools manufacture a uniform set of social signals about students. The institution of schooling ensures some measure of quality control so that strangers can judge the relative worth of a student in their effort to become a fully participating adult in the labor market.

Plus, with the development of democratic political systems based, in theory, on the idea of equality, as economist Alison Wolf (2002) pointed out, academic credentials become a "socially acceptable way of ranking people" (29). Most people in democratic societies believe that schools are merito-cratic institutions that reward individual effort and skill. However, this has never been actually been true.

In the 1960s and '70s, social scientists, like Bourdieu and Spence, dis-covered that the symbolic signal is often more important than the supposed material reality behind the signal. While educational credentials can represent productive forms of human capital, in terms of knowledge and skills, often-times students just play school, learn very little, and still earn a degree. But this empty degree will still be rewarded in the labor market because it is an important signal of social status.

This predicament doesn't make sense according to human capital theory. But according to Spence (1974) and Hirsch (1976), the symbolic and material value of a degree can diverge because there are two very different sources of value. There is the value of social status, and there is the value of human capital. Many students are rewarded in the labor market because they wear a badge of distinction, their credential, which brings higher status, not because they have learned practical knowledge or skills that makes them more eco-nomically productive. Credentials primarily represent social capital, rather than economic capital.

This is because social capital has been more important than economic capital in most societies up until the 20th century. For most of human history, social status and wealth were conveyed primarily through traditional mark-ers of distinction, such as clothing, language, family lineage, ethnicity, and consumption patterns, so there was no need for a piece of paper bearing a credential to enhance one's social status. It was easy to see powerful people. The social signals were clear. And everyone knew their place in the social hierarchy.

China invented the notion of formal credentials in schools a thousand years ago as an additional layer of social distinction for established elites, not as a meritocratic initiative to promote human capital and economic productivity. In ancient China, most credentialed scholars were rather useless, but they did have some skills as scribes and bookkeepers.

In the modern, consumer-oriented, capitalist world, we have stopped using many traditional markers of distinction. You can't often tell a rich from a poor person by clothes or language any more, although you can still identify rich people by status symbols, such as expensive cars or watches. But more important than luxury goods, educational credentials became one of the most significant "status markers" in the 20th century, signifying "membership in the educated 'caste,'" which became one of the most exclusive classes (Reynolds 2012, 36). In some cases, credentials are more important than traditional markers of distinction, especially in post-industrial democracies like the U.S. and Western Europe.

That is why wealthy parents spend so much money on their children's schooling, and why some wealthy parents lie and cheat to get their kids into the best schools (Sandel 2020). One scholar estimated that the rich spend about $10 million more per child on schooling than poor or middle-class parents (Markovits 2019, 146). That's right, $10 million *more* a child! It is also why many wealthy parents are willing to bribe officials in order to get their children into elite schools (Langlois 2019; Golden 2006). The rich are already rich, but they are willing to spend millions, and even break the law, in order to get their children exclusive college credentials.

The modern capitalist economic system is only partly based on practical forms of human capital. Instead of the principle of utility, capitalist labor markets operate more on the principle of "credentialism" (Freidson 1986, 63; Graeber 2015, 22; Levin, Beach and Kisker 2009). A credential is a symbol of social status, which was invented in Imperial China almost 1,000 years ago (Chaffee 1995). Many people, including many economists, often confuse credentialism with human capital by assuming that academic credentials represent real knowledge or practical skills, rather than just social status.

What few people understand, besides sociologists, is that credentials are mostly a symbolic currency. Schools are not economic institutions, like factories producing useful products. Schools are cultural institutions, like churches or movie studios, which produce magic symbols and rituals. A credential gives its bearer a limited and exclusionary form of social status and power. A credential's value is determined partly by the access to elite people or elite jobs it brings.. But mostly, a credential's value is magic. It is valuable because people *believe* it is valuable.

A credential's value is also tied to being exclusive. There are a restricted number of existing credentials in a given labor market. Exclusive credentials mean higher social status. A large part of the value of academic credentials has always been their scarcity. Traditionally, credentials have been luxury goods. So what happens if academic credentials become mass-produced commodities?

In a system based on credentialism, the purpose of schooling is not education. Instead, as William Deresiewicz (2014) points out, the purpose of schooling is the magic ceremony of awarding of "gold stars" (16), which enhance some students' social status by symbolically distinguishing them from others with less or no gold stars. Cultural institutions are constituted with a special type of "social magic" that can create "difference when none existed" before by symbolically "transforming people by telling them that they are different" (Bourdieu 1993, 160–61; Bourdieu [1984] 2010). A kind or a celebrity is a special type of person because we *believe* in the reality and power of these social titles.

The traditional purpose of schools has been to not only create this social magic but also ritually confer it, just like a church ritually confers a sacrament. Schools have always conferred magically social status on select students. This is the primary function of schooling. Anthropologist David Graeber (2015) explained academic credentials as "magical objects conveying power" (22). In this way, schools have always been a lot like churches, and in many cultures, these two institutions were deeply intertwined, especially in Europe and the United States.

Traditionally, in most cultures, passing through a system of schooling was more of a social rite of passage focused on ritualized moral indoctrination, rather than an educational endeavor focused on useful knowledge or skills. And traditionally, landing a job was more about social status and family connections, rather than having talent or knowledge. In almost every culture, success has always been tied to socio-economic status and the easy confidence conferred by belonging to the elite. Schooling was not invented to be a functional, meritocratic institution. Schooling was invented to be an elite institution to socially transform privileged young boys into powerful men.

A recent study found that people from higher socio-economic classes believe they are superior to everyone else so they project an air of entitled overconfidence, which other people interpret as competency, even though many elites do not actually possess any specific knowledge or skill (Murphy 2019). Schooling has always reinforced and consecrated this air of entitlement. Schools produce overconfident elites who feel they are preordained by higher powers to rule over others, whether these higher powers be school officials, political elites, or religious leaders (Sandel 2020).

Despite popular beliefs to the contrary, things haven't changed much since schooling was first invented in ncient China. Economist Brian Caplan (2018) recently demonstrated that even in the 21st century knowledge economy, the labor market still rewards playing school and looking smart just as much as, if not more than, earning real human capital through hard work and learning (See also Labaree 1997a). In fact, because playing school is much easier for everyone involved—students, teachers, and administrators—there is a perverse incentive for everyone to reject real teaching or learning because having knowledge or skill is not necessary to earn a diploma or to land a high paying job.

Plus, psychologists have found that pressure from controlling adults along with monetary incentives combine to drive out students' intrinsic enjoyment of learning (Deci and Flaste 1995, 26, 40). Thus, most students don't want an education. They endure their prison sentence because they want a fancy, magic piece of paper hanging on their wall at the end of their ordeal. This magic piece of paper will enhance their social status and make them look better than other people without it.

William Deresiewicz (2014) points out that "everybody wants their child to get an education, but nobody wants them to get an *education* education" (author's emphasis, 49). Thus, schooling in most cultures has almost always been reduced to "an empty set of rituals" that produce symbolic forms of social status, rather than real knowledge or skill (56).

Caplan (2018) and Labaree (1997a) agree: "Unfortunately, students aren't hungry for human capital. They're hungry for signals. Why? Because the labor market mainly pays for credentials acquired, not skills earned" (Caplan 2018, 220). Or in the words of a cynical high school student, "People don't go to school to learn. They go to get good grades" (qtd. in Pope 2001, 4).

Sociologist Stanley Aronowitz (2000) really got to the heart of the problem of playing school in higher education in his book criticizing the economic transformation of college:

> I used to think that most students had no idea why they were in college beyond the widely shared sense among several generations of young adults that on the other side was the abyss. Now I am pretty sure most students understand that to play the job game they need a degree, even if their expectations are often buffeted by the market's vicissitudes. From their friends and parents, they know how little a terminal high school diploma will buy. Yet they have little idea what they want to "study." In most cases, their choice of major and minor fields are informed (no, dictated) by a rudimentary understanding of the nature of the job market rather than by intellectual curiosity, let alone intellectual passion. (10)

While Aronowitz is certainly right in his analysis about directionless students playing school, there is now a much more serious problem that he didn't realize at the time. Due to the political transformation of public schooling into a political right that is freely available to all, which is slowly being extended to college, and due to the economic transformation of public schooling into a credential factory to create employees for the global labor market, there is now a structural flaw with schooling that few have been willing to acknowledge.

Academic credentials are largely symbolic, magic tokens that have historically derived their value from being exclusive luxury goods. So what happens if these exclusive social badges become free to the public? What happens if the majority of people in any given society have an academic credential? As Fred Hirsch (1976) pointed out, "To the extent that education is a screening device . . . then the possibility of general advance is an illusion"

(6). If everyone gets college credentials then they will all lose their value, and everyone will be hurt, with the most disadvantaged students getting hurt the most.

Credentialism and Degree Inflation

In the U.S. and other advanced postindustrial economies, educational credentials have offered students high rates of economic return over the 20th century. This has enticed more and more students to graduate from high school, enter into college, and earn a degree. Now in the 21st century, about 30 percent to 40 percent of the adult population in many developed countries have bachelor's degree or higher. But this achievement isn't as positive as you might think. When it comes to education, especially expensive forms of higher education, there can be too much of a good thing (Kimhi, Shahar and Harel 2019).

Over the last two decades, the price of college has skyrocketed, while the average economic return to a bachelor's degree in most fields seems to be plateauing, if not decreasing, especially in the arts and humanities. Worse, there are not enough good jobs that require a college education, so degree holders are often forced to work at jobs unrelated to their field of study, which negates most of the economic value of their degree.

Plus, the global labor market has become more unpredictable and contingent. There is now less stability and security for all workers, even well-paid workers with a college degree. In the 21st century, due to rapid technological change, especially increased automation, most people will have to go back to school to switch careers at some point in their life (Florida 2007).

Changing careers drives down the economic value of a credential in many ways. There is the financial cost, in terms of extra educational expenses for another degree. There are the forgone wages, which one loses by going back to school. And there are the lost wages during the lucrative later years in a career that tend to be the highest-paid due to promotions and bonuses based on seniority.

Despite technological challenges and growing economic risks, more and more people are still entering college, and more and more degrees are being conferred every year. And what is the end result? More and more people with college degrees are struggling to find high paying work and satisfying careers. Part of the problem is that there is not enough work. And part of the problem, as Sir Ken Robinson (2001) pointed out, is that "there is a massive gap between the skills and abilities that business needs and those that are available in the workforce" (18; see also Florida 2007; Kimhi, Shahar and Harel 2019).

But even more importantly, success in earning academic degrees does not translate into career success, especially in terms of making enough money to live well (Florida 2007; Pfeffer 2010, 55). Most academic degrees do not adequately prepare students for success in the labor market because schooling rewards ritual more than human capital formation, as we have already discussed in this book and its companion volume. But worse for students, credentials are also becoming a lot more expensive because demand is so high, and a lot less exclusive because supply is so high.

This unfortunate situation places students in an uncomfortable bind. Colleges sell symbolic social badges of distinction, which are becoming less and less valuable to consumers, socially and economically. But even though credentials are losing their value, demand for credentials is still skyrocketing. The costs of college are also skyrocketing, with more and more pundits and politicians promoting "college for all" (Rosenbaum 2001). Thus, more students than ever feel that they must have a degree to compete for a decent life and to earn a basic level of self-respect (Sandel 2020).

But the value of higher education, especially expensive private schools, seems to have become inflated beyond all economic reality. Can a BA degree from Harvard or Yale really be worth over $200,000? Thus, some critics are looking for the impending bust of the "higher education bubble" (Reynolds 2012; Kimhi, Shahar and Harel 2019). But what most people don't realize is that the calamity of credential inflation isn't new. It has happened before, with destructive consequences.

In the 19th and early 20th century, few people went to high school in the U.S. or Europe, and even fewer graduated. At this time, a high school diploma was an exclusive social badge of distinction held only by the most privileged of students. It was a rare gold star, in Deresiewicz's terms, which set its holder apart from the majority of people on the planet.

Up until the 1930s, a high school diploma opened almost every door imaginable for high-paid work in the global labor market. But as more and more people went to high school and earned a diploma over the first half of the 20th century, and as more and more people entered college and earned a bachelor's degree, the labor market value of a high school diploma decreased to nothing. Every decade, this credential opened fewer and fewer doors to higher paid work or economic security. Now it is almost worthless.

The social value of a high school diploma has also plummeted No one is impressed by a high school diploma, except parents when their child graduates. Almost all citizens in developed industrial nations now have one. This has happened with other commodities. Cars, cell phones, and flat screen televisions also used to be luxury items owned by a privileged few. Now they can all be found in almost every home. There is no social distinction to be gained by owning something that everyone else already has. Social and cultural capital is largely derived from exclusivity and rarity (Frank 1985, 151).

Economist Fred Hirsch (1976) was one of the first social scientists to explain that educational credentials were luxury goods that were based on the zero-sum game of "positional competition." He argued, "What winners win, losers lose" (52). He used the example of a crowd of people trying to look ahead. Only a few tall people can see above everyone else. Now, the first enterprising people to stand on their toes can initially get a better view too, as if they are tall. But if everyone stands on their toes then most people go back to seeing nothing, and only the tall can see again.

Except now, everyone is worse off. It takes a lot more energy and strength to stand on your toes. So now, most people still can't see *and* they have hurt feet. Even the advantaged tall people in this example are suffering too. They stand out less than they used to. In a positional competition, there is "no net benefit" if everyone adopts the behavior or secures the scarce commodity (Hirsch 1976, 52–53). Everyone is worse off.

Hirsch (1976) called this unfortunate situation "a deterioration in the social environment": "More individual effort and resources have to be expended to achieve the same result . . . everyone expends more resources and ends up with the same position" (53, 49). Thus, Hirsch concluded, "more education for all leaves everyone in the same place" (49; see also Kimhi, Shahar and Harel 2019).

Schools are treadmills, not ladders. You work to stay in place, not rise.

Where a high school diploma once opened up access to good jobs, now everyone needs a bachelor's degree to compete in the labor market (Florida 2007). Soon everyone will need a postgraduate degree, or more. Business professor Jeffrey Pfeffer (2010) explained how "with more well-qualified people competing for each step on the organizational ladder all the time, rivalry is intense and only getting more so" (5).

Thus, the privileged stay privileged. They are able to use their social and economic capital to buy higher and higher credentials, while the disadvantaged struggle to keep up, especially when higher education is not publicly subsidized, like secondary schooling. The high school diploma bubble never really burst because the once exclusive institution of high school became subsidized by the government as a public good freely available to all. However, the the high school diploma did lose almost all of its social and economic value.

The high school bubble has now been superseded by another mandatory level of public schooling: college. And while, technically, going to college is still a "choice" because it is not mandated by law, most people feel compelled to go to college because of economic necessity and the social stigma of not having a degree. This is why many policy makers in the U.S. want to make college, or at least community college, free to all citizens. But free college will not solve the political problem of economic inequality.

As Hirsch (1976) pointed out, higher levels of schooling have become a "defensive necessity" (51; see also Kimhi, Shahar and Harel 2019). He explained, "as the average level of educational qualifications in the labor force rises, a kind of tax is imposed on those lacking such qualifications, while the bounty derived from possessing a given qualification is diminished" because more and more people have the same devalued commodity (51).

In the 21st century, workers with only a high school diploma or GED will earn close to the minimum wage and are highly likely to live in poverty their whole lives (Collins 2002, 24), unless generous minimum wage laws and social safety nets are enacted. But while a high school degree is largely worthless, it is still mandatory to have. Thus, the high school curriculum has become stripped down to the lowest standards so that most students can easily graduate, often without the basic abilities to read, write, or think (Beach 2018). The question now becomes, are bachelor's degrees next to become devalued as a worthless commodity because so many people have them?

The answer is yes. They already have.

There are not enough high paying jobs in the global economy to accommodate all of the bachelor's degrees, master's degrees, and PhDs currently earned. Most of the highest paying jobs are in a small number of highly specialized fields, like computer science, engineering, or medicine. Most students do not major in these fields, primarily because they are very demanding programs of study, often offered at highly selective schools.

From an economic and human capital standpoint, the world does not need any more college-educated workers. Nor, for that matter, does the world need any more high-school-educated workers, especially since automation will be destroying many low-skill and medium-skill jobs in the near future (Ford 2016; Brynjolfsson and McAfee 2016).

All over the world, a lot of people can't find work in their field of study and productively use their college credential, so they become part of a giant pool of semiskilled white-collar workers. In many countries, including the U.S., the U.K., Europe, China, Japan, and South Korea, there is a glut of overeducated workers with college degrees, many of whom are underemployed, and a growing number are unemployed. In the U.S. the average hourly wage for college graduates when they first leave school has stalled over the past two decades, while the bottom 60 percent of these graduates are actually earning less than similar graduates did in 2000 (Hanauer 2019, 21).

China alone created 8.3 million college graduates in 2019, the highest number ever for that country, which is up from about 5.7 million ten years ago ("Idle" 2019, 31). For decades the Chinese government simply assigned college graduates a job. However, since the 1990s, the government stopped managing employment directly, so students have had to rely largely on market competition, although the public sector, which includes state-owned companies, still employs a majority of workers.

In 2014 about 77.6 percent of college graduates in China found full-time jobs within six months of graduating, but by 2018 this number had fallen to 73.6 percent ("Idle" 2019, 31). Because there is a glut of educated workers in China, average salaries are falling. A recent graduate from college in China made about 4,800 yuan a month in 2015, but by 2017 these earnings had fallen to 4,000 yuan, which is about $580 (31). The competitive labor market has hurt rural college graduates the most in China, as they have been largely shut out of the largest cities by zoning laws, which have the most jobs and pay the highest wages (32).

What is happening in China is happening everywhere, including the U.S. While the glut of college-educated workers is growing, it is still much smaller than the larger glut of underemployed and unemployed workers with only a high school diploma or less. Employers have increasingly sought to take advantage of this growing pool of semiskilled workers with a bachelor's degree.

Why hire a high school graduate when you can hire a college graduate instead for the same amount of money? While some jobs have raised credential requirements because standards are higher than the past, many employers are raising their entry-level requirements because there are too many college-educated workers for the limited number of high-skilled jobs that currently exist.

Take, for example, the field of journalism. From the invention of the printing press, most reporters have had little formal education besides the basic ability to read and write. Traditionally, Western reporters took great pride in their rough-and-tumble, hard-drinking, idiosyncratic, working-class lifestyle.

H. L. Mencken was one of the great early 20th century American reporters. He graduated from high school in 1896 and, after working for several years in his father's cigar factory, took only one college class, on the subject writing. At his first job as a reporter for a newspaper in Baltimore, Mencken noted: "at least half of [the] other reporters were drunkards or incompetents" (qtd. in Teachout 2002, 50).

Mencken didn't want, or need, a formal education. He also didn't want to go to college in order to read classic literature that would have been useless to him as a journalist. Instead, Mencken focused on "life itself" in order to observe and learn from "the worldly wisdom of a police lieutenant, a bartender, a shyster lawyer, or a midwife" (qtd. in Teachout 2002, 51).

Walter Lippmann was another one of the greatest journalists of the 20th century. He graduated from Harvard in four years with a bachelor's degree in 1910. He could have earned a master's degree, too, but he had a low opinion of academia, and he didn't think much of academic credentials. He left school early to go to work as a reporter.

While Lippmann had only a bachelor's degree and no specialized professional training, he was able to converse knowledgeably with professors and experts in many subjects, most of whom had PhDs. Despite his lack of postgraduate training, Lippmann was able to contribute insightful scholarship on a wide range of subjects, which he published in newspaper columns and books over his whole life. He published his first book at the age of 21. He also became a public policy expert, and he helped advise many government officials until he died.

Lippmann believed that traditional, ideological, and sensationalist reporting, what some derisively called "yellow" journalism, was a threat to democracy because ignorant citizens were easily manipulated by "the quack, the charlatan, the jingo, and the terrorist" (qtd. in Goodwin 2014, 29). Thus, Lippmann argued that journalists needed to be trained in science and be knowledgable about scientific methodology so as to promote objectivity in reporting.

Lippmann, and other journalistic reformers, wanted reporters to cease being paid hacks and political party shills. Instead, reformers wanted reporters to be objective "public educators" (Goodwin 2014, 85). This meant that journalists would need more formal training, which of course, meant more formal schooling. Columbia University created the first school of journalism in 1912. It offered the first graduate degrees in journalism in 1935. And in 1961, it created one of the most important professional journals in the field, the *Columbia Journalism Review*.

By the early 1970s, the profession of journalism had completely changed. At this time, almost 60 percent of journalists in the U.S. had a college degree. Most journalists now passed up the school of hard knocks to become formally credentialed in universities due to higher standards and expectations in the labor market. By the 1990s, students could major in journalism as a college degree program. Now, having a journalism or communications degree is required to get a good job as a reporter.

In the 21st century, over 90 percent of journalists have college degrees (Graeber 2015, 22), many of them with postgraduate degrees. However, it's debatable how useful these degrees actually are now. The news-media business hasn't really changed much since the days of Mencken. Sensationalist journalism is still very popular and the "quack," the "charlatan," and the "jingo" still generate a lot of print and attract large audiences ("Invisible" 2020, 60). Journalism on television, the web, and social media relies much more on acting skills and savvy marketing than any academic principles or knowledge one might learn in college.

And yet, as entry-level credential requirements have gone up for jobs in journalism over the past several decades, entry-level salaries have continued to plummet, as have the number of jobs in in the field. There were about 57,000 journalists in the U.S. in 2007, just as the internet and social media were transforming the business. By 2015, there were only 33,000 professional journalists left, and these numbers continue to decline (Banerjee and Duflo 2019, 132). To make matters worse, most of those journalists who are lucky enough to be employed make little more than the minimum wage, with tenuous job security, despite many having post-graduate degrees.

What has happened to journalism is happening in almost every profession. In 1932 only about 45 percent of corporate managers had been to college, compared with 90 percent today, many of whom have post-graduate degrees (Markovits 2019, 142). Jobs that used to only require a high school diploma or less, like a secretary, a salesman, or a factory worker, are now requiring some college or a college degree.

Jobs that used to require a bachelor's degree, like a nurse or a teacher, now require a master's degree. Jobs that used to require a master's degree, like a corporate manager or a data analyst, now require a PhD, even though most PhD degree programs take six to ten years to complete and have almost no practical utility outside of academia (Smith 2019; Markovits 2019, 139–40). Law professor Daniel Markovits (2019) points out that "the idea that a generic BA guarantees a place among the elite has become almost quaint—a holdover from an earlier age" (162).

But even when students earn post-graduate degrees, there are not enough good jobs to go around (Florida 2007). Currently, most workers with PhDs are either underemployed or unemployed. In 1960 about 9,733 PhDs were awarded. By 2016 that number had grown to 55,904 (Childress 2019, 5, 166). For at least two decades, there has been a glut of workers with PhDs who either can't find work, who are working jobs that don't require a PhD, or who are exploited by institutions of higher education through short-term adjunct positions that pay poverty-level wages (Childress 2019, 52–53; Kezar, Depaola and Scott 2019).

As Herb Childress (2019) points out in his critical book on higher education, "doctoral programs exist because of the benefits they confer upon their institutions and their tenure-track faculty, far more than because of their benefits to grad-student consumers" (56).

Sociologist Randall Collins (1979, 2002) calls this unfortunate cycle of increased levels of schooling "degree inflation." Other economists have called it "overeducation," as in students have many credentials than are actually needed to compete in the labor market for the existing pool of jobs (Wolf 2002, 51).

Collins (2002) argues that degree inflation has become the "dirty secret of modern education" (29). He explains, "Higher-level occupations require increasingly higher and more specialized academic credentials" (24). This phenomenon decreases the value of lower-level credentials. Degree inflation has made the high school diploma largely worthless, and is slowly eroding the value of the bachelor's degree.

The increase in college credentials, especially postgraduate and professional degrees, has created a polarized labor market (Florida 2007; Markovits 2019, 158–61). There has been an increase in really good, high paying jobs, but almost all of these jobs require post-graduate degrees, sometimes multiple post-graduate degrees. At the same time, medium-skilled jobs, in sectors like manufacturing and commerce, have been disappearing, while low-skilled jobs have dramatically increased.

This polarization has led to a glut of "bullshit" jobs in the middle of the labor market that serve no purpose, according to anthropologist David Graeber (2018). These jobs are "so completely pointless, unnecessary, or pernicious that even the employee cannot justify its existence" (3). Graeber estimates that about 30 to 40 percent of all current jobs are pointless "bullshit" jobs (26). He argues that the "bullshitisation" of the economy is getting worse (24). Daniel Markovits (2019) argues that these low-skill jobs are "not just boring and low paid," but they also "carry low status and afford no realistic prospects for advancement" (158).

In 2012 there were 754,229 new master's degrees awarded in the U.S. (Childress 2019, 166). That same year, about 2 million new jobs were created, but only a fraction of those jobs actually required advanced degrees. In the UK, a recent study found that 34 percent of students who graduated after 2007 were working at jobs where they were "overeducated," which means they were overqualified for the job, compared to only 22 percent of students who graduated from college before 1992 ("Over a Third" 2019).

Overeducated workers earn about 3 percent to 8 percent less than a worker with a degree that matches the qualifications of their job, to say nothing of the expense of the unnecessary degree itself, and the forgone wages while in school. As the amount of educational credentials in the labor market has increased, the social and economic value of those credentials has decreased, just like every other marketable commodity that becomes oversupplied. "Wide distribution becomes tantamount to devaluation," Lawrence A. Cremin (1990) noted at the end of the 1980s when this phenomenon was just starting to become widely recognized by economists and educators (11).

Collins (2002) explained how credential inflation "is largely supply driven, not demand driven; it is driven by the expansion of schooling, like a government printing more paper money, not from demand by the economy for an increasingly educated labor force" (26; see also Drucker 1969, 278, 283).

Thus, in an economic system based on credentialism, schools are largely serving their own purposes by playing into consumer demand, and consumer fears, but schools are not meeting the long-term needs of students or of society.

Students want to be "untouchable," in the words of journalist Thomas Friedman (2005, 237). Students want to possess "valuable, rare, and hard-to-imitate capabilities" that will be "indispensable" to employers (Florida 2007; Peng 2017, 113). But schools are turning out thousands of students with the exact same degrees, which supposedly represent the exact same knowledge and skills, although many of these degrees are nothing more than empty badges that students were awarded for playing school.

Colleges and universities have a self-serving institutional focus that is harming students and society. While institutions of higher education pander to short-sided consumer demands, consumers are not really benefiting. Printing more and more degrees creates "educational hyperinflation," which is ultimately self-defeating for students. Inflation devalues almost all existing degrees and creates enormous pressure on consumers to accumulate more and more credentials so they will stand out above the crowd (Collins 2002, 26).

However, educational hyperinflation does benefit one group of people. More degrees mean higher enrollments, which produce higher budgets for schools, especially expensive colleges and universities. Higher budgets and higher enrollments also mean increased employment for teachers, faculty, and school administrators. Business in higher education has been booming for decades. But will the bubble burst?

Collins (2002) argues that high schools' credential producing function is not as important as it used to be. Most adolescents would agree. High schools set very low bars, just passing students through the system. Many students now recognize the devalued status and ritualistic nature of K–12 schooling, which makes it less intrinsically valuable for students. This is no doubt playing a role in the stalled and decreasing achievement scores of many high school students over the past forty years.

Teachers and students don't take high school seriously anymore. Most people assume that real schooling doesn't happen until college. Instead of educational institutions, Collins (2002) argues, high schools have become "warehouses" that temporarily keep students out of the labor market because there aren't enough good jobs available (27; see also Drucker 1969, 279–283). Most community colleges and some university undergraduate programs have become warehouses as well.

Collins (2002) argued that schools now serve the political purpose of a "hidden welfare system" because they can provide social and economic support to people who do not have a job or cannot get a job in the highly competitive global labor market (27). Fred Hirsch (1976) explained how "the obstacle course of education" was lengthening into more years of schooling, which "favor[s] those best able to sustain a longer or more costly race. These are the well-off and the well-connected" (50). Everyone else gets trapped in substandard warehouse-schools until they either drop out, move into the labor market, or move higher up the ladder of schooling.

Meritocracy isn't a ladder of success. It's a lottery, a rigged lottery (Florida 2007, 193; Markovits 2019; Sandel 2020). Rather than enabling or guaranteeing success in the labor market, schools merely offer a *chance* at success to the lucky few. And the lucky few have always been predominantly rich, white, and culturally privileged (Sandel 2020). Schooling once guaranteed a better life, when few people enrolled in schools, but now "the goalposts have moved," and schooling no longer guarantees success (Florida 2007; Banerjee and Duflo 2019, 198). And the goalposts began to move in the 1970s, unfortunately, just as schools became open to all students, regardless of race, class, or gender, for the first time in U.S. history.

Peter Drucker (1969) called schooling a "passport to outside opportunities" (333), but there are different types of passports that lead to different types of opportunities. Not all opportunities are very good. While everyone theoretically now has an equal opportunity to go to school in the U.S. and other developed countries, as sociologist Daniel Bell (1973) once pointed out, not all schools are equal, nor are all students equally prepared for success in school. Therefore, there are no equality of results for successful graduates.

To make matters worse, once students graduate with a credential and enter the labor market, they face many structural barriers to success based on traditional forms of exclusion, like class, race, and gender, which make it challenging for even the most successful students to find a high paying and stable job (Pager 2007), unless they already have a privileged socioeconomic position.

For example, technology companies and venture capital firms in Silicon Valley offer some of the highest paying jobs with the best perks in the 21st century labor market, but researchers have found that African Americans and Latinos are vastly underrepresented in these jobs. African Americans, in particular, make up only 3 percent or less of the workers at technology firms, about 2 percent or less are partners with venture capital firms, and 1 percent or less are entrepreneurs backed by venture capital ("Beyond" 2020, 53).

Because K–12 schooling has largely been a symbolic institution that does not teach useful knowledge or practical skills, a high school diploma does not really represent useful human capital. Instead, Collins (2002) argues that high schools offer "little more than a ticket into a lottery where one can buy a chance at a college degree, and that in turn is becoming a ticket to a yet higher level lottery" (24). A high school diploma has now become just a gateway credential, "a way station toward acquiring" a bachelor's degree (Collins 2002, 24).

And increasingly, a bachelor's degree is becoming another gateway credential. Many of the highest paying jobs require graduate or professional degrees (Markovits 2019, 139–40). And ultimately, that is what everyone wants. A high paying job that brings security, prosperity, and wealth. But as Fred Hirsch (1976) pointed out several decades ago, "The race gets longer for the same prize" (67). There are not enough high paying jobs to go around for everyone.

Plus, disparities based on class, race, gender, and sexual orientation still matter a great deal. When it comes to winning the ultimate prize, the victors are disproportionately privileged to begin with. In the U.S. and many other countries around the world, schooling largely reinforces and reproduces the inequitable "winner-take-all" system of global capitalism where privileged "superstars" get all the gold stars and earn all the wealth (Frank 1985, 151, 189; Frank and Cook 1995; Florida 2007; Clausing 2019, 37),

Rather than providing a meritocratic ladder of opportunity that promotes upward social mobility for all people, especially for the most impoverished and racially disadvantaged, schools help advantaged people get more advantages (Markovits 2019; Carnevale, et al. 2019a; Carnevale et al. 2019b; Sandel 2020). For most poor, working-class, and even middle-class students, schooling cannot ameliorate entrenched and growing global economic inequality (Hanauer 2019; Carnevale et al. 2019b).

As Herb Childress (2019) points out, "It's not that college gets you a good job; the average wage for college degree holders has been relatively flat for thirty years. Instead, it's that the *lack of college* sets you up to have a terrible job, or no job at all" (author's emphasis, 48). While K–12 schools do offer some "equality of opportunity" to good students who follow the rules, success in K–12 schooling is not an end in-and-of-itself any more, and neither is success in college.

Schooling only opens up access to more schooling, which no longer guarantees success in the labor market or in life. The system is rigged, as sociologist and historian David Labaree (2017) pointed out: "Stratification is at the heart of American education. . . . We let everyone in, but they all get a different experience, and they all win different social benefits . . . allowing ordinary people a high possibility of getting ahead through education and a low probability of getting ahead very far" (80).

Schooling itself has always been a competitive market with winners and losers, but this has intensified over the last century. According to Labaree (2017), there is now an academic "spiral of competition" (27–29), or what economists Fred Hirsch (1976, 76) and Robert H. Frank (1985, 211) called "an educational rat race" (see also Markovits 2019, 153). Students are competing against each other to earn *more* and more *advanced* academic credentials. And each credential along the rat race becomes more expensive and more time consuming than the previous one.

This competition increasingly disadvantages poor and middle-class students and many ethnic minorities who have less economic and social capital to start with, especially when it comes to getting a good job after school ("Which traits" 2018; Carnevale et al. 2019b). In most countries, especially in the U.S., it's better to be born rich than smart (Carnevale et al. 2019b).

To make matters worse, success in school and the accumulation of educational gold stars does not guarantee anyone success in the highly competitive global labor market, especially as automation threatens to completely transform the global economy and eliminate anywhere from 30 to 50 percent of the U.S. workforce ("Angst" 2011; Ford 2016; Brynjolfsson and McAfee 2016; Frey 2019; Markovits 2019, 181).

Credentialism not only leads to the devaluation of degrees through an over-educated workforce, but it also leads to intensifying labor market competition for scarce high-paying jobs, and to the polarization of the labor market into "a winner-take-all" contest (Frank and Cook 1995). A system based on credentialism creates "positional arms races," whereby each new generation tries to accumulate more degrees and specializations than the last generation, amassing more and more gold stars at greater cost, all in an effort to climb the slippery social ladder by generating higher status and more wealth (11; see also Hirsch 1976; Markovits 2019, 152–53; Kimhi, Shahar and Harel 2019).

And credentialism also creates arm races between schools as they battle for students, faculty, and endowment dollars. And like the labor market, the educational market is also a winner-take-all contest where a small number of the best schools with the highest social status and most money disproportionately take the spoils (Markovits 2019). As law professor Daniel Markovits (2019) argues, this kind of arms race "ultimately benefits no one, not even the victors" (153; see also Kimhi, Shahar and Harel 2019).

Climbing the ladder of success has become more costly and riskier, as students and their families are being asked to contribute more and more money to pay for more and more advanced levels of schooling that no longer guarantee labor market success. Over 30 percent of college graduates leave school with student loan debt ("Nope" 2011). Some students are even selling themselves to investors through contracts taking a set percentage of their future paychecks (Boston 2019).

But about half of students who enter college end up dropping out, which means many college dropouts also leave school with student loans and credit card debt. Many of these students, as education professor David Kirp (2019) points out, "are actually worse off economically than if they hadn't started college" (3). The total amount of student debt in the U.S. now amounts to almost $1.46 trillion, with over $160 million in loan delinquencies (Tanzi 2019).

So, bottom line, is a devalued college degree in the early 21st century still worth the risk in terms of its increased cost, especially if you have to take out tens of thousands or hundreds of thousands of dollars in student loans? The answer is still yes, but a qualified yes, if you can stay in school and earn your bachelor's degree in four years. But only for certain in-demand fields, such as business, economics, engineering, computer science, or healthcare ("Which Traits" 2018).

It helps a lot if you can get into the best schools, which are disproportionately the most expensive schools, especially if you come from a lower-class family (Giani 2016). But it's not because the best schools offer the best education—they don't. It's because they offer the highest social status and the best social connections, which can really help increase the earnings of lower-class students after they graduate (Thompson 2018).

But money isn't everything. According to a Gallup poll in 2013, about 70 percent of workers in the U.S. were either "not engaged" or were "actively disengaged" with their jobs (Oettingen 2014, 30; Pfeffer 2015, 12). In a 2012 poll over 65 percent of workers said they were unhappy with their jobs (Pfeffer 2015, 12). The vast majority of workers, including some of the highest paid workers with college degrees, are not happy with the job they were able to get in the labor market, especially the hours they have to put in to earn a decent living.

Many people describe their workplace as a "toxic environment" (Pfeffer 2015, 13). Most people are "very, very unhappy" with their managers and corporate leaders (Pfeffer 2015, 13). Some elite workers have it better, but having a high-paid and high-powered job comes with its own hidden costs, especially long, long hours. Most elite workers with high paying jobs put in sixty to eighty hours a week, with some working hundred-hour weeks and are on-call 24/7 (Markovits 2019, 10). Having a high paying job can be a special kind of hell.

Earning a college degree, even a post-graduate degree, is a hallow victory. A degree is only a ticket to an even more competitive lottery, the labor market. In this arena, the vast majority of workers fail to secure a good job that pays a decent wage and treats you as a human being. Even if you are lucky enough to find a decent job that pays good, as anthropologist David Graeber (2018) points out, "most people hate their jobs" and are miserable at work (241).

While getting a college degree can help lift your lifetime earnings under the right circumstances, it does not necessarily help you get a job you will like, even if you go into the field you majored in during college. It is exceptionally hard to find not only a good job that pays well and provides full benefits, but also a job that is enjoyable, important, or meaningful. And even if you are lucky enough to find a good job that you love, you will have to be constantly learning more knowledge and new skills to stay competitive with an increasing amount of people who want to take your job away (Hagel, Brown and Davison 2010, 13, 49, 126).

There does not seem to be any solution to the problem of the educational rat race, especially since it is a global phenomenon. As economist Robert Frank (1995) and many other scholars have pointed out, "success-breeds-success" (Frank and Cook 1995, 19). Winners with the most gold stars in one generation are now much more likely to pass along their social status, wealth, and educational attainment to their children, a system which is increasingly solidifying social and economic inequality and creating a new aristocratic "caste," especially in the U.S. (Markovits 2019, 19, 25, 115; see also Hochschild and Scrovronick 2003; Bartels 2008; Putnam 2015).

Schooling exacerbates socio-economic inequality rather than ameliorating it (Markovits 2019, 72–73). Only about 11 percent of lower-class students in the U.S. will complete college and earn a bachelor's degree. However, even with a college degree, about 38 percent of these students will remain in the bottom 40 percent of the income distribution (Goldrick-Rab 2016, 100), especially if they attend a nonselective college (Giani 2016, 457). Similar trends can be seen in the U.K. ("Which Traits" 2018).

With the educational arms race escalating, rich students are disproportionately able to enroll in graduate school, especially elite programs, and they capture most of the economic advantages of advanced degrees (Markovits 2019, 139–40; see also Mullen, Goyette and Soares, 2003).

One study found that lower-class students with a graduate degree earned only 60 percent as much as upper-class students, although this effect was partly due to the fact that upper-class students were more likely to earn an advanced degree in higher paying fields, like business, law, or medicine (Torch 2011).

We are now living in what political scientist Larry M. Bartels (2008) and others have called the "new gilded age" (1–2). Economic and political inequality is reaching extremes not seen since the late 19th century (Markovits 2019, ch. 3–4; Scheidel 2017). Recent trends in the global labor market due to the pandemic of 2020 seem to be exacerbating these trends ("Zoomers" 2020, 54).

Winners in the 21st century globalized economy currently take all the spoils and pass along their status and fortune to their children, creating a new hereditary aristocracy (Markovits 2019, 19, 25, 72). The poor and middle-class are becoming less and less able to compete in the labor market and climb the ladder of success.

Schooling will not help to ameliorate this situation. Never in human history have educational institutions ever reliably contributed to a reduction in socio-economic inequality (Scheidel 2017, 376, 361). Schools do not promote meritocracy or reduce inequality. Most forms of schooling, especially higher education, have always reproduced and reinforced, if not exacerbated, socio-economic inequality (Markovits 2019; Scheidel 2017, 412). To fully understand this point, we need to look at the history of China and East Asia.

Chapter 8

The Myth of Meritocracy

The Cautionary Examples of Ancient China and Modern South Korea

While state-sponsored public schooling, standardized tests, credentialism, and the educational rat race are relatively new phenomenon in Europe and the U.S., in East Asia they have been venerated traditions for over a thousand years. One could argue that ancient China invented the whole notion of a "knowledge economy" populated with credentialed elites about two thousand years ago (Jacques 2012, 15; Chaffee 1995; Acemoglu and Robinson 1994, 70).

China developed its own philosophical tradition about a century before the ancient Greeks, and Chinese philosophers had more influence on politics and the economy because many were employed as bureaucrats in the civil administration of various Chinese states. And well before Western Europe developed formal schooling or the printing press, China was "the most literate and numerate society in the world" (Jacques 2012, 15; Chaffee 1995).

By the 6th century C.E. the ancient Chinese had invented the multilevel, state education system, which included primary schools all the way up to universities. These academic institutions awarded a complex array of credentials that were one of the primary markers of class distinction in Chinese society, especially in the Imperial bureaucracies. Western democracies did not invent the notion of "meritocracy" in the 20th century (Horowitz 2006; Sandel 2020). The Chinese invented this concept sometime around 589 C.E. (Chaffee 1995, 15; Acemoglu and Robinson 1994, 70).

Due to the regional power of various Chinese dynasties, which reached all over Asia, the Chinese system of schooling and credentialism was adopted in many other East Asian cultures, long before this notion ever developed in Europe. Perhaps most notably, the Koreans developed their own distinctive version of Confucian culture, graded schooling, and credentialism, and

125

Koreans independently developed the printing press, and later in the 15th century, they developed their own alphabet (Cumings 2005).

Because of China's long history with schooling and reverence for academic credentials, some Asian American educational critics have pointed to China and East Asia as a model that other countries should follow in the 21st century (Chua 2011; Loh 2011). Even some education professors, like Linda Darling-Hammond (2010) have praised the "deep respect for knowledge and teaching" in East Asian culture (173).

While these pundits are right to applaud China's longstanding respect for schooling, they suffer from a selective, superficial, and nostalgic understanding of Chinese culture. The original purpose of Imperial schools was authoritarian control (Chaffee 1995), not education. Chinese schooling created and maintained sociopolitical inequality, and it continues to do so today (Mu, Dooley and Luke 2019).

Upon a close examination of the evidence, East Asian schooling prefigured many of the problems that we have discussed in this book and its companion volume, *Can We Measure What Matters Most?* For over a thousand years, schooling in China and Korea has been a rigged, ritualistic charade that provided only the "myth of opportunity" for most students (Chaffee 1995, 17; Mu, Dooley and Luke 2019).

The Chinese aristocracy invented schooling as an ideological façade that facilitated the maintenance of a hereditary aristocracy and the virtual enslavement of the majority of laborers in the imperial economy (Chaffee 1995). This is similar in many respects to how the 21st century meritocratic system operates in the U.S. and other developed democracies, as well as in modern, communist China.

Yes, East Asian cultures have traditionally venerated learning and academic success. Many educational pundits in the U.S. have celebrated Chinese culture for this emphasis, and perhaps rightly so (Chua 2011; Loh 2011). But that does not justify the Chinese concept of schooling, nor does it make it a model for other countries to follow.

While Asian American students in the U.S. currently work harder than other students and have higher levels of academic success, on average (Steinberg 2014, 119; Steinberg, 1996), research has shown that the "autocratic" parenting and teaching styles advocated by Amy Chua (2011) and others, the so-called "tiger" parenting, does not promote healthy child development or empower all Asian American students (Lee 1996; Steinberg 2014, 136). Nor does East Asian schooling guarantee human capital formation or labor market success (Mu, Dooley and Luke 2019).

Rather than a model to be emulated, the Chinese concept of schooling should serve as a warning to the rest of the world.

A RIGGED MERITOCRACY IN ANCIENT CHINA

For most of Chinese history, educational institutions stressed rote memorization of classical Chinese texts, ritualized socialization, writing, and the arts
(Mote 1971; Chaffee 1995). While some Confucian educational doctrines did
recognize the importance of individual development, the emphasis of formal
schooling in China and Korea, especially in later neo-Confucian institutions,
focused more on preparing a select few for service within the hierarchical
bureaucracy of Chinese and Korean monarchies.

Thus, much of a student's instruction was geared toward a highly ritualized and controlled socialization process. Students learned proper social
values and ritualistic behaviors, including how to dress, eat, walk, and draw.
Most importantly, students learned how to properly communicate as Imperial
officials, with a highly formal oral and written discourse (Jacques 2012, 96;
Chaffee 1995).

In ancient China, most students spent decades in private and public schools,
sometimes many decades. The average age of a graduated scholar who passed
the state exam was 36 years old, but degree recipients ranged from 19 to 66
(Chaffee 1995, 4). Chinese and Korean schooling culminated in a high stakes
and very stressful final examination that served as the gateway to a social title
and an elite position in the state bureaucracy.

But the vast majority of scholars, many of whom spent decades in school,
would end up failing the final exam. This was by design because there simply
were not enough jobs to go around (Chaffee 1995, 8). The Chinese educational system produced a small, elite population of bureaucrats who were
trained in a traditional and largely unchanging body of ethical knowledge,
classic literature, and political discourse.

However, the official Chinese school curriculum was not practically ori-
ented, and it was not designed to actually help students fulfill their duties as
civil servants. Schooling was focused on ancient ritual and socialization, not
human capital formation.

The literate and credentialed elite served as the administrative center of
vast Chinese empires, writing and implementing the decrees of the various
emperors and their ministers. Historian John W. Chaffee (1995) has documented how "status, power, and wealth were intimately linked to government service" (4; see also Scheidel 2017, 68). However, Chaffee (1995)
also pointed out that one shouldn't confuse social status with class. While
scholars enjoyed high social status, and their own distinctive caste, which
offered access to wealth and power, these civil servants were not part of the
aristocracy, which meant that they occupied a middle-management sector of
Chinese society between the nobility and peasantry (10).

Credentialed Chinese elites enjoyed a better life than the vast majority of Chinese peasant laborers, but these educated elites certainly did not enjoy the best life that Chinese aristocracy had to offer. Ancient China was a rigidly unequal and autocratic society ruled by a "stable imperial elite" who maintained a high "concentration of income and wealth" (Scheidel 2017, 63, 68). In most premodern societies, argues historian Walter Scheidel (2017), income and wealth "regularly owed more to political power than to economic prowess" (84).

Because China developed a relatively open system of schooling that was ostensibly available to almost everyone, some people have assumed that this system was meritocratic and that it allowed some measure of upward social mobility for lower class Chinese peasants. It is true that some students from modest social backgrounds were able to use schooling and the government exam to gain a measure of upward mobility, which meant rising slightly above the peasantry into which the vast majority of Chinese people were born.

However, the ancient Chinese and Korean systems of schooling had only the outward veneer of meritocracy (Chaffee 1995, 11). While many were allowed into the system, only a few graduated out of the system with a credential, and fewer still were given a stable, good paying job. Schooling in ancient China could only take one so far. In Chinese society, social lineage and marriage largely determined one's socioeconomic standing, not schooling. As Chaffee (1995) points out: "Marriage, not examinations, was the critical criterion for entrance into a socially-defined elite" (11, 16).

The Chinese system of schooling was *relatively* open to all, which meant that many classes of people were socially prohibited from attending school, or structurally hindered from being successful if they were lucky enough to get their foot in the door. First of all, few boys actually became students, as most people were born peasants and staid peasants their whole lives. Girls were prohibited from attending school because China was a deeply patriarchal society. Women were regarded as property and they were owned and controlled by men, which was similar to the status of women in the middle east and Europe for two thousand years (Lerner 1986, 99; Lerner 1993, ch. 2).

One scholar estimated that out of over a hundred million people, there were only about 200,000 students a year in ancient Chinese schools, which comprised around 0.2 percent of the total population or 0.4 percent of the male population (Chaffee 1995, 78). The majority of these boys would drop out of school or fail the exam. Thus, schooling did relatively little, if anything, to raise the socioeconomic status of most students.

Even worse, the academic system was rigged in favor of established elites who were politically connected to powerful despots. As more and more students entered the school system and sat for exams, competition dramatically increased for a limited number of spots. Eventually, quotas became initiated to reduce the numbers of students who could take the final exam (Chaffee 1995, 35).

Plus, as more and more students took and passed the state examination, the educated caste initiated special, easier examinations that were only available to relatives of officials, which helped "subvert the essential fairness of the system" (Chaffee 1995, 17, 105). This was a type of affirmative action for the privileged, a sneaky type of inequity and entitlement that we still see in modern systems of schooling, especially in the U.S. (Golden 2006; Markovits 2019).

And then there was good old-fashioned cheating. Many rich and powerful families found ways to cheat on behalf of their sons. This included bribing officials, bribing other students, changing exam answers, and getting exams ahead of time to prepare answers in advance (Chaffee 1995, 114). Sound familiar? Cheating and schooling have always gone hand in hand.

The recent cheating scandal in U.S. higher education, where parents bribed school officials to get their children into elite schools, is just the most recent manifestation of a long, long legacy of rich parents doing everything in their power to enable their privileged sons (and sometimes daughters) to maintain their elite status (Golden 2006; Markovits 2019; Sandel 2020).

Chaffee (1995) and many other historians have argued that the expansion of formal schooling in China, and the opening of state exams to more and more students, resulted not in a meritocratic society, but in a "politically useful but false promise of mobility to non-elites," and to "the contraction of opportunity and the growth of privilege" (xxvii, 183, xxv). Most peasants in ancient China never became students, and most students dropped out.

And what about the successful students who made their way through the educational rat race? Most got little more than exalted social status through the pomp, ceremony, and symbols of belonging to an elite academic culture. Only some successful students actually got a good government job. But these jobs enabled only a little power and not much wealth. And yet, a job did bring an additional layer of ceremonial status by being affiliated with the monarchy.

Ancient China was not the only society to engineer a rigged meritocratic system of schooling. The false promise of meritocracy can also be seen several centuries later in early modern England (Chaffee 1995, xxvii, 183, xxv). And now this same type of rigged meritocracy is in full effect in the 21st century all over the world, but perhaps most auspiciously in the U.S., Europe, China, and South Korea.

THE FALSE PROMISE OF SCHOOLING AND MERITOCRACY IN SOUTH KOREA

The small country of Korea was largely unnoticed by the rest of the world until the mid-20th century when it was thrust into the limelight due to the invasion of the United States to stop the advance of communist China. For much of its three-thousand-year history, Korea was an autonomous kingdom, conquered briefly only three times: by the T'ang dynasty of China in the 9th century, by the Mongols in the 13th century, and finally by Imperial Japan in the early 20th century (Cumings 2005).

The Korean War never formally ended, but the U.S. helped a despotic South Korea with foreign aid and economic advisors for many decades after a ceasefire was declared. Since then, South Korea has transformed itself into a developed, quasi-democratic country that has one of the world's most vibrant economies, especially in the technology and manufacturing sectors, with global champions like Samsung, LG, and Hyundai. From 1965 to 1978, South Korea's GNP grew around 9 percent annually, which decreased slightly to 8 percent from 1978 to 1997, hence its designation as a "tiger" economy in the 1990s (Cumings 2005).

While South Korea is now a democracy, it remains an authoritarian and rigidly class-based society with deep social, political, and economic inequalities, similar in many ways to both China and the U.S. (Cumings 2005; Lett 1998; Mu, Dooley and Luke 2019). For much of its independent existence in the 20th century, military dictators and repressive presidents ruled South Korea as an autocratic state. Authoritarianism is still very ingrained in Korean culture.

The foundation of South Korea's vibrant economy is based on a history of Western investment, state-sponsored capitalism, police state repression, and the oligarchic control of major industries by wealthy families. These aristocratic families are called *chaebol*. This exclusive group comprises a super-elite that largely controls the economy, and members of this group are often above the rule of law (Cumings 2005, 205, 317, 373; Lee 1984, 383–84; "Return" 2010).

The Asian financial crisis in 1997–1998 was only a temporary setback to Korean economic growth. Since then, the South Korean economy has greatly expanded, due in part to an increase in the public consumption of goods and the expansion of public education, especially access to higher education, which has become one of the dominant markers of class distinction in Korean society (Lett 1998; Seth 2002).

But not everyone has benefited from Korea's expanding economy and increased access to educational institutions. Inequality has intensified over the past couple of decades, and there is "a growing disparity" between rich and poor as measured by consumption patterns, residential segregation, and access to quality education, especially higher education (Koo 2007; Lim 2005). The correlation between parental income and social class in South Korea is higher than in any of the other 34 countries in the OECD, a group mostly composed of economically developed democracies ("One Country" 2019, 41).

Traditional gender inequality and pervasive sexism also persist in full-force, limiting social mobility for many women, even those with college degrees. According to *The Economist*, "Only 60 percent of female South Korean graduates aged between 25 and 64 are working—making educated South Korean women the most underemployed in OECD countries" ("Profiting" 2010). In 1994 women constituted only 8.6 percent of the workers in the top fifty corporations and in 1997 women held only 27 percent of all the professional jobs (Nelson 2000; Seth 2002, 245).

Not only are the numbers of impoverished and underemployed still a problem in 21st century South Korea, but there has also been increasing unemployment and growing job insecurity for white-collar workers with college degrees. Over the past two decades, Koreans have suffered setbacks from less protective labor laws, increased competition in the skilled labor market for fewer full-time jobs, and the introduction of neoliberal business models, like increased use a flexible, contingent, and low-paid labor force that can be easily hired and fired in reaction to business cycles (Koo 2007; Kim and Park 2006; Lett 1998).

Plus, the educationally driven culture of South Korea turns out many more college graduates than can be adequately employed in the economy (UNESCO 2006). While South Korea is near the top in producing college-educated students each year, it ranks near the bottom in terms of actually employing these college graduates.

As Michael J. Seth (2002) pointed out, "In 1995, only 61 percent of college graduates were able to find jobs within six months of receiving their degrees, despite the booming economy and a labor shortage" (247). While South Korea has made some improvement with employing college graduates, it still lags behind most other developed economies.

A recent OECD report found that only 77.1 percent of South Korean college graduates in 2008 were employed, compared to 87.8 percent in the U.K. and 83.1 percent in the U.S. (Jae-eun, 2010). Like other developed countries, the best jobs and highest paying jobs go to students who graduate from prestigious universities, while students from less prestigious universities are stuck with lower-paying work and higher levels of unemployment (Jung and Lee, 2016).

The official youth unemployment rate is around 10.4 percent, but some researchers estimate that it could be as high as 25 percent ("One Country"

2019, 42). The problem is now getting worse because economic growth has been slowing over the past decade, while the number of students graduating from college each year keeps increasing. The private rate of return for a college degree in South Korea has been declining, although the symbolic social status of a credential remains undiminished (Lett 1998).

Today, South Korea has one of the highest percentages of school-age population enrolled in both K–12 schooling and higher education, with around 99 percent enrollment in middle school, over 96 percent in high school, and close to 70 percent in some form of higher education (UNESCO 2006; Lee 2009). For most Koreans, public schooling is seen not only as an economic ladder to the middle class, but academic achievement in and of itself also confreres social status and prestige because of the traditional veneration of schooling in East Asian cultures (Robinson 1994; Lett 1998, 159).

However, public schools in Korea have a bad reputation for poor quality due to lack of funding, outdated curriculum, exam-oriented classes, autocratic and untrained teachers, large classes, and ancient pedagogical techniques that include rote memorization, standardized tests, and corporeal punishment. Korean schools are also highly tracked from middle-school on up, and they relentlessly sort students based on a variety of standardized tests. Student start preparing for high stakes tests in primary school (Seth 2002, 157).

It should be no surprise that superior achievement scores in Korean schools are highly correlated with socioeconomic status, as wealthier families can afford more private education to prepare students for high stakes tests (Robinson 1994; Seth 2002, 88–90, 142; Koo 2007). In 1970 there were about 1,421 *hagwons* in South Korea, which is the name for a private school, but most of these closed during the 1980s. The autocratic President Chun Doo-hwan decreed that private education was illegal so as to promote an equal educational playing field, but this ban was later ruled unconstitutional.

Hagwons were legalized in a regulated market in 1991, and by 1996 private tutoring was also legal (Lartigue 2000; Card 2005; Seth 2002, 185). In 1980, before the ban took place, about 1/5 of Korean students received some form of private education: 13 percent of elementary school students, 15 percent of middle school students, and 26 percent of high school students. In 1997 over half of Korean students were being privately educated: 70 percent of elementary students and 50 percent of middle and high school students. Those numbers have kept growing into the 21st century.

By 2003 Koreans were spending around $12.4 billion on private education, which was more than half the national budget for public schooling (Koo 2007, 12, 14). In 2003 about 72.6 percent of Korean students were privately educated and parents were spending between 10 to 30 percent of family income on private schools (Yi 2009; Lartigue 2000). By 2008 there were around 70,213 *hagwons* and Koreans spent almost 21 trillion won (around $17 billion) on private education (Gwang-lip 2009; "Lee" 2009).

Because the state has never funded much of the educational system, parents bear most of the burden of educating their children in the private educational market. Because of this, South Korean families spend more on education than in most other countries, around 69 percent of the total price, making South Korea, in the estimate of one scholar, "possibly the world's costliest educational system" (Seth 2002, 172, 187).

Every level of South Korean schooling is punctuated by high stakes exams, even in extracurricular *hagwons*, which has led Koreans to call their system of schooling "*sihom chiok*," "examination hell" or "examination mania" (Seth 2002, 140). The pinnacle of K–12 public schooling is the National University Entrance Examination, and only the best and brightest students make it into the top-tier Korean universities, which are the exclusive gateways to the best jobs.

Some have dubbed the South Korean educational system a "testocracy," rather than a meritocracy (Sorensen 1994, 17; Sah-Myung 1983, 229). If a student gets into a top-tier university, then they are a success. If not, they are seen by most people as a failure—and not only for themselves, but for their whole extended family. As one scholar summarized the predicament of schooling in South Korea, "The crux of the matter is that this system is too competitive, too exam-oriented with a single preoccupation to prepare students for college entrance exams" (Koo 2007, 11; Seth 2002, 140).

In South Korea, as in other Asian countries, education is seen as an intense social competition for prestige and wealth, not as a process of individual development, nor as a tool for national economic development. Family and society push students to succeed for the glory of the family, where success is measured in exam scores, English language acquisition, placement at elite universities, white-collar jobs at corporate firms, and all the trimmings of Western consumer capitalism.

This institutionalized drive for academic, social, and economic success has been captured in a Korean phrase "*kyoyungnyol*," which can be translated as "education mania" or "education fever" (Seth 2002; Ellinger and Beckam 1997; Sorensen 1994, 21, 23). The system of schooling in South Korea perfectly fits Frank's (1985) definition of an "educational rat race" (211). South Korean society is consumed by "education fever," which is a social epidemic fed by stark inequality and the scramble for social status and wealth. This phenomenon is a threat to the well-being of Korean youth who are psychologically and physically harmed by this intense competition.

First of all, students don't learn anything of value in Korean schools. From kindergarten to college, most Korean schools use a "teach-for-the-test" curriculum that focuses on the memorization of information, standardized multiple-choice tests, and test-taking techniques. Educational historian Diane Ravitch (2010) has insightfully critiqued this kind of school curriculum, which reduce student learning to "test-taking skills" (107–8). Ravitch argued that students "master the art of filling in the bubbles on multiple-choice tests, but [cannot] express themselves, particularly when a question requires them to think about and explain what they had just read" (107–8, 159).

Linda Darling-Hammond (2010) has also noted the limitations of the high stakes, standardized testing, which Koreans practice:

Researchers consistently find that instruction focused on memorizing uncon-nected facts and drilling skills out of context produces inert rather than active knowledge that does not transfer to real-world activities or problem-solving situations. Most of the material learned in this way is soon forgotten and cannot be retrieved or applied when it would be useful later. (70)

With a narrow, teach-for-the-test curriculum, students are "trained, not edu-cated," as Darling-Hammond (2010, 109) pointed out. This type of training rewards students for endurance, short-term memorization, and trickery, not useful learning or personal development. With this type of training, students rarely understand the information being taught to them because they are not taught how to critically analyze information or think for themselves. Students also find it difficult to apply information learned in school to other contexts where it might be useful.

Students simply become "expert memorizers" of "decontextualized" facts that can only be used to take standardized tests (Senior, 2009; Card 2005). The teach-for-the-test curriculum of most Korean schools "stifle[s] creativ-ity, hinder[s] the development of analytical reasoning, ma[kes] schooling a process of rote memorization of meaningless facts, and drain[s] all the joy out of learning" (Seth 2002, 170). High stakes exams also lead to widespread cheating, grade inflation, and outright bribery (Card 2005).

But there is a much more serious problem with Korean schooling, and with "education fever" more broadly. It does a lot of damage to children and adolescents. Korean culture places a lot of emphasis on success in school, especially on passing exams and college placement, which creates a "pressure-cooker atmosphere" for students, starting in kindergarten (Seth 2002, 192).

Students already spend a lot of time studying for regular school exams, but the addition of *hagons* and private tutors takes up a lot of time during the week, leaving most students with little to no free time. Students routinely are in school, studying, or engaged in private education for up to 18 hours a day, seven days a week. One student explained, "I have to get up at 7 in the morning. I have to be at school by 8, and lessons finish at 4. Then you to to a *hagwon and when you arrive home, it's around 1 o'clock in the morning"* *(qtd. in* Khang, 2001).

Doctors have found that "rates of curvature of the spine have more than doubled in the last decade" for Korean students because they are sitting at school desks for so long (Markovits 2019, 154). Korean doctors have also discovered a new disorder they call "turtleneck syndrome," which is when a "child's head hunches forward anxiously" (154).

The Korean Teachers and Education Worker's Union claims that high school students sleep on average only 5.4 hours a day, although a recent academic study found that the average sleep time was slightly higher, around 6.5 hours a day (Joo et al. 2005). The Ministry of Health, Welfare and Family Affairs has issued warnings about student's irregular meals and lack of sleep (Ji-sook 2008).

About 40 percent of elementary and middle school students skip meals because they lack a break in their busy daily schedule (Ji-sook 2008). There is a popular student proverb in Korea, that students repeat often, "If you sleep for four hours a night, you'll get into the college of your choice—if you sleep for five hours, you fail" (qtd. in Khang 2001).

This pressure to perform leads to serious physical harm and psychological distress. Parents and teachers routinely beat students that do not perform well academically. A study published in 1996 found that "97 percent of all children reported being beaten by parents and/or teachers, many of them frequently" (Seth 2002, 168).

Many students turn to suicide as the only escape from this relentless pressure to perform. Statistics are not routinely kept on this issue, but limited data are frightening. South Korea has the highest suicide rate among all OECD countries (Koretz 2017, 22). Around 50 high school students committed suicide after failing the college entrance exam in 1987. An academic study published in 1990 revealed, "20 percent of all secondary students contemplated suicide and 5 percent attempted it" (Seth 2002, 166).

And the problem seems to be getting worse. Two recent surveys found that between 43–48 percent of Korean students have contemplated suicide. From 2000 to 2003 over 1,000 students between the ages of 10 and 19 committed suicide. Families also suffer. In 2005 a father was so distressed over his son's bad grades that he lit himself on fire outside his son's school, along with his wife and their daughter, because the family could not live with the shame (Card 2005).

WHAT'S THE POINT OF SCHOOLING IN KOREA?

From a distance, the South Korean systems of schooling looks attractive. South Korea has one of the highest percentages of school-age population enrolled in both K–12 and higher education, and it has been the site of a "miracle" socioeconomic transformation from an underdeveloped, autocratic third-world backwater into a developed, free-market, high-skilled economy and democratizing society.

But schooling in South Korea, as it was in ancient China, has traditionally been about social status and class, not employment in the labor market, and especially not individual development through useful learning or self-fulfillment (Seth 2002, 100). Furthermore, South Korean schooling is a literal hell that students have to endure seven days a week for almost twenty years. When I taught in South Korea, one grade school student told me that schooling "feels like dying inside" (Beach 2011b).

Anthropologist Denise Potrzeba Lett (1998) documented how the South Korean system of schooling confirms the signaling theory of credentials rather than the human capital theory (Spence 1974; Caplan 2018). Lett (1998) argued that South Koreans don't care much about useful knowledge or skills. She argued that "the primary motivation" behind Koreans pursuit of education is not personal development or economic mobility; it is social status (159).

Koreans see schooling, "more than anything else," as a "pursuit of status" (Lett 1998, 159, 164). Lett (1998) calls this the "yangbanization" of Korean society, after Korea's traditional cultured caste of scholars who were an official part of the Korean aristocracy (212, 215). The pursuit of formal education in South Korea, as it was in ancient China, has always been focused on credentials and class distinction, not education. This is why the latter 20th century expansion of schooling, and the proliferation of credentials in Korea, have only served to reinforce traditional inequalities, rather than to enable socioeconomic mobility.

We are seeing the same pattern in the U.S. (Markovits 2019) and other postindustrial countries around the world. This is ironic because in Western democracies, like the U.S., public schooling was invented to supposedly ameliorate socioeconomic inequalities and enable all children from every social and economic background to get an equal chance at success through hard work and merit. This was the American Dream (Sandel 2020).

But the democratic and meritocratic mission for schools, which John Dewey ([1916] 1966) famously articulated, has always struggled to take hold in the U.S. (see also Ryan 1995; Gutmann, 1987). The Chinese model of schooling is far older and it has been much more influential in most societies.

Schooling has always institutionalized the consecration of social status in the service of aristocratic power. Changing schools into meritocratic institutions that enable social mobility has proven to be very difficult, and in most societies, this political program has failed. It may even be impossible. The practice of schooling may be naturally autocratic and inequitable, which would explain why it has been so difficult to change.

Conclusion

Can Schools Become
Meritocratic Institutions?

In 1939 Newton Edwards, professor of education at the University of Chicago, published a report for the American Council on Education (Tyack 1974, 272). Having seen the recent devastation caused by the Great Depression in the 1930s, he noted the inequitable social, economic, and educational resources available to American citizens to train themselves adequately for economic success and job security, especially access to high quality schools with the best teachers.

Edwards explained that no matter what the idealistic purpose of a school may be, it would always be embedded in larger social, political, and economic networks. Up until the early 20th century, scholars called this complex social system the *political economy*.

Social, political, and economic forces have always shaped and constrained schooling. And they always will. The political economy has always limited the ability of teachers to educate students. It has also structurally prevented most poor and working-class students from gaining much, if any, social mobility through schooling in any country.

In a highly stratified and unequal society, as most cultures have always been, Edwards argued that "education becomes an instrument of social stratification and of regional and racial inequality," not a progressive tool for meritocracy (qtd. in Tyack 1974, 272). Edwards went on to say that in the U.S., which was supposed to be "the bulwark of democracy," public schools "may in fact become an instrument for creating those very inequalities they were designed to prevent" (qtd. in Tyack 1974, 272–73).

When looking at the social, political, and economic data, especially labor market outcomes and the generation of wealth, schooling has rarely been a meritocratic institution. Whether it be in the U.S., the U.K., Europe, South

139

Korea, or China, one point remains crystal clear. Far from ameliorating socioeconomic inequalities, schools have almost always maintained, if not exacerbated, existing inequalities for most people, especially institutions of higher education.

And if that is indeed the case, then the recent accountability movement, which started in the U.S. in the later 20th century, may not really be about reforming schools to make them more effective educational institutions. This point was explored in this book's companion volume, *Can We Measure What Matters Most?* Despite calls for reform and accountability over the past century, most schools in the U.S. are not doing much of anything to improve student learning or to create learning organizations.

So let's revisit the basic conclusions we have arrived at in both volumes.

The accountability movement in the U.S. is *not* about education. It's *not* even about accountability. It's about economics. It's about politics. It's about money, social status, control, and power. It's also about the administrative coup d'état of education, which started in the 19th century.

Rather than improve schools, accountability reforms have often been used to justify ineffective managerialism and the top-down authority of school administrators, while delegitimizing the professional judgment and skilled practices of teachers.

If everyone is focused on short-term efficiency metrics, and competing against each other for the best numbers, then often those accountability markers get manipulated for personal gain, since long-term organizational goals don't really matter.

As many critics have pointed out over the past couple of decades, the current overreliance on accountability measurements in schools, like grades, student evaluation surveys, and awarded credentials, are not focused on the authentic practice of education. Accountability measures and procedures are about playing school, cutting costs, management gimmicks, and the illusions (if not delusions) of managerial authority.

Student evaluation surveys in particular are a prime example of administrative malfeasance. Student surveys reflect a cost-conscious administrative decision to outsource management responsibilities onto the consumer so that administrators can save time and money, and pretend to look effective in the process.

It is too difficult and too expensive for school administrators to actually evaluate teachers using valid measurement techniques, such as observing teachers in the act of teaching, or paying teachers to conduct classroom observations of each other, or setting up formal peer-to-peer discussions of teaching, or engaging teachers in quality professional development opportunities from trained experts instead of consultants pushing useless fads.

Educational researchers have already identified effective practices to improve teaching and student learning, but school administrators simply choose not to implement or support these practices, often because they feel there is no time, money, or organizational will to do so.

Most school administrators, policy makers, and even students don't understand the difference between education and playing school, they can't tell the difference between real learning and pretending to learn, and they can't tell the difference between effective teaching and merely acting like a teacher.

In order for accountability metrics to work, and for broader school reforms to be successful, innovations must originate from within the classroom and be directed by committed and experienced teachers who are trying to reach the needs of specific groups of students. Schools should be managed by teachers, not administrators or business consultants. Teachers should hold themselves accountable to their students, just like students should be held accountable to their teachers.

The practices of empirical research and evidence-based evaluation in both theory and practice are very important and useful. But there are some things that just cannot be measured. We need to learn how to be more comfortable with our collective ignorance about teaching and learning, and what that means for the management of schools. We cannot substitute technocratic engineering and management for the messy and imperfect personal judgments of professional educators, who need to be part of the process of evaluating their work as teachers.

We need to imagine something much more radical than administrative reforms through faddish management theory, privatization, or government decree. Ivan Illich (1970) suggested a half-century ago that there was an important distinction between education and schooling. Illich argued schools were getting in the way of students' education, and so he proposed that educational reformers needed to think about how they might "deschool" our culture.

Illich argued that we "confuse teaching with learning, grade advancement with education, [and] a diploma with competence" (1). Further, he argued, "We cannot begin a reform of education unless we first understand that neither individual learning nor social equality can be enhanced by the ritual of schooling" (55).

The problem of schooling in the 21st century is urgent. Where a high school diploma once opened up access to good jobs, now everyone needs a bachelor's degree to compete in the labor market. Soon everyone will need a postgraduate degree, or more. Business professor Jeffrey Pfeffer (2010) explained how "with more well-qualified people competing for each step on the organizational ladder all the time, rivalry is intense and only getting more so" (5).

From an economic and human capital standpoint, the world does not need any more college-educated workers. Nor, for that matter, does the world need any more high-school-educated workers, especially since automation will be destroying many low-skill and medium-skill jobs in the near future.

Colleges and universities have a self-serving institutional focus that is harming students and society. While institutions of higher education pander to short-sided consumer demands, consumers are not really benefiting. Printing more and more degrees creates "educational hyperinflation," which is ultimately self-defeating for students.

Sociologist Randal Collins (2002) argued that schools now serve the political purpose of a "hidden welfare system" because they can provide social and economic support to people who do not have a job or cannot get a job in the highly competitive global labor market (27).

Economist Fred Hirsch (1976) explained how "the obstacle course of education" was lengthening into more years of schooling, which "favor[s] those best able to sustain a longer or more costly race. These are the well-off and the well-connected" (50). Everyone else gets trapped in substandard warehouse-schools until they either drop out, move into the labor market, or move higher up the ladder of schooling.

Because K–12 schooling has largely been a symbolic institution that does not teach useful knowledge or practical skills, a high school diploma does not really represent useful human capital. Instead, Collins (2002) argues that high schools offer "little more than a ticket into a lottery where one can buy a chance at a college degree, and that in turn is becoming a ticket to a yet higher level lottery" (24). A high school diploma has now become just a gateway credential, "a way station toward acquiring" a bachelor's degree (Collins 2002, 24).

Credentialism not only leads to the devaluation of degrees through an over-educated workforce, but it also leads to intensifying labor market competition for scarce high-paying jobs, and to the polarization of the labor market into "a winner-take-all" contest (Frank and Cook 1995). A system based on credentialism creates "positional arms races," whereby each new generation tries to accumulate more degrees and specializations than the last generation, amassing more and more gold stars at greater cost, all in an effort to climb the slippery social ladder by generating higher status and more wealth.

Meritocracy isn't a ladder of success. It's a lottery, a rigged lottery. Rather than enabling or guaranteeing success in the labor market, schools merely offer a chance at success to the lucky few. And the lucky few have always been predominantly rich, white, and culturally privileged.

Schooling once guaranteed a better life, when few people enrolled in schools, but now "the goalposts have moved," and schooling no longer guarantees success. And the goalposts began to move in the 1970s, unfortunately, just as schools became open to all students, regardless of race, class, or gender, for the first time in U.S. history.

Plus, disparities based on class, race, gender, and sexual orientation still matter a great deal. When it comes to winning the ultimate prize, the victors are disproportionately privileged to begin with. In the U.S. and many other countries around the world, schooling largely reinforces and reproduces the inequitable "winner-take-all" system of global capitalism where privileged "superstars" get all the gold stars and earn all the wealth.

Schooling will not help to ameliorate this situation. Never in human history have educational institutions ever reliably contributed to a reduction in socio-economic inequality. Schools do not promote meritocracy or reduce inequality. Most forms of schooling, especially higher education, have always reproduced and reinforced, if not exacerbated, socio-economic inequality. To fully understand this point, we need to remember the history of China and East Asia.

If democratic nations, like the U.S., are going to take the ideals of meritocracy and political equality seriously, then schools need to be refashioned into institutions of learning and human development, rather than institutions of political power and social reproduction. If schools are going to be meritocratic institutions, then teachers and students need to be the heart and soul of the practice of education, not bureaucrats, economists, or politicians. This is a tall order. To do this, schools will need to realign organizational priorities to focus on the practices of teaching and learning instead of playing school, competition, and awarding social status.

The statistician and management professor W. Edwards Deming (1994) once argued that we need to create a "system of education in which pupils from toddlers on up through the university take joy in learning, free of fear of grades and gold stars, and in which teachers take joy in their work, free from fear in ranking" (62–63). This wonderful vision is very similar to the educational vision of John Dewey, which inspired me to become a teacher. Because I never experienced an authentic learning institution as a student, I wanted to become a teacher and try to give students the type of educational experience I never had. I am grateful that I was able to do this successfully with many students over my long career as an educator, although I failed more often that I was successful because most of my students never wanted to learn.

For most of human history, schools have been organizations focused on authority, peer pressure, and social status. If schools became educational institutions, as Deming and Dewey argued, then they would need to be re-focused on creating mutually beneficial relationships that promote learning and understanding, which would, in turn, promote individual and organizational change the likes of which the world has rarely seen (Argyris 1993; Senge [1990] 2006; Kellerman 2012; Keltner 2016). In an educational organization, teachers would teach and guide students, instead of trying to command and control them (Rogoff 2003, 207). And administratorswould need to get out of the way of teachers so they could focus on educating students

Is this ideal even possible on large scale?

It may not be. The early 20th century sociologist and political economist Max Weber argued that the need for social status is deeply engrained in all human cultures. He explained that "the fortunate [person] is seldom satisfied with the fact of being fortunate" (qtd. in Sandel 2020, 42). Weber went on to explain that human beings want to know that they have a "right" to their "good fortune," and they want "to be convinced" that they "deserve" their fortune, and "above all," that they "deserve it in comparison with others" (42).

Philosopher Michael J. Sandel (2020) argues in his most recent book that there is a "triumphalist aspect of meritocracy" that is a "kind of providentialism without God (42). In many countries, including the U.S., China, and South Korea, prosperity "is a sign of salvation, suffering is a sign of sin" (48, 59). Thus, schooling, and other types of meritocratic contests, have become "the last acceptable prejudice" to not only socially and economically sort people, but also to politically and morally judge people as worthy or unworthy (81).

The root of the problem, as Sandel points out, is that in every human society, merit and distinction have always been tied to social, economic, and political advantages. It is hard to "disentangle" merit from privilege (10). Thus, when societies have tried to create schools to promote equality or meritocracy, schools have almost always degenerated into traditional institutions that promote and reproduce competition, ranking, status, power, inequality, and privilege. As Sandel rightly concludes, "today's meritocracy has hardened into a hereditary aristocracy" (24).

Is it possible to create a meritocratic system of schools focused on education and personal development that won't harden into a hereditary aristocracy? Is it possible to get human beings to stop competing for social status and wealth? Is it possible to get all students to learn, and want to learn, so they can personally grow into fully capable and thriving human beings ?

Maybe. But maybe this circle may never be squared. Maybe the principle of education, learning, and student development are more aspirational ideals than they are programmatic ends for schooling, especially national systems of schools. The evidence is discouraging, but not devoid of hope.

Can We Measure What Matters Most? offered a somewhat optimistic conclusion. This book does not. Without fundamental changes to the larger political economy, and perhaps to human nature, the reformation of schools into educational institutions may not be possible. Sadly, most students don't want an education. They prefer to be entertained by actors, or to cynically play school until they can get their gold star and enter the labor market.

But that doesn't mean that visionary educators shouldn't try. John Dewey's ([1916] 1966) idealistic concept of education is an enticing vision of what may, one day, come to pass (see also Ryan 1995 Gutmann, 1987). Failure is inevitable, as the companion volume discussed at length in the chapter on teaching and learning, but if we as a species can collectively learn from our mistakes and do better, then who knows how far we can get in reforming and refashioning the institutions of schooling and higher education.

As William James once pointed out, there are no natural limits if we chose to *believe* a better future is possible, and then act *as if* we can succeed (Wiseman 2012). Many people over the past century have taken the first brave, bold steps to build better educational organizations and reform existing institutions. There have been some successes and many failures. I know we can we do better.

These two companion volumes represent more than three decades of my passionate struggle against schooling in a fight to promote education and learning. I have distilled almost everything that I have learned as a student, a teacher, and a scholar. I spent 24 years as a student in formal schooling and over 20 years as a teacher in various types of schools.

I have been continually inspired over the years by the French philosopher Albert Camus' (1955) myth of Sisyphus, the titan who was tortured by the Greek gods for rebelling against their authority. Sisyphus was condemned to roll a rock up and down a hill for an eternity of mindless drudgery and failure. But Camus argued that despite the meaninglessness of this torture, Sisyphus was able to find happiness in the struggle because "the struggle itself toward the heights is enough to fill a man's heart" (123). Camus argued, "there is so much stubborn hope in the human heart" (103).

It may be impossible to refashion all bureaucratic schools into learning organizations. It may be impossible to inspire every human being to become lifelong learners. It may be impossible to overcome centuries of hatred, social exclusion, and socio-political inequality to build more equitable social, economic, and political institutions. But that is no reason not to try. And while succeeding in these endeavors at scale may be impossible, there is no reason why we can't achieve smaller measures of localized success.

There is so much stubborn hope in the human heart.

References

Abrami, Philip C., Les Leventhal, and Raymond P. Perry. 1982. "Educational Seduction." *Review of Educational Research* 52 (3): 446–64.

Acemoglu, Daron, and James A. Robinson. 2019. *The Narrow Corridor: States, Societies, and the Fate of Liberty*. New York: Penguin.

Aguayo, Rafael. 1990. *Dr. Deming: The American Who Taught the Japanese about Quality*. New York: Carol Publishing Group.

Alexander, Kern. 1996. "The Value of an Education." In Breneman, David W., Larry L. Leslie, and Richard E. Anderson, eds. *Assessing Teacher Quality: Understanding Teacher Effects on Instruction and Achievement*, 85–111. ASHE Reader on Finance in Higher Education. Needham Heights, MA: Simon & Schuster. Originally published 1976 in *Journal of Education Finance* 1 (4): 429–67.

Ambady, Nalini, and Robert Rosenthal. 1993. "Half a Minute: Predicting Teacher Evaluations from Thin Slices of Nonverbal Behavior and Physical Attractiveness." *Journal of Personality and Social Psychology* 64 (3): 431–41.

Anderson, Chris. 2008. *The Long Tail: Why the Future of Business Is Selling Less of More. 2nd ed.* New York: Hachette Books.

"Angst for the Educated." 2011, Sep 3. *The Economist*, 66.

Anonymous. 2019, March 25. "What Happens after Rich Kids Bribe Their Way into College? I Teach Them." *The Guardian*. Retrieved from www.theguardian.com

Argyris, Chris. 1993. *Knowledge for Action: A Guide to Overcoming Barriers to Organizational Change*. San Francisco: Jossey-Bass.

Ariely, Dan. 2008. *Predictably Irrational: The Hidden Forces That Shape Our Decisions*. New York: Harper Perennial.

———. 2012. *The Honest Truth About Dishonesty: How We Lie to Everyone—Especially Ourselves*. New York: Harper Perennial.

Aronowitz, Stanley. 2000. *The Knowledge Factory: Dismantling the Corporate University and Creating True Higher Learning*. Boston, MA: Beacon Press.

Atack, Jeremy, and Peter Passell. 1994. *A New Economic View of American History from Colonial Times to 1940. 2nd ed.* New York: W.W. Norton & Company.

Atteberry, Allison, and Daniel Mangan. 2020, June/July. "The Sensitivity of Teacher Value-Added Scores to the Use of Fall or Spring Test Scores." *Educational Researcher*, 495: 335–349.

"Backs to the Future: Briefing—Chronic Pain." 2020, Jan 18. *The Economist*, 17–19.

Bain, Ken. 2004. *What the Best College Teachers Do*. Cambridge, MA: Harvard University Press.

Baker, Wayne. 2020. *All You Have to Do Is Ask: How to Master the Most Important Skill for Success*. New York: Currency.

Banaji, Mahzarin R., and Anthony G. Greenwald. 2013. *Blindspot: Hidden Biases of Good People*. New York: Bantam Books.

Banerjee, Abhijit V., and Esther Duflo. 2019. *Good Economics for Hard Times.* New York: Public Affairs.

"Barely Managing." 2018, June 30. *The Economist*, 65.

Bartels, Larry M. 2008. *Unequal Democracy: The Political Economy of the New Gilded Age*. New York: Russell Sage Foundation.

Barton, Paul E. 2008. "How Many College Graduates Does the US Labor Force Really Need?" *Change.* Retrieved from www.carnegiefoundation.org.

Beach, Josh M. 2007. "Ideology of the American Dream: Two Competing Philosophies in Education, 1776–2006." *Educational Studies: A Journal of the American Educational Studies Association*, 41 (2): 148–64.

———. 2009. "A Critique of Human Capital Formation in the US and the Economic Returns to Sub-Baccalaureate Credentials." *Educational Studies: A Journal of the American Educational Studies Association,* 45 (1): 24–38.

———. 2011a. *Gateway to Opportunity: A History of the Community College in the United States.* Sterling, VA: Stylus Publishing, LLC.

———. 2011b. *Children Dying Inside: A Critical Analysis of Education in South Korea*. Austin, TX: West by Southwest.

———. 2018. *How Do You Know? The Epistemological Foundations of 21st Century Literacy*. London: Routledge.

Bell, Daniel. 1973. *The Coming of Post-Industrial Society: A Venture in Social Forecasting*. New York: Basic Books.

Benedict, Ruth. 1934. *Patterns of Culture: An Analysis of Our Social Structure as Related to Primitive Civilization*. New York: Penguin Books.

Berman, Jillian. 2019, May 15. "America's Educational System Is an 'Aristocracy Posing as a Meritocracy.'" *Marketwatch.* Retrieved from www.marketwatch.com.

Bernays, Edward L. 2005. *Propaganda*. Brooklyn, NY: IG. Originally published 1928.

———. 2011. *Crystallizing Public Opinion*. Brooklyn, NY: IG. Originally published 1923.

Berrett, Dan. 2014, Sept 26. "Scholars Take Aim at Student Evaluations' 'Air of Objectivity.'" *The Chronicle of Higher Education*. Retrieved from www.universityworldnews.com.

Berry, Christopher R., and Anthony Fowler. 2019. "How Much Do Coaches Matter?" *13th Annual MIT Sloan Sports Analytics Conference, MIT*. Boston, MA. Paper ID: 12549.

"Beyond the Pale." 2020, June 20. *The Economist*, 53–54.

Bills, David B. 2003, Winter. "Credentials, Signals, and Screens: Explaining the Relationship between Schooling and Job Assignment." *Review of Educational Research* 73 (4): 441–69.

Birnbaum, Robert. 2000. *Management Fads in Higher Education: Where They Come from, What They Do, Why They Fail*. San Francisco, CA: Jossey-Bass.

Bok, Derek. 2003. *Universities in the Marketplace: The Commercialization of Higher Education*. Princeton: Princeton University Press.

Boston, Claire. 2019, April 9. "College Grads Sell Stakes in Themselves to Wall Street." *Bloomberg Businessweek*. Retrieved from www.bloomberg.com.

Botstein, Leon. 2013, summer. "Resisting Complacency, Fear, and the Philistine: The University and Its Challenges." *The Hedgehog Review* 15 (2): 70–78.

Bourdieu, Pierre. 1993. *Sociology in Question*. London: Sage.

———. 2010. *Distinction: A Social Critique of the Judgement of Taste*. London: Routledge. Originally published 1984.

Boydston, Jeanne. 1990. *Home and Work: Housework, Wages, and the Ideology of Labor in the Early Republic*. Oxford: Oxford University Press.

Brackett, Marc. 2019. *Permission to Feel: Unlocking the Power of Emotions to Help Our Kids, Ourselves, and Our Society Thrive*. New York: Celadon.

Brafman, Ori, and Rom Brafman. 2008. *Sway: The Irresistible Pull of Irrational Behavior*. New York: Crown Business.

Braga, Michela, Marco Paccagnella, and Michele Pellizzari. 2014. "Evaluating Students' Evaluations of Professors." *Economics of Education Review* 41: 71–88.

———. 2016. "The Impact of College Teaching on Students' Academic and Labor Market Outcomes." *Journal of Labor Economics* 34 (3): 781–822.

Brantlinger, Ellen A. 1993. *The Politics of Social Class in Secondary School*. New York: Teachers College Press.

Breit, William, and Roger L. Ransom. 1998. *The Academic Scribblers*, 3rd ed. Princeton: Princeton University Press.

Breneman, David W. 2001. "The Outputs of Higher Education." In *Ford Policy Forum 2001*. Cambridge, MA: Forum for the Future of Higher Education, Massachusetts Institute of Technology.

Brint, Steven. 2008. "No College Student Left Behind?" *Research & Occasional Paper Series*. Center for Studies in Higher Education, University of California Berkeley, CSHE.9.2008

Brint, Steven, and Jerome Karabel. 1989. *The Diverted Dream: Community Colleges and the Promise of Educational Opportunity in America, 1900–1985*. Oxford: Oxford University Press.

Brown, David K. 1995. *Degrees of Control: A Sociology of Educational Expansion and Occupational Credentialism*. New York: Columbia Teachers College Press.

Bruner, Jerome. 1983. *In Search of Mind: Essays in Autobiography*. New York: Harper & Row.

Brynjolfsson, Erik, and Andrew McAfee. 2016. *The Second Machine Age: Work, Progress, and Prosperity in a Time of Brilliant Technologies*. New York: W. W. Norton.

Buckman, Ken. 2007, Fall. "What Counts as Assessment in the 21st Century?" *Thought & Action*, 23: 29–37.

Bunge, Nancy. 2018. "Students Evaluating Teachers Doesn't Just Hurt Teachers. It Hurts Students." *The Chronicle of Higher Education*. Retrieved from www. chronicle.com.

Campbell, Shanyce. 2014. "Quality Teachers Wanted: An Examination of Standards-Based Evaluation Systems and School Staffing Practices in North Carolina Middle Schools." ProQuest Dissertations and Theses. Retrieved from https://search.proquest.com.

Campbell, Shanyce L., and Matthew Ronfeldt. 2018. "Observational Evaluation of Teachers: Measuring More Than We Bargained For?" *American Educational Research Journal,* in press, 1–35.

Camus, Albert. 1955. *The Myth of Sisyphus and Other Essays*. Trans. Justin O'Brien. New York: Vintage International.

Caplan, Bryan. 2007. *The Myth of The Rational Voter: Why Democracies Choose Bad Policies*. Princeton, NJ: Princeton University Press.

———. 2018. *The Case Against Education: Why the Education System Is a Waste of Time and Money*. Princeton, NJ: Princeton University Press.

Card, James. 2005, Nov 30. "Life and Death Exams in South Korea." *Asia Times Online*.

Carnevale, Anthony P., Jeff Strohl, Artem Gulish, Martin Van Der Werf, and Kathryn Peltier Campbell. 2019a. *The Unequal Race for Good Jobs: How Whites Made Outsized Gains in Education and Good Jobs Compared to Blacks and Latinos*. McCourt School of Public Policy, Georgetown University. Retrieved from www. cew.georgetown.edu.

Carnevale, Anthony, Megan Fasules, Michael Quinn, and Kathryn Peltier Campbell. 2019b. *Born to Win, Schooled to Lose. Why Equally Talented Students Don't Get Equal Chances to Be All They Can Be*. Center on Education and the Workforce. McCourt School of Public Policy, Georgetown University. Retrieved from www. cew.georgetown.edu.

Cavanagh, Sarah Rose. 2016. *The Spark of Learning: Energizing the College Classroom with the Science of Emotion*. Morgantown, WV: West Virginia University Press.

Chaffee, John W. 1995. *The Thorny Gates of Learning in Sung China: A Social History of Examinations*. New Ed. Albany, NY: State University of New York Press.

Chen, Pauline W. 2013, Feb 29. "Why Failing Med Students Don't Get Failing Grades." *The New York Times.* Retrieved from well.blogs.www.nytimes.com.

Childress, Herb. 2019. *The Adjunct Underclass: How America's Colleges Betrayed Their Faculty, Their Students, and Their Mission*. Chicago: University of Chicago Press.

Chua, Amy. 2011. *Battle Hymn of the Tiger Mother*. New York: Penguin.

Cialdini, Robert B. 2007. *Influence: The Psychology of Persuasion*. New York: Collins Business.

Clausing, Kimberly. 2019. *Open: The Progressive Case for Free Trade, Immigration, and Global Capital*. Cambridge, MA: Harvard University Press.

Clayson, Dennis E. 2009. "Student Evaluations of Teaching: Are They Related to What Students Learn?" *Journal of Marketing Education* 31 (1): 16–30.

Cohen, David K., James P. Spillane, and Donald J. Peurach. 2018, April. "The Dilemmas of Educational Reform." *Educational Researcher* 47 (3): 204–212.

Cohen, Lizabeth. 2003. *A Consumers' Republic: The Politics of Mass Consumption in Postwar America*. New York: Alfred A. Knopf.

Cohen, Peter A. 1987. "A Critical Analysis and Reanalysis of the Multisection Validity Meta-Analysis." *1987 Annual Meeting of the American Educational Research Association*.

Cohen, Rachel D. 2018, Oct 3. "Patients Give Doctors High Marks for Prescribing Antibiotics for Common Sniffles." *NPR*. Retrieved from www.npr.org

Collins, Randall. 1979. *The Credential Society: An Historical Sociology of Education and Stratification*. New York: Academic Press.

———. 2002. "Credential Inflation and the Future of Universities." In Steven G. Brint, ed. *The Future of the City of Intellect: The Changing American University*. Stanford, CA: Stanford University Press. 23–46.

Cremin, Lawrence A. 1961. *The Transformation of The School: Progressivism in American Education, 1876–1957*. New York: Vintage Books.

———. 1990. *Popular Education and Its Discontents*. New York: Harper & Row.

Cuban, Larry. 2013. *Inside the Black Box of Classroom Practice: Change Without Reform in American Education*. Cambridge, MA: Harvard Education Press.

Cumings, Bruce. 2005. *Korea's Place in the Sun: A Modern History*. New York: Norton.

"Cut-Price Economics." 2019, Aug 10. *The Economist*, 62.

Dale, Stacy Berg, and Alan B. Krueger. 1999. "Estimating the Payoff to Attending A More Selective College: An Application of Selection on Observables and Unobservables." Working Paper 7322. Cambridge, MA: National Bureau of Economic Research.

Damasio, Antonio. 1994. *Descartes' Error: Emotion, Reason, and the Human Brain*. New York: Penguin.

———. 1999. *The Feeling of What Happens: Body and Emotion in the Making of Consciousness*. New York: Harcourt.

Darling-Hammond, Linda. 2010. *The Flat World and Education: How America's Commitment to Equity Will Determine Our Future*. New York: Teachers College Press.

Dawley, Alan. 1991. *Struggles for Justice: Social Responsibility and the Liberal State*. Cambridge, MA: Harvard University Press.

De Waal, Frans. 2016. *Are We Smart Enough to Know How Smart Animals Are?* New York: W. W. Norton.

Deci, Edward L., and Richard Flaste. 1995. *Why We Do What We Do: Understanding Self-Motivation*. New York: Penguin.

Delbanco, Andrew. 2007. "Scandals of Higher Education." *New York Review of Books*, March 29, 2007. Retrieved from www.nybooks.com.

Deming, W. Edwards. 1994. *The New Economics for Industry, Government, Education*. 2nd ed. Cambridge, MA: The MIT Press.

Dench, Geoff, ed. 2006. *The Rise and Rise of Meritocracy*. Oxford: UK: Blackwell.

Deresiewicz, William. 2014. *Excellent Sheep: The Miseducation of the American Elite and the Way to a Meaningful Life*. New York: Free Press.

Dewey, John. 1966. *Democracy and Education*. New York: Free Press. Originally published 1916.

Dey, Judy Goldberg, and Catherine Hill. 2007. *Behind the Pay Gap*. American Association of University Women Educational Foundation. Washington, DC: Author.

Domjan, Michael. 2010. *The Principles of Learning and Behavior*. 6th ed. Belmont, CA: Wadsworth.

"Don't Even Ask! Economic Statistics." 2018, May 26. *The Economist*, 54–55.

Dougherty, Kevin J. 2001. *The Contradictory College: The Conflicting Origins, Impacts, and Futures of the Community College*. Albany, NY: State University of New York Press, Originally published 1994.

Dougherty, Kevin J., Sosanya M. Jones, Hana Lahr, Rebecca S. Natow, Lara Pheatt, and Vikash Reddy. 2016. "Looking Inside the Black Box of Performance Funding for Higher Education: Policy Instruments, Organizational Obstacles, and Intended and Unintended Impacts." *RSF: The Russell Sage Foundation Journal of the Social Sciences* 2 (1): 147–173.

Drucker, Peter. F. 1969. *The Age of Discontinuity: Guidelines to Our Changing Society*. New York: Harper & Row.

Duckworth, Angela. 2016. *Grit: The Power of Passion and Perseverance*. New York, NY: Scribner.

Dweck, Carol S. 2002. "Beliefs That Make Smart People Dumb." In Robert J. Sternberg, ed., *Why Smart People Can Be So Stupid*. New Haven: Yale University Press.

Eaton, Judith S. 1994. *Strengthening Collegiate Education in Community Colleges*. San Francisco: Jossey-Bass.

Ebenstein, Lanny. 2015. *Chicagonomics: The Evolution of Chicago Free Market Economics*. New York: St. Martin's Press.

Eberhardt, Jennifer L. 2020. *Biased: Uncovering the Hidden Prejudice That Shapes What We See, Think, and Do*. New York: Penguin Books.

"#Economists Too: Women in Economics." 2019, March 23. *The Economist*. Retrieved from www.economist.com.

Edmondson, Amy C. 2012. *Teaming: How Organizations Learn, Innovate, and Complete in the Knowledge Economy*. San Francisco: Jossey-Bass.

———. 2019. *The Fearless Organization: Creating Psychological Safety in the Workplace for Learning, Innovation, and Growth*. New York: Wiley.

Edwards, Richard C. 1979. *Contested Terrain: The Transformation of the Workplace in the Twentieth Century*. New York: Basic Books.

Ellinger, Thomas R., and Garry M. Beckham. 1997. "South Korea: Placing Education on Top of the Family Agenda." *Phi Delta Kappan* 78 (8): 624–625.

Engelke, Matthew. 2018. *How to Think Like an Anthropologist*. Princeton: Princeton University Press.

Evans, Jonathan St. B. T. 1989. *Bias in Human Reasoning: Causes and Consequences*. Hove: Lawrence Erlbaum.

Ewen, Stuart. 1996. *PR!—A Social History of Spin*. New York: Basic Books.

"Face Blind." 2020, Feb 22. *The Economist, 77.*

Fish, Stanley. 1980. *Is There a Text in This Class? The Authority of Interpretive Communities*. Cambridge, MA: Harvard University Press.

———. 2010, June 21. *"Deep in the Heart of Texas." New York Times*. Retrieved from www.nytimes.com.

———. 2019. *The First: How to Think about Hate Speech, Campus Speech, Fake News, Post-Truth, and Donald Trump*. New York: One Signal Publishers.

Florida, Richard. 2007. *The Flight of the Creative Class*. New York: HarperCollins.

Ford, Martin. 2016. *Rise of the Robots: Technology and the Threat of a Jobless Future*. New York: Basic Books.

Foster, William T. 1911. "Scientific Versus Personal Distribution of College Credits." *Popular Science Monthly* LXXVIII, 388–408.

Frank, Robert H. 1985. *Choosing the Right Pond: Human Behavior and the Quest for Status*. Oxford: Oxford University Press.

Frank, Robert H. and Philip J. Cook. 1995. *The Winner-Take-All Society: Why the Few at the Top Get So Much More Than the Rest of Us*. New York: Penguin.

Freedman, David H. 2019, July. "The Worst Patients in the World." *The Atlantic*, 28–30.

Freidson, Eliot. 1986. *Professional Powers: A Study of the Institutionalization of Formal Knowledge*. Chicago: University of Chicago Press.

Frey, Carl Benedikt. 2019. *The Technology Trap: Capital, Labor, and Power in the Age of Automation*. Princeton: Princeton University Press.

Friedman, Milton M. 2002. *Capitalism and Freedom*. Chicago: The University of Chicago. Originally published 1962.

Friedman, Thomas L. 2005. *The World Is Flat*. New York: Farrar, Straus, and Giroux.

Friesen, Norm. 2011. "The Lecture as a Transmedial Pedagogical Form: A Historical Analysis." *Educational Researcher*, 40 (3): 95–102.

Gaither, Gerald., B. Nedwek, and J. E. Neal. 1994. *Measuring Up: The Promises and Pitfalls of Performance Indicators in Higher Education*. ASHE-ERIC Higher Education Report No. 5. Washington, DC: George Washington University, Graduate School of Education and Human Development.

Gannon, Kevin. 2018, May 6. "In Defense (Sort of) of Student Evaluations of Teaching." *The Chronicle of Higher Education*. Retrieved from www.chronicle.com.

Gardner, Howard. 1993. *Multiple Intelligences: The Theory in Practice*. New York: Basic Books.

———. 2011a. *Frames of Mind: The Theory of Multiple Intelligences*. New York: Basic Books. Originally published 1983.

———. 2011b. *The Unschooled Mind: How Children Think and How Schools Should Teach*. New York: Basic Books. Originally published 1995.

Garrett, Rachel, Martyna Citkowicz, and Ryan Williams. 2019. "How Responsive Is a Teacher's Classroom Practice to Intervention? A Meta-Analysis of Randomized Field Studies." *Review of Research in Education: Changing Teaching Practice in P–20 Educational Settings* 43 (1): 106–137.

Geddes, Jennifer L., ed. 2000, Fall. *What's the University For? The Hedgehog Review, 23.*

Geertz, Clifford. 1973. *The Interpretation of Cultures: Selected Essays by Clifford Geertz.* New York: Basic Books.

Gerstle, Gary. 2001. *American Crucible: Race and Nation in the Twentieth Century.* Princeton: Princeton University Press.

Gerzema, John, and Edward Lebar. 2008. *The Brand Bubble: The Looming Crisis in Brand Value and How to Avoid It.* San Francisco: Jossey-Bass.

Giani, Matt S. 2016, Spring. "Are All Colleges Equally Equalizing? How Institutional Selectivity Impacts Socioeconomic Disparities in Graduates' Labor Outcomes." *The Review of Higher Education* 39 (3): 431–461.

Gigliotti, Richard J., and Foster S. Buchtel. 1990. "Attributional Bias and Course Evaluations." *Journal of Educational Psychology* 82 (2): 341.

Ginsberg, Benjamin. 2011. *The Fall of the Faculty. The Rise of the All-Administrative University and Why It Matters.* Oxford: Oxford University Press.

Golden, Daniel. 2006. *The Price of Admission: How America's Ruling Class Buys Its Way into Elite Colleges—and Who Gets Left Outside the Gates.* New York: Crown.

Goldin, Claudia. 1990. *Understanding the Gender Gap: An Economic History of American Women.* Oxford: Oxford University Press.

Goldrick-Rab, Sara. 2016. *Paying the Price: College Costs, Financial Aid, and the Betrayal of the American Dream.* Chicago: University of Chicago Press.

Goleman, Daniel. 1995. *Emotional Intelligence.* New York: Bantam.

———. 2013. *Focus: The Hidden Driver of Excellence.* New York: Harper.

Goodman, Nelson. 1978. *Ways of Worldmaking.* Indianapolis, IN: Hackett Publishing Company.

Goodwin, Craufurd D. 2014. *Walter Lippmann: Public Economist.* Cambridge, MA: Harvard University Press.

Gopnik, Alison. 2009. *The Philosophical Baby: What Children's Minds Tell Us about Truth, Love and the Meaning of Life.* New York: Picador.

———. 2016. *The Gardener and the Carpenter: What the New Science of Child Development Tells Us about the Relationship Between Parents and Children.* New York: Picador.

Gottschall, Jonathan. 2012. *The Storytelling Animal: How Stories Make Us Human.* New York: Mariner Books.

Graeber, David. 2015. *The Utopia of Rules: On Technology, Stupidity, and the Secret Joys of Bureaucracy.* Brooklyn, NY: Melville House.

———. 2018. *Bullshit Jobs: A Theory.* New York: Simon & Schuster.

Gray, John. 2018. *Seven Types of Atheism.* New York: Farrar, Straus and Giroux.

Greene, Joshua D. 2013. *Moral Tribes: Emotion, Reason, and the Gap Between Us and Them.* New York: Penguin.

Greene, Maxine. 1988. *The Dialectic of Freedom.* New York: Teachers College Press.

Greenwald, Anthony G., and Gerald M. Gillmore. 1997. "Grading Leniency Is a Removable Contaminant of Student Ratings." *American Psychologist* 52 (11): 1209–1217.

Gregorian, Vartan. 2005. "Six Challenges to the American University." In Richard H. Hersh and John Merrow. *Declining by Degrees: Higher Education at Risk.* 77–96. New York: Palgrave Macmillan.

Gregory, Sean. 2016, April 25. "The Obamacare Quirk That Is Fueling the Opioid Epidemic." *Time, 19–20.*

Grimes, Howard. 2018, Nov 14. "Inquiry, Academic Management of Classroom for BIO 2053, Fall 2018." San Antonio, TX: The University of Texas, San Antonio.

Grove, Andrew S. 2015. *High Output Management.* New York: Vintage Books.

Grubb, W. Norton. 1985. "The Convergence of Educational Systems and the Role of Vocationalism." *Comparative Education Review* 29 (4): 526–548.

———. 1992. "The Economic Returns to Baccalaureate Degrees: New Evidence from the Class of 1972." *The Review of Higher Education* 15 (2): 213–231.

———. 1996a. *Working in the Middle: Strengthening Education and Training for the Mid-Skilled Labor Force.* San Francisco: Jossey-Bass.

———. 1996b. *Learning to Work: The Case for Reintegrating Job Training and Education.* Russell Sage Foundation, 1996.

———. 1999. *Learning and Earning in the Middle: The Economic Benefits of Sub-Baccalaureate Education.* Community College Research Center, Teachers College, Columbia University. New York: Author.

Grubb, W. Norton, and Marvin Lazerson. 2004. *The Education Gospel: The Economic Power of Schooling.* Cambridge, MA: Harvard University Press.

Gutek, Gerald Lee. 1984. *George S. Counts and American Civilization: The Educator as Social Theorist.* Mercer University Press.

Gutmann, Amy. 1987. *Democratic Education.* Princeton: Princeton University Press.

Gwang-lip, M. 2009, Dec 15. "Statistics Paint Korean Picture." *Joong Ang Daily.*

Hacker, Andrew, and Claudia Dreifus. 2010. *Higher Education? How Colleges are Wasting Our Money and Failing Our Kids—And What We Can Do About It.* New York: St. Martin's Griffin.

Hagel III, John, John Seely Brown, and Lang Davison. 2010. *The Power of Pull: How Small Moves, Smartly Made, Can Set Big Things in Motion.* New York: Basic Books.

Haidt, Jonathan. 2001. "The Emotional Dog and Its Rational Tail: A Social Intuitionist Approach to Moral Judgment." *Psychological Review* 108 (4): 814–34.

———. 2006. *The Happiness Hypothesis.* New York: Basic Books.

Hammersley, Martyn, and Paul Atkinson. 1995. *Ethnography: Principles in Practice.* 2nd ed. London: Routledge.

Hanauer, Nick. 2019, July. Better Schools Won't Fix America. *The Atlantic.*

Handy, Charles. 1990. *The Age of Unreason.* Boston, MA: Harvard Business School Press.

———. 1993. *Understanding Organizations.* 4th ed. New York: Penguin Books.

Harris, Judith Rich. 1999. *The Nurture Assumption: Why Children Turn Out the Way They Do.* New York: Touchstone.

Harvey, David. 2005. *A Brief History of Neoliberalism*. Oxford: Oxford University Press.

Hattie, John, and Helen Timperley. 2007. "The Power of Feedback." *Review of Educational Research* 77 (1): 81–112.

Heckman, James J. 2013. *Giving Kids a Fair Chance*. Cambridge, MA: MIT Press.

Heckman, James J., Jora Stixrud, and Sergio Urzua. 2006. "The Effects of Cognitive and Noncognitive Abilities on Labor Market Outcomes and Social Behavior." *Journal of Labor Economics* 24 (3): 411–482.

Hersh, Richard, and John Merrow, eds. 2005. "Introduction." In Richard Hersh and John Merrow, eds., *Declining by Degrees: Higher Education at Risk* 1–9. New York: Palgrave Macmillan.

Hertz, Tom. 2006. *Understanding Mobility in America*. Washington, DC: Center for American Progress. Retrieved from http://www.americanprogress.org.

Hibbing, John R., Kevin B. Smith, and John R. Alford. 2014. *Predisposed: Liberals, Conservatives, and the Biology of Political Differences*. London: Routledge.

Hirsch, Fred. 1976. *Social Limits to Growth*. Cambridge, MA: Harvard University Press.

Hochschild, Jennifer L., and Nathan Scovronick. 2003. *The American Dream and the Public Schools*. Oxford: Oxford University Press.

Homes, David S. 1972. Effects of Grades and Disconfirmed Grade Expectancies on Students' Evaluations of their Instructor. *Journal of Educational Psychology* 63 (2): 130–133.

Horowitz, Irving Louis. 2006. "The Moral Economy of Meritocracy: Or, the unanticipated Triumph of Reform and the Failure of Revolution in the West. In Geoff Dench, ed. *The Rise and Rise of Meritocracy*. Oxford, UK: Blackwell. 127–133.

"How One Restaurant Fought Yelp's Alleged Extortion." 2014, Oct 13. *New York Post*. Retrieved from www.nypost.com.

Huff, Darrel. 1954. *How to Lie with Statistics*. New York: W. W. Norton.

Hyman, Ray. 2002. "Why and When Are Smart People Stupid." In Robert J. Sternberg, ed. *Why Smart People Can Be So Stupid*. New Haven: Yale University Press.

"I Am Number 0.6." 2020, Feb 8. *The Economist*, 55.

"Idle Hands." 2019, Aug 3. *The Economist*, 31–32.

Igo, Sarah E. 2007. *The Averaged American: Surveys, Citizens, and the Making of a Mass Public*. Cambridge: Harvard University Press.

Illich, Ivan, 1970. *Deschooling Society*. New York: Harper and Row.

Inglehart, Ronald, and Christian Welzel. 2005. *Modernization, Cultural Change, and Democracy: The Human Development Sequence*. Cambridge: Cambridge University Press.

"Invisible Men." 2020, July 18. *The Economist*, 60–61.

Isaacs, William. 1999. *Dialogue and the Art of Thinking Together: A Pioneering Approach to Communicating in Business and in Life*. New York: Currency.

Jacob, Brian A., and Elias Walsh. 2011. "What's in a Rating?" *Economics of Education Review* 30 (3): 434–448.

Jacobs, Lawrence R., and Theda Skocpol, eds. 2005. *Inequality and American Democracy: What We Know and What We Need to Learn*. New York: Russell Sage Foundation.

Jacoby, Susan. 2009. *The Age of American Unreason*. Revised ed. New York: Vintage.

Jacques, Martin. 2012. *When China Rules the World: The End of the Western World and the Birth of a New Global Order*. New York: Penguin.

Jae-eun, Cho. 2010, Oct 18. "Too Many Grads Fight for Too Few Jobs." *Joong Ang Daily*.

Jarvis, Will. 2019, July 22. "LSU Just Unveiled a $28-Million Football Facility. The Flood-Damaged Library Is Still 'Decrepit.'" *The Chronicle of Higher Education*. Retrieved from www.chronicle.com.

Ji-sook, Bae. 2008, March 13. "Should *Hagwon* Run Round-the-Clock?" *Korea Times*.

Jiang, Jennie Y., and Susan E. Sporte. 2016. *Teacher Evaluation in Chicago: Differences in Observation and Value-Added Scores by Teacher, Student, and School Characteristics*. Chicago, IL: University of Chicago Consortium on School Research.

Jillson, Cal. 2004. *Pursuing the American Dream: Opportunity and Exclusion over Four Centuries*. Lawrence, KS: University Press of Kansas.

Johnson, Valen E. 2003. *Grade Inflation: A Crisis in College Education*. New York: Springer.

Jolls, Christine, Cass R. Sunstein, and Richard Thaler. 1998. "A Behavioral Approach to Law and Economics." *Stanford Law Review* 50 (5): 1471–1550.

Joo, Soonjae, Chol Shin, Jinkwan Kim, Hyeryeon Yi, Yongkyu Ahn, Minkyu Park, Jehyeong Kim, and SangDuck Lee. 2005. "Prevalence and Correlates of Excessive Daytime Sleepiness in High School Students in Korea." *Psychiatry and Clinical Neurosciences* 59 (4): 433–440.

Jung, Jisun, and Soo Jeung Lee. 2016. "Influence of University Prestige on Graduate Wage and Job Satisfaction: The Case of South Korea." *Journal of Higher Education Policy and Management* 38 (3): 297–315.

Kahneman, Daniel. 2011. *Thinking, Fast and Slow*. New York: Farrar, Straus and Giroux.

Kamenetz, Anya. 2014, Sept 26. "Student Course Evaluations Get an F." *NPR*. Retrieved from www.npr.org.

Kantor, Harvey A. 1988. *Learning to Earn: School, Work, and Vocational Reform in California, 1880–1930*. Madison: The University of Wisconsin Press.

Kaplan, Robert S., and David P. Norton. 1996. *The Balanced Scorecard: Translating Strategy into Action*. Boston, MA: Harvard Business School Press.

Keeling, Richard, and Richard Hersh. 2012. *We're Losing Our Minds: Rethinking American Higher Education*. New York: Palgrave Macmillan.

Kellerman, Barbara. 2008. *How Followers Are Creating Change and Changing Leaders*. Boston, MA: Harvard School Press.

———. 2012. *The End of Leadership*. New York: Harper Business.

———. 2015. *Hard Times: Leadership in America*. Stanford University Press.

Kelly, Sean, ed. 2012. *Assessing Teacher Quality: Understanding Teacher Effects on Instruction and Achievement.* New York: Teachers College Press.

Keltner, Dacher. 2016. *The Power Paradox: How We Gain and Lose Influence.* New York: Penguin.

Kezar, Adrianna, Tom DePaola, and Daniel T. Scott. 2019. *The Gig Academy: Mapping Labor in the Neoliberal University.* Baltimore: Johns Hopkins University Press.

Khang, Hyunsung. 2001, Aug 5. "Education Obsessed South Korea." *Radio Netherlands Wereldomroe.*

Khurana, Rakesh. 2002. *Searching for a Corporate Savior: The Irrational Quest for Charismatic CEOs.* Princeton: Princeton University Press.

———. 2007. *From Higher Aims to Hired Hands: The Social Transformation of American Business Schools and the Unfulfilled Promise of Management as a Profession.* Princeton: Princeton University Press.

Kim, Andrew Eungi, and Innwon Park. 2006, May/June. "Changing Trends of Work in South Korea: The Rapid Growth of Underemployment and Job Insecurity." *Asian Survey* 46 (3): 437–456.

Kimhi, Omer, Ben Shahar, and Tammy Harel. 2019, Jan 20. "Higher Education: Too Much of a (Potentially) Good Thing." Paper presented at Debt, Degrees and Democracy: A Critical Look at the Value of College Completion. Boston College Law School. Retrieved from www.academia.edu.

Kindlon, Daniel J. 2001. *Too Much of a Good Thing: Raising Children of Character in an Indulgent Age.* New York: Hyperion.

Kirp, David. 2019. *The College Dropout Scandal.* Oxford: Oxford University Press.

Kliebard, Herbert M. 1999. *Schooled to Work. Vocationalism and the American Curriculum, 1876–1946.* New York: Teachers College Press.

———. 2004. *The Struggle for the American Curriculum, 1893–1958.* New York: Routlege Falmer.

Kling, A. 2017, Aug 16. "College Customers vs. Suppliers." *EconLog.* Retrieved from www.econlog.econlib.org.

Koo, Hagen. 2007. "The Changing Faces of Inequality in South Korea in the Age of Globalization." *Korean Studies* 3 (1): 1–18.

Koon, Jeff, and Harry G. Murray. 1995. "Using Multiple Outcomes to Validate Student Ratings of Overall Teacher Effectiveness." *The Journal of Higher Education* 66 (1): 61–81.

Koretz, Daniel. 2017. *The Testing Charade: Pretending to Make Schools Better.* Chicago: The University of Chicago Press.

Kotler, Philip, and Kevin Lane Keller. 2012. *Marketing Management.* 14th ed. Boston, MA: Prentice Hall.

Kozol, Jonathan. 1991. *Savage Inequalities: Children in America's Schools.* New York: Harper Perennial.

Kraft, Matthew A., and John Papay. 2014. "Can Professional Environments in Schools Promote Teacher Development? Explaining Heterogeneity in Returns to Teaching Experience." *Educational Evaluation and Policy Analysis* 36 (4): 476–500.

Kuper, Adam. 1999. *Culture: The Anthropologists' Account.* Cambridge, MA: Harvard University Press.

Labaree, David. 1984. "Setting the Standard: Alternative Policies for Student Promotion." *Harvard Educational Review* 54 (1): 67–88.

———. 1992. "Power, Knowledge, and the Rationalization of Teaching: A Genealogy of the Movement to Professionalize Teaching." *Harvard Educational Review* 62 (2): 123–154.

———. 1997a. *How to Succeed in School without Really Learning: The Credentials Race in American Education.* New Haven, CT: Yale University Press.

———. 1997b. "Public Goods, Private Goods: The American Struggle over Educational Goals." *American Educational Research Journal* 34 (1): 39–81.

———. 2000, May/June. "On the Nature of Teaching and Teacher Education." *Journal of Teacher Education,* 51 (3): 228–233.

———. 2004. *The Trouble with Ed Schools.* New Haven, CT: Yale University Press.

———. 2005, Feb. "Progressivism, Schools and Schools of Education: An American Romance." *Paedagogica Historica* 41 (1–2): 275–288.

———. 2010. *Someone Has to Fail: The Zero-Sum Game of Public Schooling.* Cambridge, MA: Harvard University Press.

———. 2011. "The Lure of Statistics for Educational Researchers." *Educational Theory* 61 (6): 621–632.

———. 2012. "School Syndrome: Understanding the USA's Magical Belief that Schooling Can Somehow Improve Society, Promote Access, and Preserve Advantage." *Journal of Curriculum Studies* 44 (2): 143–163.

———. 2017. *A Perfect Mess: The Unlikely Ascendancy of American Higher Education.* Chicago: University of Chicago Press.

Langlois, Shawn. 2019, Mar 13. "Meet the YouTube Star Caught in the Admissions Scam." *Marketwatch.* Retrieved from www.marketwatch.com.

Lartigue, Casey, Jr. 2000, May 28. "You'll Never Guess What South Korea Frowns Upon." *Washington Post.* Retrieved from www.washingtonpost.com.

Lauren, Douglas Lee, and S. Michael Gaddis. 2013. "Exposure to Classroom Poverty and Test Score Achievement: Contextual Effects or Selection?" *American Journal of Sociology* 118 (4): 943–979.

Le Bon, Gustav. 1995. *The Crowd.* New Brunswick, NJ: Transaction Publishers. Originally published 1895.

Lears, Jackson. 1994. *Fables of Abundance: A Cultural History of Advertising in America.* New York: Basic Books.

Lebergott, Stanley. 1993. *Pursuing Happiness: American Consumers in the Twentieth Century.* Princeton: Princeton University Press.

"Lee Seeks to Cut Educational Costs." 2009, Aug 14. *Korea Herald.*

Lee, H. J. 2009, Feb. *Higher Education in Korea.* Center for Teaching and Learning, Seoul National University. Seoul: Seoul National University.

Lee, Ki Baik. 1984. *A New History of Korea.* Seoul: Ilchokak.

Lee, Stacey J. 1996. *Unraveling the "Model Minority" Stereotype: Listening to Asian American Youth.* New York: Teachers College Press.

Lerner, Gerda. 1986. *The Creation of Patriarchy.* Oxford: Oxford University Press.

———. 1993. *The Creation of Feminist Consciousness: From the Middle Ages to Eighteen-Seventy.* Oxford: Oxford University Press.

Leslie, Ian. 2014. *Curious: The Desire to Know and Why Your Future Depends on It.* New York: Basic Books.

Leslie, Larry L., and Paul T. Brinkman. 1988. *The Economic Value of Higher Education.* New York: American Council on Education.

Lett, Denise Potrzeba. 1998. *In Pursuit of Status: The Making of South Korea's "New" Urban Middle Class.* Cambridge: Harvard University Press, 1998.

Levin, John S., Josh M. Beach, and Carrie B. Kisker. 2009. "Educational Attainment Skewed in California Community Colleges?" *Community College Journal of Research and Practice* 33 (3–4): 256–269.

Levine, Arthur. 2005. "Worlds Apart; Disconnects Between Students and Their Colleges." In Richard H. Hersh and John Merrow, eds., *Declining by Degrees: Higher Education at Risk.* 155–167. New York: Palgrave Macmillan.

Lewis, Michael. 2017. *The Undoing Project: A Friendship That Changed Our Minds.* New York: W. W. Norton.

Lewis, Sarah. 2014. *The Rise: Creativity, the Gift of Failure, and the Search for Mastery.* New York: Simon & Schuster.

Lichtenstein, Nelson. 2002. *State of the Union: A Century of American Labor.* Princeton: Princeton University Press.

Lim, Jae Hoon. 2005. "Class Reproduction and Competing Ideologies in Korean Education." In Young-Key Kim-Renaud, Roy Richard Grinker, and Kirk W. Larsen, eds., *Korean Education.* Washington, DC: The George Washington University, The Elliot School of International Affairs.

Lindstrom, Martin. 2010. *Buy-ology: Truth and Lies about Why We Buy.* New York: Crown.

———. 2011. *Brandwashed: Tricks Companies Use to Manipulate Our Minds and Persuade Us to Buy.* New York: Crown.

Lippman, Walter. 1997. *Public Opinion.* New York: Free Press. Originally published 1922.

Lodge, Milton, and Charles S. Taber. 2013. *The Rationalizing Voter.* Cambridge: Cambridge University Press.

Loftus, Elizabeth F. 1996. *Eyewitness Testimony.* Cambridge, MA: Harvard University Press.

Loh, Sandra Tsing. 2011, April. "My Chinese American Problem—and Ours. *The Atlantic,* 83–91.

Lortie Dan C. 2002. *Schoolteacher: A Sociological Study,* 2nd ed. Chicago: University of Chicago Press.

Lucas, Christopher J. 1994. *American Higher Education: A History.* New York: St. Martin's Griffin.

Lukianoff, Greg, and Jonathan Haidt. 2018. *The Coddling of the American Mind: How Good Intentions and Bad Ideas Are Setting up a Generation for Failure.* New York: Penguin.

Maheshwari, Sapna. 2019, Nov 28. "When Is a Star Not Always a Star? When It's an Online Review." *New York Times.* Retrieved from www.nytimes.com.

Marchand, Roland. 1985. *Advertising the American Dream: Making Way for Modernity, 1920–1940*. Berkeley, CA: University of California Press.

Markovits, Daniel. 2019. *The Meritocracy Trap: How America's Foundational Myth Feeds Inequality, Dismantles the Middle Class, and Devours the Elite*. New York: Penguin.

Marsh, Herbert W. 1984. "Students' Evaluations of University Teaching: Dimensionality, Reliability, Validity, Potential Baises, And Utility." *Journal of Educational Psychology* 76 (5): 707–754.

Marsh, Herbert W., and Michael J. Dunkin. 1992. "Students' Evaluations of University Teaching: A Multidimensional Perspective." *Higher Education: Handbook of Theory and Research* 8: 142–233.

Matthews, Anne. 1998. *Bright College Years: Inside the American College Today*. Chicago: University of Chicago Press.

McGrath, Dennis, and Martin B. Spear. 1991. *The Academic Crisis of the Community College*. Albany, NY: State University of New York.

McGregor, Douglas. 1960. *The Human Side of Enterprise*. New York: McGraw-Hill.

McLaughlin, Brian P., and Amélie Rorty, Eds. 1988. *Perspectives on Self-Deception*. Berkeley, CA: University of California Press.

Mele, Alfred R. 2001. *Self-Deception Unmasked*. Princeton: Princeton University Press.

Melguizo, Tatiana, and Federick Ngo. 2020. "Mis/Alignment Between High School and Community College Standards." *Educational Researcher* 49 (2): 130–133.

Menand, Louis. 2001. *The Metaphysical Club: A Story of Ideas in America*. New York: Farrar, Straus, and Giroux.

Mercedes, Cheryl. 2019, April 25. "Broken Ribs, Kicked and Punched: Reports Show Houston School Teachers Bullied by Their Students." *KVUE ABC*. Retrieved from www.kvue.com.

Mercier, Hugo, and Dan Sperber. 2017. *The Enigma of Reason*. Cambridge, MA: Harvard University Press.

Milner, Murray. 1994. *Status and Sacredness: A General Theory of Status Relations and an Analysis of Indian Culture*. Oxford: Oxford University Press.

———. 2006. *Freaks, Geeks, and Cool Kids: American Teenagers, Schools, and the Culture of Consumption*. New York: Routledge.

Milton, Ohmer, Howard R. Pollio, and James A. Eison. 1986. *Making Sense of College Grades*. San Francisco, CA: Jossey-Bass.

Mischel, Walter. 2014. *The Marshmallow Test: Why Self-Control Is the Engine of Success*. New York: Little, Brown and Company.

Mishel, Lawrence R., Jared Bernstein, and Sylvia A. Allegretto. 2007. *The State of Working America 2006/2007*. An Economic Policy Institute Book. Ithaca, NY: ILR Press, an imprint of Cornell University Press.

Mitchell, Kevin J. 2018. *Innate: How the Wiring of Our Brains Shapes Who We Are*. Princeton: Princeton University Press, 2020.

Moretti, Enrico. 2012. *The New Geography of Jobs*. Boston: Mariner Books.

————. 2015. "Are Cities the New Growth Escalator?" In A. Joshi-Ghani and E. Glaeser, eds., *The Urban Imperative: Toward Competitive Cities*. Oxford: Oxford University Press.

Morris, Paul. 1996, March. "Asia's Four Little Tigers: A Comparison of the Role of Education in Their Development." *Comparative Education* 32 (1): 95–110.

Mote, Frederick W. 1971. *Intellectual Foundations of China*. New York: Knopf.

Mu, Guanglun Michael, Karen Dooley, and Allan Luke. 2019. *Bourdieu and Chinese Education: Inequality, Competition, and Change*. New York: Routledge.

Mullen, Ann L., Kimberly A. Goyette, and Joseph A. Soares. 2003. "Who Goes to Graduate School? Social and Academic Correlates of Educational Continuation After College." *Sociology of Education* 7 (6): 143–169.

Muller, Jerry Z. 2018. *The Tyranny of Metrics*. Princeton, NJ: Princeton University Press.

Murphy, Heather. 2019, May 20. "Why High-Class People Get Away with Incompetence." *New York Times*. Retrieved from www.nytimes.com.

Murphy, Michelle. 2017. *The Economization of Life*. Durham, NC: Duke University Press.

Naftulin, Donald H., John E. Ware, and Frank A. Donnelly. 1973. "The Doctor Fox Lecture: A Paradigm of Educational Seduction." *Journal of Medical Education* 48 (7): 630–635.

National Governors Association. 1991. *Time for Results: The Governors' 1991 Report on Education*. Washington, DC: Author.

Nelson, Laura C. 2000. *Measured Excess: Status, Gender, and Consumer Nationalism in South Korea*. New York: Columbia University Press.

Nichols, Tom. 2017. *The Death of Expertise: The Campaign Against Established Knowledge and Why It Matters*. Oxford: Oxford University Press.

Nisbett, Richard E., and Timothy D. Wilson. 1977. "Telling More Than We Can Know" *Psychological Review* 84 (1): 231–59.

"Nope, Just Debt." 2011, Oct 29. *The Economist*, 83–85.

Oettingen, Gabriele. 2014. *Rethinking Positive Thinking: Inside the New Science of Motivation*. New York: Portfolio/Penguin.

Olson, Methew H., and B. R. Hergenhahn. 2009. *An Introduction to Theories of Learning*, 8th ed. Upper Saddle River, NJ: Pearson-Prentice Hall.

"One Country, Two Systems." 2019, Oct 12. *The Economist*, 41–42.

"Over a Third of Graduates in Britain Are Too Educated for Their Jobs: Daily Chart." 2019, May 6. *The Economist*. Retrieved from www.economist.com

Painter, Nell Irvin. 1987. *Standing at Armageddon: The United States, 1877-1919*. New York: W. W. Norton.

Pager, Devah. 2007. *Marked: Race, Crime, and Finding Work in an Era of Mass Incarceration*. Chicago: The University of Chicago Press.

Pascarella, Ernest T., and Patrick T. Terenzini. 2005. *How College Affects Students: A Third Decade of Research. Volume 2*. San Francisco: Jossey-Bass.

Patterson, James T. 2001. *Brown v. Board of Education: A Civil Rights Milestone and Its Troubled Legacy*. Oxford: Oxford University Press.

Paulsen, Michael B. 2001. "The Economics of Human Capital and Investment in Higher Education." *The Finance of Higher Education: Theory, Research, Policy, and Practice.* Michael B. Paulsen and J. C. Smart, Eds., 55–94. New York: Agathon Press.

Payne, Charles M. 2008. *So Much Reform, So Little Change: The Persistence of Failure in Urban Schools.* Cambridge, MA: Harvard Education Press.

Peng, Mike W. 2017. *Global Business.* 4th ed. Boston, MA: Cengage.

Peterson, Hayley. 2019, May 10. "Millions of Students Are Buying 'Plagiarism-Free' Essays for as Little as $13." *Business Insider.* Retrieved from www.businessinsider. com.

Peterson, Paul E. 1985. *The Politics of School Reform, 1870–1940.* Chicago: University of Chicago Press.

Peurach, Donald J., David K. Cohen, Maxwell M. Yurkofsky, and James P. Spillane. 2019. "From Mass Schooling to Education Systems: Changing Patterns in the Organization and Management of Instruction." *Review of Research in Education: Changing Teaching Practice in P–20 Educational Settings,* 43 (1): 32–67.

Pfeffer J. 1992. *Managing with Power: Politics and Influence in Organizations.* New York: Harper Business.

———. 2010. *Power: Why Some People Have It—and Other Don't.* New York: Harper Business.

———. 2015. *Leadership BS: Fixing Workplaces and Careers One Truth at a Time.* New York: Harper Business.

Phillips, Kristine. 2018, Nov 30. "They Had Us Fooled: Inside Payless' Elaborate Prank to Dupe People into Paying $600 for Shoes." *The Washington Post.* Retrieved from www.washingtonpost.com.

Pianta, Robert C., and Arya Ansari. 2018. "Does Attendance in Private Schools Predict Student Outcomes at Age 15? Evidence from a Longitudinal Study." *Educational Researcher* 47 (7): 419–434.

Pinker, Steven. 1997. *How the Mind Works.* New York: W. W. Norton.

———. 2002. *The Blank Slate: The Modern Denial of Human Nature.* New York: Penguin.

———. 2011. *The Better Angels of Our Nature: Why Violence Has Declined.* New York: Penguin.

Polanyi, Michael. 1962. *Personal Knowledge: Towards a Post-Critical Philosophy.* Chicago: University of Chicago Press.

———. 1967. *The Tacit Dimension.* New York: Doubleday.

Pollan, Michael. 2008. *In Defense of Food: An Eater's Manifesto.* New York: Penguin.

Pope, Denise Clark. 2001. *Doing School: How We Are Creating a Generation of Stressed Out, Materialistic, and Miseducated Students.* New Haven, CT: Yale University Press.

Popkin, Samuel L. 1994. *The Reasoning Voter: Communication and Persuasion in Presidential Campaigns.* 2nd ed. Chicago: University of Chicago Press.

"Profiting from Sexism." 2010, Oct 21. *The Economist.* Retrieved from www. economist.com.

"Purblind Prejudice." 2017, Sept 23. *The Economist,* 74.

Putnam, Robert D. 2015. *Our Kids: The American Dream in Crisis*. New York: Simon & Schuster.

Ransom, Roger L., and Richard Sutch. 2001. *One Kind of Freedom: The Economic Consequences of Emancipation*, 2nd ed. Cambridge: Cambridge University Press.

Ravitch, Diane. 2010. *The Death and Life of the Great American School System: How Testing and Choice Are Undermining Education*. New York: Basic Books.

Remmers, Hermann H. 1928. "The Relationship Between Students' Marks and Student Attitude Toward Instructors." *School & Society* 28: 759–760.

———. 1930. "To What Extent Do Grades Influence Student Ratings of Instructors?" *The Journal of Educational Research* 2 (1): 314–316.

Remmers, Hermann H., F. D. Martin, and Donald N. Elliott. 1949. "Are Students' Ratings of Instructors Related to Their Grades?" *Purdue University Studies in Higher Education* 6 (6): 17–26.

"Return of the Overlord." 2010, April 3. *The Economist,* 71–73.

Reynolds, Glenn Harlan. 2012. *The Higher Education Bubble*. New York: Encounter Books.

Rhoades, Gary. 1987. "Higher Education in a Consumer Society." *The Journal of Higher Education* 58 (1): 1–24.

Richardson, Ken. 1999. *The Making of Intelligence*. London: Weidenfeld and Nicolson.

Robinson, James. 1994. "Social Status and Academic Success in South Korea." *Comparative Education Review* 38 (4): 506–530.

Robinson, Ken. 2001. *Out of Our Minds: Learning to Be Creative*. Chichester, UK: Capstone.

Rodin, Miriam, and Burton Rodin. 1972. "Student Evaluations of Teachers." *Science* 177 (4055): 1164–1166.

Roediger, David R. 2003. *The Wages of Whiteness: Race and the Making of the American Working Class.* Rev. ed. London: Verso.

Rogoff, Barbara. 1990. *Apprenticeship in Thinking: Cognitive Development in Social Context*. Oxford: Oxford University Press.

———. 2003. *The Cultural Nature of Human Development*. Oxford University Press.

Ronfeldt, Matthew. 2015. "Field Placement Schools and Instructional Effectiveness." *Journal of Teacher Education* 66 (4): 304–320.

Rosenbaum, James E. 2001. *Beyond College for All: Career Paths for the Forgotten Half*. New York: Russell Sage Foundations.

Rosenberg, Shawn W. 1988. *Reason, Ideology and Politics*. Princeton: Princeton University Press.

———. 2017, Dec. "Unfit for Democracy? Irrational, Rationalizing, and Biologically Predisposed Citizens." *Critical Review* 29 (3): 362–387.

———. Forthcoming. "Democracy Devouring Itself: The Rise of The Incompetent Citizen and the Appeal of Right-Wing Populism." In Domenico Uhng Hur and José Manuel Sabucedo, eds., *Psychology of Political and Everyday Extremisms*. Retrieved from www.researchgate.net.

Rosovsky, Henry, and Matthew Hartley. 2002. *Evaluation and the Academy: Are We Doing the Right Thing. Grade Inflation and Letters of Recommendation.* The American Academy of Arts and Sciences. Cambridge, MA: Author.

Rothschild, David, and Sharad Goel. 2016, Oct 5. "When You Hear the Margin of Error Is Plus or Minus 3 Percent, Think 7 Instead." *The New York Times.* Retrieved from www.nytimes.com.

Ryan, Alan. 1995. *John Dewey and the High Tide of American Liberalism.* New York: W. W. Norton.

Sacks, Oliver. 2012. *Hallucinations.* New York: Vintage Books.

———. 2017. *The River of Consciousness.* New York: Vintage Books.

Sah-Myung, Hong. 1983. "The Republic of Korea." In R. Murray Thomas and T. Neville Postlethwaite, eds. *Schooling in East Asia: Forces of Change.* Oxford, UK: Pergamon Press.

Salsburg, David. 2001. *The Lady Tasting Tea: How Statistics Revolutionized Science in the Twentieth Century.* New York: Henry Holt and Company.

Sandel, Michael J. 2012. 1996. *Democracy's Discontent: America in Search of a Public Philosophy.* Cambridge, MA: Harvard University Press.

———. 2012. *What Money Can't Buy: The Moral Limits of Markets.* New York: Farrar, Straus and Giroux.

———. 2020. *The Tyranny of Merit.* New York: Farrar, Straus and Giroux.

Sanders, William L., and June C. Rivers. 1996. *Cumulative and Residual Effects of Teachers on Future Student Academic Achievement. Research Progress Report.* Knoxville, TN: University of Tennessee Value-Added Research and Assessment Center.

Santoro, Doris A. 2018. *Demoralized: Why Teachers Leave the Profession They Love and How They Can Stay.* Cambridge, MA: Harvard University Press.

Sapolsky, Robert M. 2004. *Why Zebras Don't Get Ulcers,* 3rd ed. New York: St. Martin's Griffin.

———. 2017. *Behave: The Biology of Humans at Our Best and Worst.* New York: Penguin.

Sass, Tim, Jane Hannaway, Zeyu Xu, David N. Figlio, and Li Feng. 2012. "Value Added of Teachers in High-Poverty Schools and Lower-Poverty Schools." *Journal of Urban Economics* 72 (2): 104–122.

Scheidel, Walter. 2017. *The Great Leveler: Violence and the History of Inequality from the Stone Age to the Twenty-First Century.* Princeton, NJ: Princeton University Press.

Schneider, Jack. 2017. *Beyond Test Scores: A Better Way to Measure School Quality.* Cambridge, MA: Harvard Education Press.

Schultz, Theodore W. 1961. "Investment in Human Capital." *The American Economic Review* 5 (11): 1–17.

Schwartz-Chrismer, Sara, Shannon T. Hodge, and Debby Saintil, eds. 2006. "Assessing NCLB: Perspectives and Prescriptions." *Harvard Educational Review* 76 (4).

Seife, Charles. 2010. *Proofinesss: How You're Being Fooled by the Numbers.* New York: Penguin.

"Seize the Memes." 2019, Dec 21. *Economist*, 85–87.

Sen, Amartya. 1999. *Development as Freedom*. New York: Anchor Books.

Senge, Peter M. 2006. *The* Fifth Discipline*:* The Art and Practice of the Learning Organization, 2nd ed. New York: Currency. Originally published 1990.

Senior, Rose. 2009, January 15. "Korean Students Silenced by Exams." *The Guardian.* Retrieved from https://www.theguardian.com/world/2009/jan/15/south-korea-students.

Seth, Michael J. 2002. *Education Fever: Society, Politics, and the Pursuit of Schooling in South Korea.* Honolulu, HI: University of Hawai'i Press.

Shenkman, Rick. 2008. *Just How Stupid Are We? Facing the Truth about the American Voter.* New York: Basic Books.

———. 2016. *Political Animals: How Our Stone-Age Brain Gets in the Way of Smart Politics.* New York: Basic Books.

Sigmund, Karl. 2017. *Exact Thinking in Demented Times: The Vienna Circle and the Epic Quest for the Foundations of Science.* New York: Basic Books.

Silver, Nate. 2012. *The Signal and the Noise: Why So Many Predictions Fail—But Some Don't.* New York: Penguin.

———. 2017, Feb 20. "Why Polls Differ on Trump's Popularity: It's Cherry-Picking Season Already." *FiveThirtyEight*, Retrieved from https://fivethirtyeight.com/features/why-polls-differ-on-trumps-popularity/.

Sizer, Theodore R. 1992. *Horace's Compromise: The Dilemma of the American High School*. Boston: Houghton Mifflin.

Sklansky, Jeffrey. 2002. *The Soul's Economy: Market Society and Selfhood in American Thought, 1820–1920*. Chapel Hill, NC: The University of North Carolina Press.

Sloman, Steven, and Philip Fernbach. 2017. *The Knowledge Illusion: Why We Never Think Alone*. New York: Riverhead.

Smith, Noah. 2019, March 27. "American Employers Are Hung Up on Hiring Ph.D.s." *Bloomberg*. Retrieved from https://www.bloomberg.com.

Sniderman, Paul M., Richard A. Brody, and Philip E. Tetlock. 1991. *Reasoning and Choice. Explorations in Political Psychology*. Cambridge, UK: Cambridge University Press.

Sodexo. 2019, May 7. "More Than Bricks and Mortar." *The Chronicle of Higher Education*. Retrieved from https://www.chronicle.com.

Sokol, Alan, and Jean Bricmont. 1998. *Fashionable Nonsense: Postmodern Intellectuals' Abuse of Science*. New York: Picador.

Soo-yeon, Lee. 2009, Aug 17. "Hagwon Close, But Late-Night Education Goes On." *Joong Ang Daily*.

Sorensen, Clark W. 1994, Feb. "Success and Education in South Korea." *Comparative Education Review* 38 (1): 10–35.

Spellings Commission. 2006. *A Test of Leadership: Charting the Future of US Higher Education*. Washington, DC: US Department of Education.

Spence, Michael A. 1974. *Market Signaling: Informational Transfer in Hiring and Related Screening Processes*. Cambridge: Harvard University Press.

Sperber, Murray. 2000. *Beer and Circus: How Big-Time College Sports Is Crippling Undergraduate Education.* New York: Henry Holt and Company.

———. 2005. "How Undergraduate Education Became College Lite—and a Personal Apology." In *Declining by Degrees: Higher Education at Risk,* edited by Richard H. Hersh and John Merrow, 131–143. New York: Palgrave Macmillan.

Spindler, Michael. 2002. *Veblen and Modern America: Revolutionary Iconoclast.* London: Pluto Press.

St. John, Edward P., Kimberly A. Kline, and Eric H. Asker. 2001. "The Call for Public Accountability: Rethinking the Linkages to Student Outcomes." In *The States and Public Higher Education Policy: Affordability, Access, and Accountability,* edited by Donald E. Heller, 219–242. Baltimore: The Johns Hopkins University Press.

Stanovich, Keith E. 2009. *What Intelligence Tests Miss: The Psychology of Rational Thought.* New Haven: Yale University Press.

———. 2010. *Decision Making and Rationality in the Modern World.* Oxford: Oxford University Press.

Stark, Philip B., and Freishtat, Richard. 2014, Sept 26. *An Evaluation of Course Evaluations.* University of California, Berkeley. Retrieved from www.stat.berkeley.edu/~stark/Preprints/teachEval14.pdf.

Starr, Douglas. 2020, Jan 2. "This Italian Scientists Has Become a Celebrity by Fighting Vaccine Skeptics." *Science.* Retrieved from www.sciencemag.org

Starr, Paul. 2017. *The Social Transformation of American Medicine.* Updated Edition. New York: Basic Books.

Steinberg, Lawrence D. 1996. *Beyond the Classroom: Why School Reform Has Failed and What Parents Need to Do.* New York: Simon & Schuster.

———. 2014. *Age of Opportunity: Lessons from the New Science of Adolescence.* New York: Mariner Books.

Steinberg, Matthew P., and Rachel Garrett. 2016. "Classroom Composition and Measured Teacher Performance: What Do Teacher Observation Scores Really Measure?" *Educational Evaluation and Policy Analysis,* 38 (2): 293–317.

Stephens-Davidowitz, Seth. 2017. *Everybody Lies: Big Data, New Data, and What the Internet Can Tell Us about Who We Really Are.* New York: Dey Street Books.

Sternberg, Robert J. 1988. *The Triarchic Mind: A New Theory of Human Intelligence.* New York: Viking.

———. 2002. *Why Smart People Can Be So Stupid.* New Haven: Yale University Press.

Stewart, Matthew. 2009. *The Management Myth: Debunking Modern Business Philosophy.* New York: W. W. Norton.

Sunstein, Cass R. 1997. *Free Markets and Social Justice.* Oxford: Oxford University Press.

———. 2019. *Conformity: The Power of Social Influences.* New York: New York University Press.

Supiano, Beckie. 2019, April 7. "Digital Distraction Is a Problem Far Beyond the Classroom. But Professors Can Still Help." *The Chronicle of Higher Education.* Retrieved from www.chronicle.com.

———. 2019, Sept 9. "Sociologists Caution Colleges Not to Over-Rely on Student Evaluations of Teaching." *The Chronicle of Higher Education*. Retrieved from www.chronicle.com

Swartz, David. 1997. *Culture and Power: The Sociology of Pierre Bourdieu*. Chicago: University of Chicago Press.

Taleb, Nicholas. 2012. *Antifragile: Things That Gain from Disorder*. New York: Random House.

Tanzi, Alexandre. 2019, Feb 16. "U.S. Student Debt in 'Serious Delinquency' Tops $166 Billion." *Bloomberg*. Retrieved from www.bloomberg.com.

Tavris, Carol, and Elliot Aronson. 2015. *Mistakes Were Made but Not by Me: Why We Justify Foolish Beliefs, Bad Decisions, and Hurtful Acts*. Boston: Mariner Books.

Teachout, Terry. 2002. *The Skeptic: A Life of H. L. Mencken*. New York: HarperCollins.

Tetlock, Philip E., and Dan Gardner. *Superforecasting: The Art and Science of Prediction*. New York: Broadway.

Thaler, Richard H. 2015. *Misbehaving: The Making of Behavioral Economics*. New York: W. W. Norton.

Thaler, Richard H., and Cass R. Sunstein. 2008. *Nudge: Improving Decisions about Health, Wealth, and Happiness*. New Haven, CT: Yale University Press.

"The New AI-ssembly Line." 2020, Feb 22. *The Data Economy: A Special Report. The Economist*, 8–9.

Thelin, John R. 2004. *A History of American Higher Education*. Baltimore, MD: Johns Hopkins University Press.

Thompson, Derek. 2018, Dec 11. "Does It Matter Where You Go to College?" *The Atlantic*. Retrieved from theatlantic.com

Tomasello Michael. 2014. *A Natural History of Human Thinking*. Cambridge, MA: Harvard University Press.

Torch, Florencia. 2011. "Is a College Degree Still the Great Equalizer? Intergenerational Mobility across Levels of Schooling in the United States." *American Journal of Sociology* 117 (3): 763–807.

Tough, Paul. 2008. *Whatever It Takes: Geoffrey Canada's Quest to Change Harlem and America*. Boston: Houghton Mifflin Company.

Turner, James. 2014. *Philology: The Forgotten Origins of the Modern Humanities*. Princeton: Princeton University Press.

Tversky, Amos, and Daniel Kahneman. 1982. "The Framing of Decisions and the Psychology of Choice." In *New Directions in Methodology of Social and Behavioral Sciences: Question Framing and Response Consistency*, edited by Robin Hogarth. San Francisco: Jossey-Bass.

Tversky, Barbara. 2019. *Mind in Motion: How Action Shapes Thought*. New York: Basic Books.

Twain, Mark. 1962. *Mark Twain on the Damned Human Race*. J. Smith, ed. New York: Hill and Wang.

Twenge, Jean Marie. 2017. *iGen: Why Today's Super-Connected Kids Are Growing Up Less Rebellious, More Tolerant, Less Happy—and Completely Unprepared for Adulthood*. New York: Altria Books.

Twenge, Jean Marie, and William Keith Campbell. 2009. *The Narcissism Epidemic: Living in the Age of Entitlement.* New York: Free Press.

Twitchell, James B. 2004. "Higher Ed, Inc." *Wilson Quarterly* 28 (3): 46–59.

Tyack, David B. 1974. *The One Best System: A History of American Urban Education.* Cambridge, MA: Harvard University Press.

Tyack, David B., and Larry Cuban. 1995. *Tinkering Toward Utopia: A Century of Public School Reform.* Cambridge, MA: Harvard University Press.

Tyack, David, B., and Elisabeth Hansot. 1982. *Managers of Virtue: Public School Leadership in America, 1820–1980.* New York: Basic Books.

Tye, Larry. 1998. *The Father of Spin: Edward L. Bernays and the Birth of Public Relations.* New York: Crown Publishers.

UNESCO. 2006, Oct. *South Korea.* Revised Version. *World Data on Education.* 6th ed. Paris: UNESCO.

Uttl, Bob, Carmela A. White, and Daniela Wong Gonzalez. 2017. "Meta-Analysis of Faculty's Teaching Effectiveness: Student Evaluation of Teaching Ratings and Student Learning Are Not Related." *Studies in Educational Evaluation* 54: 22–42.

van Doorn, Evert A., Gerben A. van Kleef, and Joop van der Pligt. 2014. "How Instructors' Emotional Expressions Shape Students' Learning Performance: The Role of Anger, Happiness, and Regulatory Focus." *Journal of Experimental Psychology General* 143 (3): 980–84.

Waller, Willard. 1932. *The Sociology of Teaching.* New York: J. Wiley and Sons.

Walton, Mary. 1986. *The Deming Management Method.* New York: Perigee Books.

Ware, John E., and Reed G. Williams. 1975. "The Dr. Fox Effect: A Study of Lecturer Effectiveness and Ratings of Instruction." *Journal of Medical Education* 50: 149–156.

———. 1976. "Validity of Student Ratings of Instruction under Different Incentive Conditions." *Journal of Educational Psychology* 68: 48–56.

———. 1977. "An Extended Visit with Dr. Fox: Validity of Student Satisfaction with Instruction Ratings after Repeated Exposures to a Lecturer." *American Educational Research Journal* 14 (4): 449–57.

Washburn Jennifer. 2005. *University, Inc.: The Corporate Corruption of American Higher Education.* New York: Basic Books.

Weissberg, Robert. 2002. *Polling, Policy, and Public Opinion: The Case Against Heeding the Voice of the People.* New York: Palgrave.

"Which Traits Predict Graduates' Earnings?" 2018 June 15. *The Economist.* Retrieved from www.theeconomist.com.

Willer, Robb, Ko Kuwabara, and Michael W. Macy. 2009. "The False Enforcement of Unpopular Norms." *American Journal of Sociology* 115 (2): 451–90.

Williams, Wendy. M., and Stephen J. Ceci. 1997, Sept. "How'm I Doing?" 13–23.

Wilson, David Sloan. 2002. *Darwin's Cathedral: Evolution, Religion, and the Nature of Society.* Chicago: University of Chicago Press.

Wilson, E. O. 1978. *On Human Nature.* Cambridge, MA: Harvard University Press.

Winsor, Jerry L. 1977. "A's, B's, But Not C's?: A Comment." *Contemporary Education* 48 (2): 82–84.

Wiseman, Richard. 2012. *The As If Principle: The Radically New Approach to Changing Your Life*. New York: Free Press.

Wolf, Alison. 2002. *Does Education Matter? Myths About Education and Economic Growth*. London: Penguin.

Wolverton, Brad. 2016, Aug 28. "The New Cheating Economy." *The Chronicle of Higher Education.* Retrieved from www.chronicle.com

Wrangham, Richard, and Dale Peterson. 1996. *Demonic Males: Apes and the Origins of Human Violence*. New York: Mariner.

Yi, Joseph E. 2009, Oct 2. "Academic Success at Any Cost?" *KoreAm: The Korean American Experience.*

Young-Eisendrath, Polly. 2008. *The Self-Esteem Trap: Raising Confident and Compassionate Kids in an Age of Self-Importance*. New York: Little, Brown, and Company.

"Zoomers, Zeros and Gen Z." 2020, May 23. *The Economist*, 54.

Zuckerman, Gregory. 2019. The Man Who Solved the Market. New York: Portfolio/ Penguin.

Preview of This Book's Companion Volume

Can We Measure What Matters Most?
Why Educational Accountability
Metrics Lower Student Learning
and Demoralize Teachers

Rather than believing in the traditional value of education, in the 21st century, most schools now have to prove their worth with quantitative data, while also being cost effective organizations, just like businesses (Friedman [1962] 2002; Drucker 1969; Muller 2018). Organizational accountability schemes have been advertised as fact-based, results-oriented assessments of institutional goals and organizational performance. But under the veneer of scientific legitimacy and economic efficiency lie irrational assumptions based on unexamined political myths. The purpose of this book is to critically examine some of those myths.

This book will be examining the very notion of organizational accountability. The idea of keeping public institutions accountable, especially schools, has become a new "secular gospel," which has been documented and deconstructed by several insightful scholars over the past couple decades, especially by Diane Ravitch (2010), Jerry Z. Muller (2018), and Daniel Koretz (2017). These critics have pointed out, "There is an often-unexamined faith that amassing data and sharing it widely . . . will result in improvements of some sort" (Muller 2018, 47; see also Taleb 2012, 307; Schneider 2017, 62).

In the 19th century, educational reform in the U.S. was focused on lofty, messianic missions to promote democracy, knowledge, equality, public spirit, self-discipline, and self-sacrifice. Naïve in many ways, but based on ideals of the greater good. In the 21st century, according to Diane Ravitch (2010), educational reform has devolved into a technocratic "measurement strategy" that has "no underlying educational vision at all" (16). Test-based accountability, according to Daniel Koretz (2017) has "become an end in itself . . . unmoored from clear thinking about what should be measured, how it should be measured, or how testing can fit into a rational plan for evaluating and improving our schools" (5).

Schools are now drowning in accountability data (Schneider 2017, 62). Most of this data is trivial. And a lot of it compromised by invalid methodology. But few policy makers or school administrators have bothered to ask if their accountability programs actually work. Do accountability policies or accountability data actually make schools any better at what they do? Or is this just a myth?

Schools in the U.S. have been subjected to wave after wave of accountability reforms over the past century. But almost every initiative has been ineffective, so the notion that accountability measurements improve schools seems to be a myth (Elmore and McLaughlin 1988; Tyack and Cuban 1995; Payne 2008; Cuban 2013; Labaree 2012; Koretz 2017). Part of the problem is that reformers have often relied on "bad measures of school quality," which has usually misidentified both the actual problems and the needed solutions (Schneider 2017, 4).

This is tragically ironic given that educational researchers have known about core best practices for almost 50 years (Argyris 1993, 30).

Because of this record of failure, historian and sociologist David F. Labaree (1992) quipped that reforming schools has been "steady work" for enterprising crusaders (130). The central problems of schooling never seem to get solved. New reform proposals seem to pop up every year. However, most schools never actually get reformed, especially the most challenged schools that serve the neediest students. For about half a century, educational researchers have documented and warned that schools have been "producing the very consequences of ineffective schooling that they decry" (Argyris 1993, 29).

Index

Abrami, Philip C., 85
academic malpractice, 38–42
accountability measurements: as
    conventional wisdom, xxiii;
    discouragement around, xxv–xxvi;
    examination of important, xviii–xix;
    inflation of, 39; key problem with,
    xiii; myths of, investigating, xxi–
    xxviii. *See also specific topics*
accountability movement: higher
    education as target of, xiii;
    purpose of, xvii
acting: seductive communication
    techniques, 83–84; teaching
    compared to, 82–83
adolescents: consumer training of,
    59; fragility of, 34–35, 55–56; life
    purpose for, 81; lying by, 75–76;
    peer culture influencing, 31;
    pessimistic belief about future of,
    2–3; poor judgment of, 71
advertising. *See* marketing/advertising
agency, individual, 9–11
Alexander, Kern, 101
anti-learning techniques, 22
Archives of Internal Medicine, 87
aristocracy: hereditary, 124, 126,
    127–29, 130; meritocracy posing as,
    xxviii, 96; power in, 107

Aristotle, 4
arms race, 121–22
Aronowitz, Stanley, 109
Asian American students, 126
attractiveness, 84–85
attribution theory, 20–26
authentic learning: resentment of, 36;
    stress of, 53
automatic-thinking reflexes, 65–66
automation, 111, 114, 121

bachelor's degree, 111, 113–15, 120
Bell, Daniel, 100
Benedict, Ruth, 9–10
Bernays, Edward, 3, 5
bias: of cognitive miser, 65–67;
    confirmation, 90; consumer
    feedback, 17; from culture, 10;
    gender, 51–52; group-centered, 11;
    groupthink furthering, 25; individual
    agency and, 9–11; likability, 79–81;
    of memory, 72, 73–74; root cause
    of, 72; self-centered, 11; self-
    serving, 21–22, 24–25; student
    evaluation surveys influenced by,
    19–20, 24, 25–26, 27, 43, 46; from
    subjectivity, 10
brands: emotion, price and, 61–64;
    importance of, 60–61

bribery, 35, 108, 129
businesses, xxii–xxiii, 60–61

Can We Measure What Matters Most,
    xvii, 1, 140, 141
Caplan, Bryan, xxvii, 68
career change, 111
chaebol, 130
cheating economy, 31–32
children: educational reform focusing
    on, 32; love of learning, 33; natural
    learning capacities of, 89. *See also*
    adolescents
China: college graduate increase in,
    114; credentialism origins in, 108,
    125; hereditary aristocracy in, 126,
    127–29; Korea influenced by, 125–
    26; meritocracy and schooling rigged
    in ancient, 127–29; meritocracy
    concept invented in, 125; myth of
    opportunity for students in, xxvii–
    xxviii, 126; social status of women
    in ancient, 128
Chua, Amy, 126
churches, 109
cognitive miser, 65–69
cognitive shortcuts, 61–64
college. *See* higher education;
    specific topics
Collins, Randall, 117, 119
Columbia Journalism Review, 116
community college, 64, 95–96
conditioning, 21
confabulations, 73
confirmation bias, 90
consumerism mantra, 31, 89
consumer-rating systems, 16–17
consumers: adolescents trained as, 59;
    cognitive shortcuts and, 61–64;
    confusion about popularity, 80;
    control of, 6–7; culture hacking
    of, 62–63; ignorance of, 79;
    preferences toward student, xiv–xv,
    42; product evaluation accuracy of,
    questioning, 59–61

consumer satisfaction: assumptions
    about, 78; corruption of education
    and, 17; health care influenced by,
    87–89; product value confused
    with, 57; school administrators
    commitment to, 86–87; teaching in
    relation to, 86–91
consumer sovereignty, 16
control: of consumers, 6–7; public
    opinion manipulated for, 2–9;
    teachers loss of classroom, 13–14
corporate managers, xxii
craftsmen, 98
credentialism: arms race created
    from, 121–22; defining, 93; degree
    inflation and, 111–24; meritocracy in
    relation to, 93–94; origins in China,
    108, 125; as secular faith, 94
credentials: career change and, 111; as
    currency, 104; demand increase for,
    111–12; factories, xxi, xxiii; gateway,
    120; high school diploma, 112,
    113, 114–15, 120; human capital in
    relation to, xxvii; journalism and,
    115–16; labor market outcomes in
    relation to, xxvi; as magical objects,
    109; purpose of, 105–6; social status
    in relation to, xxvi–xxvii, 106, 108;
    value of, 108–9. *See also* degrees
critical thinking, 65, 66
cultural capital, xxvi
culture: bias from, 10; peer, 31; of truth-
    telling, 24
culture hacking, 62–63

Darling-Hammond, Linda, 134
DCX Growth Accelerator, 62–63
debt, 122
defensive teaching, 33
degree inflation, 111–24
degrees: bachelor, 111, 113–15, 120;
    economic return from, 94–95,
    102–3, 111; as magic piece of
    paper, 31; meaninglessness of, 41;

medical, 106; PhD, 116–17; as value
proposition, 60
Deming, W. Edwards, 47, 140
demoralization, 38–42
discrimination: in labor market, 97–98,
103; student evaluation surveys
influenced by, 51–52
dissonance theory, 23
doctors: consumer satisfaction
influencing, 87–89; medical degree,
106; in South Korea, 135
Donnelly, Frank A., 82–83
dropout factories, xxiii
Drucker, Peter F., xxi, 100
dual-process theory, 65
Dunning-Kruger Effect, 90

economic efficiency, xvii
economic return, 94–95, 102–3, 111
economic value: of education, 96–104;
measurements of, xxvi
economy: cheating, 31–32; knowledge,
99, 100, 125; political, 139
education: belief in transformative
power of, xix; consumer satisfaction
and corruption of, 17; economic
value of, 96–104; entertainment over,
81, 83, 85–86; hope for future, 141–
42; human capital theory devaluing,
101–2; mantra, 31, 89; mystery of,
90–91; propaganda in relation to, 3;
social stratification at heart of, 121,
139. *See also* higher education
educational credentials. *See*
credentialism; credentials
educational hyperinflation, 118–19
educational rat race, 121, 123
educational reform: children as
focus of, 32; higher education as
focus of, xxiii
Edwards, Newton, 139
emotion: brands, price and, 61–64;
human brain influenced by, 67–68;
student learning in relation to, 53–55
employees, xxii

enrollment: educational hyperinflation
increasing, 118–19; marketing for
college, xiv, 62
entertainment, 81, 83, 85–86
equality legality, 99

fear: free of, 140; self-esteem in relation
to, 23; of students, 41, 56
Fish, Stanley, 90–91
Fitzhugh, George, 4
Fox, Myron L., 82
Fox Effect, 79–86
fragility, 34–35, 55–56
fraud: academic malpractice and, 38–42;
student evaluation surveys as, 36
Freishtat, Richard, 46
Friedman, Milton, xxi
funding restrictions, xiv

gender bias, 51–52
Generation Snowflake, 55
grades: assumptions and truth about, 21;
false sense of competence regarding,
55; fear influencing, 41; inflation of,
xv; self-esteem in relation to, 22–23,
24; student evaluation surveys
in relation to, 17–19, 27, 43–46;
unreliability of, 1
grade-satisfaction theory: defining,
27–30; support of, 43–46
Grimes, Howard, 16
group-centered bias, 11
groupthink, 25
Grove, Andy, xxiii

hagwons, 132–33, 134–35
harassment, 37
Harvard University, 63
Harvey, David, xxii
health care, 87–89
helicopter parents, 34
herd management, 2–9
hereditary aristocracy: in China, 126,
127–29; creation of new, 124; in
South Korea, 130

higher education: core characteristics of, xiv–xv; educational reform focusing on, xxiii; outcomes desired from, xiii; sacred truths about, xxv; scandal of, xxiv. *See also specific topics*

high school diploma, 112, 113, 114–15, 120

Hirsch, Fred, 112–13

Holmes, David S., 44–45

honesty: conflict regarding, 74; student evaluation surveys issue of, 72, 76; teachers fear of, 41, 56. *See also* lying

human brain: as cognitive miser, 65–69; dual-process theory of, 65; emotion influencing, 67–68; subjectivity rooted in, 72

human capital: credentials in relation to, xxvii; education devalued by, 101–2; measurement of, xxvi; meritocracy in relation to, 100; schools producing, xxii, 99; social status signaling and, 104–10; students earning and using, xxv

human capital theory, 96–104

hypersensitivity, 52

ignorance: of consumers, 79; inability to acknowledge own, 73, 90; rational, 68

individual agency, 9–11

internet: journalism changes from, 116; student evaluation surveys, 15–16

irrationality of truth, 67–68

Jefferson, Thomas, 3

Johnson, Valen E., 43–44, 45–46, 84

journalism, 115–16

Journal of Medical Education, 81–82

joy, 140

knowledge: assumptions about attaining, xxvi; as currency, 99; entitlement over, 109; personal, 20–21

knowledge economy, 99, 100, 125

Korea: China influencing, 125–26; conquering of, 130; myth of opportunity for students in, xxvii–xxviii, 126; South, 130–35, 136–37

Korean War, 130

Labaree, David, xiii–xv

labor market: automation impacting, 111, 114, 121; credentials in relation to outcomes in, xxvi; discrimination in, 97–98, 103; exclusion from, 119–20; inequality of, 123–24; journalism in, 115–16; as lottery, 123; meaningless jobs in middle of, 117–18; net national product growth and, 96–97; overeducation of workers in, 118; polarization of, 117, 121; slavery compared to, 97–98; social institutions forever changing, 98–99; in South Korea, 130–32; unhappiness of workers in, 122–23; unpredictability of global, 111; women invisibility in, 97

labor unions, 98

ladder of opportunity, 93–94

Law of the Excluded Middle, 47

learning: authentic, 36, 53; children's natural capacities in, 89; children's natural love of, 33; joy of, 140; playing school as opposite of real, 30; psychologists questioning process of, 13; student evaluation surveys ineffectively measuring, 44–51; student resistance to, 28–29; students forced into, 32–33. *See also* student learning

Le Bon, Gustave, 5

legal equality, 99

Leventhal, Les, 85

life-expectancy improvements, 89

likability heuristic, 79–81

Lincoln, Abraham, 98

Lippmann, Walter, 3, 5, 115–16

lottery: labor market as, 123; meritocracy as, 119

Louisiana State University football, 42
lying: by adolescents, 75–76; frequency
    of, 74; about nutrition, 75; reasons
    for, 26, 71–72; self-deception as,
    74–75; with statistics, 76–77; by
    teachers, xxv–xxvi

malpractice, academic, 38–42
mantra: of consumerism and education,
    31, 89; of playing school, 30
marketing/advertising: brands, 60–64;
    for college enrollment, xiv, 62; for
    consumer control, 6–7
market principles, xxii
Marx, Karl, 98
"Mathematical Game Theory as Applied
    to Physical Education," 81–82
medical degree, 106
memory: bias rooted in, 72, 73–74;
    confabulations, 73; emotion
    prioritizing, 67; as fictionalization of
    past experience, 73; self-deception
    in relation to, 75; subjectivity in
    relation to, 73–74
Mencken, H. L., 115
meritocracy: as aristocracy in disguise,
    xxviii, 96; China inventing concept
    of, 125; China rigged schooling and,
    127–29; credentialism in relation
    to, 93–94; human capital in relation
    to, 100; as lottery, 119; South
    Korea false promise of schooling
    and, 130–35
meritocratic institutions, 139–42
Mill, John Stuart, 6
moral blackmail, 40
moral violence, 39–40

Naftulin, Donald H., 80–81
narcissism, 23
National Governors Association
    (NGA), xxiii
negative feedback, 54–56
neoliberalism: model of schooling, xxii;
    political agendas of, xvii

net national product, 96–97
NGA. *See* National Governors
    Association
Nisbett, Richard, 59–60
No Child Left Behind legislation, xxiv
nutrition science, 75

organizational accountability, xvii

pandemic of 2020, 124
paradox, 28
parents: approval ratings of school
    from, 29; bribes from, 35, 108, 129;
    helicopter, 34; self-esteem influenced
    by, 23–24; South Korea pressure on,
    135; tiger, 126
Patient Preference and Adherence, 87
Payless Shoe Source, 62–63
peer culture, 31
Perry, Raymond P., 85
personal knowledge, 20–21
PhDs, 115–16
Pinker, Steven, 22
playing school: compromise of,
    negotiated, 30–38; definition of, 30;
    incentives for, 109–10
Polanyi, Michael, 20–21
polarization: of labor market, 117,
    121; of student evaluation survey
    responses, 46
political conflict, 27
political economy, 139
political polling, 77–78
popularity, 79–81
positive feedback, 53–54
positive illusions, 22
power: in aristocracy, 107; belief in
    educations transformative, xix;
    schools solidifying, 96
pretend achievement, 32–33
price, 61–64
prison sentence, 34
privilege: schools solidifying, 96; social
    class, 103, 109; tiers of service
    regarding, 61

products: consumers accurate evaluation of, questioning, 59–61; consumer satisfaction confused with value of, 57
propaganda: education in relation to, 3; school surveys as, 2
Prussia, xxviii
psychologists: on conditioning, 21; on individual agency and bias, 9–11; on self-deception, 74–75; teaching and learning process questioned by, 13
psychology of price, 62–64
public opinion surveys: for herd management, 2–9; neutrality missing from, 48–49; questioning trust of, 72–79

ratemyprofessors.com, 15–16
rational ignorance, 68
rat race, 121, 123
Remmers, Hermann Henry, 17–20
research: background on, xvii–xviii; conclusion, 139–42; focus of, xviii–xix; hope for, xix
ritualization. *See* playing school
Rodin, Burton, 44
Rodin, Mirum, 44
Ross, Edward A., 3–4

Sacks, Oliver, 73–74
Sandel, Michael J., 141
Santoro, Doris A., 39–40
school administrators: consumer satisfaction as duty of, 86–87; as corporate managers, xxii; student evaluation surveys favored by, 15, 16; teachers pressured by, 39–40
schooling: assumptions about, 104; China rigged meritocracy and, 127–29; as educational rat race, 121, 123; faith in sacred value of, xvii–xviii; inefficiency of public, xxi; inequality in benefits of, 103–4; ladder of opportunity from, 93–94; myth of opportunity in, xxvii–xxviii;

126; neoliberal model of, xxii; as passport to outside opportunities, 119; political conflict essential to, 27; political economy influencing, 139; purpose of, 104–10; for social status, 136–37; South Korea false promise of meritocracy and, 130–35; South Korea purpose of, 136–37; sub-baccalaureate, 95–96; tax dollars wasted on, xxi; vocationalization of, 93
schools: arms race between, 121–22; as businesses, xxii–xxiii, 60–61; cheating economy in, 31–32; as credential factories, xxi, xxiii; human capital produced in, xxii, 99; market principles applied to, xxii; as meritocratic institutions, 139–42; myth about, xviii; paradox for, 28; parent and student approval ratings of, 29; power and privilege solidified in, 96; as prison sentence, 34; purpose of early 20th century, 3; social magic created in, 109; as warehouses, 119
school survey origins, 2
Schultz, Theodore W., 99–100
seductive communication techniques, 83–84
self-centered bias, 11
self-deception, 74–75
self-esteem, 22–24, 26
self-serving bias: defining, 21–22; experiment, 24–25
skills: assumptions about attaining, xxvi; entitlement over, 109
slavery: belief in, 4; labor market compared to, 97–98
social capital, xxvi
social class privilege, 103, 109
Social Control (Ross), 3–4
social magic, 109
social scientists: on individual agency and bias, 9–11; on public opinion manipulation, 2–9

social status: of aristocrats, 107;
credentials in relation to, xxvi–
xxvii, 106, 108; human capital and
signaling, 104–10; need for, 104–5,
141; schooling for, 136–37; survival
in regard to, 105; of women in
ancient China, 128; of women in
South Korea, 131
social stratification, 121, 139
South Korea: *chaebol*, 130; doctor
concerns in, 135; *hagwons*, 132–33,
134–35; hereditary aristocracy
in, 130; labor market in, 130–32;
purpose of schooling in, 136–37;
schooling and meritocracy false
promises in, 130–35; social status of
women in, 131; suicide rates in, 135;
testocracy, 133–34
Spellings Commission, xxiv
Stark, Philip B., 46
Steinberg, Laurence D., 29, 31, 71
stress, 53
student achievement: predictors of, 86;
pretend, 32–33
student aide, 64
student debt, 122
student evaluation surveys:
attractiveness of teacher influencing,
84–85; bias influencing, 19–20,
24, 25–26, 27, 43, 46; contextual
issues regarding results of,
49–50; defining types of, 14–15;
discrimination influencing, 51–52;
as foundation of assessment, xxv;
Fox Effect and, 79–86; as fraud,
36; grade-satisfaction theory and,
27–30, 43–46; grades in relation
to, 17–19, 27, 43–46; honesty
issue with, 72, 76; hypersensitivity
impacting, 52; increase in use
of, 13–14; index number, 47;
internet, 15–16; likability heuristic
influencing, 79–81; mathematical
issues regarding results of, 46–47;
over-reliance on, 51; response rate

selectivity and polarization, 46;
school administrators in favor of,
15, 16; seductive communication
techniques influencing, 83–84;
teacher-effectiveness theory and,
17–20, 27, 43–45; teaching and
learning ineffectively measured by,
44–51; unfairness to teachers, 51–57;
validity problem with, 17, 38, 43–44
student learning: emotion in relation
to, 53–55; factors influencing, 13;
problem of measuring, xvii; self-
esteem in relation to, 22–24, 26
students: approval ratings of school
from, 29; Asian American, 126;
cooperation needed between
teachers and, xiii–xiv; entertainment
preferred by, 81, 83, 85–86; false
sense of competence, 55; human
capital earned and used by, xxv;
joy of, 140; learning forced upon,
32–33; learning resistance from,
28–29; motivation loss for, 32–33;
narcissism, 23; negative feedback
for, 54–56; positive feedback for,
53–54; preferences toward consumer,
xiv–xv, 42; self-esteem, 22–24, 26;
South Korean, 131–35, 136; teachers
fear of, 41, 56; teachers harassed by,
37; teachers lying to, xxv–xxvi
sub-baccalaureate schooling, 95–96
subjectivity: bias from, 10; human
brain as root cause of, 72;
memory in relation to, 73–74;
rediscovery of, 20–21
suicide rates, 135
Sunstein, Cass R., 50

tax dollars, xxi
teacher-effectiveness theory:
contradiction of, 43–45; defining,
17–20; turning away from, 27
teachers: attractiveness of, 84–85;
cooperation needed between
students and, xiii–xiv; discrimination

against female, 51–52; distrust of, presumptive, 42; doctors compared to, 88–89; as employees, xxii; fear of students, 41, 56; fight lost by, 69; harassment of, 37; joy of, 140; likability of, 79–81; loss of classroom control, 13–14; moral blackmail against, 40; moral violence impacting, 39–40; negative feedback from, 54–56; in political bind, 28; positive feedback from, 53–54; pressure to please impacting, 38–42; seductive communication techniques used by, 83–84; student evaluation surveys unfairness to, 51–57; students lied to by, xxv–xxvi
teach-for-the-test curriculum, 133–34
teaching: academic malpractice and demoralization in, 38–42; acting compared to, 82–83; consumer satisfaction in relation to, 86–91; defensive, 33; playing school as opposite of real, 30; psychologists questioning process of, 13; student evaluation surveys ineffectively measuring, 44–51
testocracy, 133–34
theory: attribution, 20–26; dissonance, 23; dual-process, 65; essentialness of valid, 48; grade-satisfaction, 27–30, 43–46; human capital, 96–104; incompleteness of, 49; teacher-effectiveness, 17–20, 27, 43–45
tiger parenting, 126

toxic environments, 122
Trump, Donald, 77–78
Trump University, 62, 63
truth: culture of telling, 24; about grades, 21; higher educations sacred, xxv; irrationality of, 67–68

United States presidential election of 2000, 78
University of Texas at San Antonio, 16
Uttl, Bob, 50–51

vocationalization, 93

wage discrimination, 97
Waller, Willard, 27–28, 33, 52
Ware, John E., 82–83
warehouse-schools, 119
wealthy parents, 108
weather, 78
Weber, Max, 141
Weissbergm, Robert, 48
Wilkomirski, Binjamin, 73
Williams, Reed G., 83
Wilson, Tim, 59–60
Winsor, Jerry L., 38
women: discrimination against teachers as, 51–52; labor market invisibility of, 97; social status in ancient China, 128; social status in South Korea, 131

Yelp, 15, 75

About the Author

J. M. Beach is a scholar, teacher, entrepreneur, investor, and a poet. He is the founder and director of 21st Century Literacy, a nonprofit organization focused on literacy education and teacher training. The organization offers a free web textbook and other educational materials. Beach is available for workshops, teacher training seminars, and consulting. For more information, visit www.21centurylit.org.

Beach has advanced degrees in the fields of English, history, philosophy, and education and is finishing degrees in business administration and marketing. He was a lecturer in higher education for more than twenty years in the U.S., South Korea, and China. Beach is a member of the American Educational Research Association and the American Association for the Advancement of Science. His scholarly research focuses on several distinct, but interrelated subjects: the philosophy of knowledge, the science of culture and society, the history and philosophy of education, and literature.

Beach has two new books coming out this year: *Can We Measure What Matters Most? Why Educational Accountability Metrics Lower Student Learning and Demoralize Teachers* and *The Myths of Measurement and Meritocracy: Why Accountability Metrics in Higher Education Are Unfair and Increase Inequality.* Some of Beach's previous books include *How Do You Know? The Epistemological Foundations of 21st Century Literacy* (2018), *Gateway to Opportunity? A History of the Community College in the United States* (2011), *Children Dying Inside: Education in South Korea* (2011), and *Studies in Poetry: The Visionary* (2004).

For more information, visit the author's website at www.jmbeach.com.